STECK-VAUGHN

CONNECTIONS

Reading & Literature

Mohamed

REVIEWERS

Rochelle Kenyon
Assistant Principal
School Board of Broward County
Fort Lauderdale, Florida

Margaret A. Rogers
Vice-Principal
San Juan Unified School District
Sacramento, California

Dee Akers Prins
Resource Specialist
Richmond Public Schools
Richmond, Virginia

Lois J. Sherard
Instructional Facilitator
New York City Board of Education
New York, New York

Danette S. Queen
Instructional Facilitator
New York City Public Schools
New York, New York

STECK-VAUGHN
COMPANY
ELEMENTARY • SECONDARY • ADULT • LIBRARY

Acknowledgments

Executive Editor: Elizabeth Strauss
Supervising Editor: Carolyn Hall
Design Director: D. Childress
Design Coordinator: Cynthia Ellis
Cover Design: D. Childress
Editorial Development: McClanahan & Company, Inc.
Project Director: Mark Moscowitz
Writer/Editor: Virginia Lowe, Olive H. Collen
Design/Production: McClanahan & Company, Inc.

Photograph Credits: p. 12   © Ken Regan/Camera Five
p. 106   New York Public Library
p. 164   ABC Visual Communication

Cover Illustration: Rhonda Childress

Literary Acknowledgments

Grateful acknowledgment is made to the following publishers, authors, and agents for permission to use copyrighted material.

p. vi   "Sympathy" by Paul Dunbar. 1896, Dodd, Mead Co.
p. 2   Excerpt from ENTER TALKING by Joan Rivers. Copyright © 1986 Joan Rivers. Used by permission of Dell Books, a division of Bantam Doubleday Dell Publishing Group, Inc.
p. 4   Excerpt from Act III of A DOLL'S HOUSE by Henrik Ibsen, translated by R. Farquharson Sharp and E. Marks-Aveling. Reprinted with permission of David Campbell Publishers Ltd., publishers of Everyman Library.
p. 6   Excerpt from ENTERPRISE/THE FIRST ADVENTURE. Copyright © 1986 by Paramount Pictures. All Rights Reserved.
p. 8   Excerpt from Jay Cocks' review of Shirley Horn, "Taking Her Own Sweet Time" in TIME Magazine, 3/25/91. Copyright © 1991 by the Time Inc. Magazine Company. Reprinted by permission.

Acknowledgments for literary selections continue on pages 241-243, which are an extension of this copyright page.

ISBN 0-8114-5601-3

Copyright © 1992 Steck-Vaughn Company.

Table of Contents

Unit 1 — Popular Literature — Page 12

To the Student

The reading passages in this book are from popular literature, classical literature and commentary on the arts. You will read and analyze these passages.

Popular literature is what most people are reading today. It includes novels, short stories, essays, and poems. Classical literature is literature that has stood the test of time. It is about experiences that are important to people of all cultures and time periods. Commentary is someone's opinion about another person's work. You will read reviews of popular books, movies, plays, and concerts.

Inventory and Posttest

The Inventory is a self-check of what you already know and what you need to study. After you complete this book, you will take a Posttest. Compare your Posttest and Inventory scores to see your progress.

Sections

Each section gives you a passage to read actively. *Active reading* means doing something before reading, during reading, and after reading. By reading actively, you will improve your reading comprehension skills.

Setting the Stage. This is the activity you do *before reading*. First, determine what you already know about the subject of the article. Then, you preview the passage by reading the first few sentences. Finally, write your prediction of what the passage will be about.

The Passage. The passages you will read are taken from well-known works of popular and classical literature as well as commentary selections. As you read each passage, you will see a feature called *Applying Your Skills and Strategies*. It explains a reading skill and gives you a short activity. After completing the activity, continue reading the passage. *Applying Your Skills and Strategies* occurs two or three times in every passage. These are the activities you do *during reading*.

Thinking About the Passage. These are the activities you do *after reading*. Here you answer fill-in-the-blank, short-answer, and multiple-choice questions. Answering these questions will help you decide how well you understood what you just read.

Answers and Explanations

Answers and explanations to all exercise items begin on page 213. The explanation for multiple-choice exercises tells you why one answer choice is correct and why the other answer choices are incorrect.

INVENTORY

Use this Inventory before you begin Section 1. Don't worry if you can't easily answer all the questions. The Inventory will help you determine which areas you are already strong in and which you need to study further.

Read each passage and answer the questions that follow. Check your answers on pages 213–214. Then enter your scores on the chart on page 10. Use the chart to figure out which content areas to work on and where to find them in this book.

Read the following poem, "Sympathy," by Paul Laurence Dunbar.

I know what the caged bird feels, alas!
　When the sun is bright on the upland slopes;
When the wind stirs soft through the springing
　　grass,
And the river flows like a stream of glass;
　When the first bird sings and the first bud opes,
And the faint perfume from its chalice steals—
I know what the caged bird feels!

I know why the caged bird beats his wing
　Till its blood is red on the cruel bars;
For he must fly back to his perch and cling
When he fain would be on the bough a-swing;
　And a pain still throbs in the old, old scars
And they pulse again with a keener sting—
I know why he beats his wing!

I know why the caged bird sings, ah me,
　When his wing is bruised and his bosom sore,—
When he beats his bars and would be free;
It is not a carol of joy or glee,
　But a prayer that he sends from his heart's deep
　　core,
But a plea, that upward to Heaven, he flings—
I know why the caged bird sings!

To learn more about this poem, turn to page 237.

Items 1–6 refer to the poem on page vi.

Fill in the blanks with the word or words that best complete the statements.

1. The bird _____ itself when it beats its wings against the bars of the cage.

2. The caged bird in the poem wants to be _____.

3. The words *like a stream of glass* suggest that the river looks very

   _____.

Circle the number of the best answer for each question.

4. What general truth about life is suggested by this poem?

   (1) All creatures suffer when they are trapped.

   (2) People should protest against cruelty to animals.

   (3) Caged birds should not be allowed to see what they are missing.

   (4) The only true happiness is what people can find inside themselves.

   (5) Music solves all problems.

5. Which emotion does the author probably want the reader to experience while reading the poem?

   (1) joy

   (2) hope

   (3) yearning

   (4) fear

   (5) love

6. What kind of song would a person who feels like the caged bird be most likely to sing?

   (1) a song of thanksgiving

   (2) a patriotic march

   (3) a children's song

   (4) the blues

   (5) a rock 'n' roll tune

Read the following passage from the autobiography *Enter Talking* by Joan Rivers with Richard Meryman.

Beginners are constantly being used and abused. Desperately eager to be noticed, they are the perfect, defenseless victims. The biggest scam ever pulled on me was that summer of 1960. An agent called up and offered me fifteen dollars to emcee a Catholic church bazaar in Queens, Long Island—draw raffle tickets out of the bowl, do my act, etc. I said yes, thrilled to do it. The agent came with me—which was unusual—and at the stage door of the school auditorium, we were met by ladies with corsages and acetate dresses and blue hairdos. They kept saying to the agent, "Where is she? Where is she?" And he said, "Don't worry she'll be along."

I could hear a little band playing out front and feel a humming excitement and electricity in the air. As I was about to walk onstage, the agent said, "Good luck—and one more thing. When you get out there, tell them your name is Rosalind Russell."

I said, "Excuse me?"

He said, "When you get out there, just say your name is Rosalind Russell. I'll explain it to you later." He pushed me onstage.

The room was jammed with kids and parents and priests and nuns, crowds of people standing along the walls where banners read, WELCOME ROSALIND RUSSELL TO ST. IGNATIUS. YOU'RE OUR WOMAN OF THE YEAR. WE LOVE YOU, ROZ. And here I was, this short chunko standing there. I went to the microphone and said, "Hi, my name is Rosalind Russell also. I'm the other one. Isn't it a coincidence? I get this all the time."

They did not take it well. The place went crazy! A wave of hate rose over the footlights—yelling, stamping on the floor. Have you ever seen screaming priests? Nuns shaking their fists?

I tried to sing "I'll Never Forget What's His Name," but there was so much noise, my accompanist could not even hear my cue. Pretty soon I said, "I'm terribly sorry. Good night." And got off. The agent, who did not want to be lynched, had disappeared. I felt *terrible*. I had ruined their night. Can you imagine the anticipation, thinking that Rosalind Russell at her height as an actress is going to show up in Queens to close your bazaar? For fifteen dollars? Think of all the ladies figuring they were going home with a Polaroid shot of themselves with Rosalind Russell.

I called the agent up the next day and said, "How could you do that?" He said a lot of performers make a buck doing it. "How would you like to be Marilyn Monroe on Tuesday?"

To learn more about this passage, turn to page 240.

Items 7–11 refer to the passage on page 2.

Write your answers in the space provided.

7. Who is telling this story?

_____

8. The author concludes that the audience was not happy when they realized she was not Rosalind Russell. What details does the author give to support this conclusion?

_____

_____

Circle the number of the best answer for each question.

9. Which of the following sentences best states the main idea of the passage?

    (1) "The biggest scam ever pulled on me was that summer of 1960."

    (2) "When you get out there, tell them your name is Rosalind Russell."

    (3) "And here I was, this short chunko standing there."

    (4) "The place went crazy!"

    (5) "He said a lot of performers make a buck doing it."

10. Which word best describes how Joan Rivers felt when she was on-stage?

    (1) excited

    (2) angry

    (3) successful

    (4) sad

    (5) embarrassed

11. How does the author now seem to feel about this experience?

    (1) amused

    (2) bitter

    (3) angry

    (4) sad

    (5) disappointed

HELMER.   Oh, you think and talk like a heedless child.

NORA.   Maybe. But you neither think nor talk like the man I could bind myself to. As soon as your fear was over—and it was not fear for what threatened me, but for what might happen to you—when the whole thing was past, as far as you were concerned it was exactly as if nothing at all had happened. Exactly as before, I was your little skylark, your doll, which you would in future treat with doubly gentle care, because it was so brittle and fragile. (*Getting up.*) Torvald [his first name]—it was then it dawned upon me that for eight years I had been living here with a strange man, and had borne him three children—. Oh, I can't bear to think of it! I could tear myself into little bits!

HELMER (*sadly*).   I see, I see. An abyss has opened between us—there is no denying it. But, Nora, would it not be possible to fill it up?

NORA.   As I am now, I am no wife for you.

HELMER.   I have it in me to become a different man.

NORA.   Perhaps—if your doll is taken away from you.

HELMER.   But to part!—to part from you! No, no, Nora, I can't understand that idea.

NORA (*going out to the right*).   That makes it all the more certain that it must be done. (*She comes back with her cloak and hat and a small bag which she puts on a chair by the table.*)

HELMER.   Nora, Nora, not now! Wait till to-morrow.

NORA (*putting on her cloak*).   I cannot spend the night in a strange man's room.

HELMER.   But can't we live here like brother and sister—?

NORA (*putting on her hat*).   You know very well that would not last long. (*Puts the shawl around her.*) Good-bye, Torvald. I won't see the little ones. I know they are in better hands than mine. As I am now, I can be of no use to them.

HELMER.   But some day, Nora—some day?

NORA.   How can I tell? I have no idea what is going to become of me.

HELMER.   But you are my wife, whatever becomes of you.

NORA.   Listen, Torvald. I have heard that when a wife deserts her husband's house, as I am doing now, he is legally freed from all obligations towards her. In any case I set you free from all your obligations. You are not to feel yourself bound in the slightest way, any more than I shall. There must be perfect freedom on both sides. See, here is your ring back. Give me mine.

To find out more about this passage, turn to page 238.

Items 12–16 refer to the passage on page 4.

Write your answers in the space provided.

12. How long has the couple been married?

_____

13. Based on the stage directions, what will Nora probably do after she gets her ring back? How can you tell?

_____

_____

Circle the number of the best answer for each question.

14. Which word gives the best meaning for *abyss*?

    (1) agreement

    (2) argument

    (3) gap

    (4) road

    (5) family

15. What do you learn about Torvald Helmer?

    (1) He has become a different man.

    (2) He does not really understand what Nora wants.

    (3) He understands why his wife is upset.

    (4) He has been a cruel husband.

    (5) He is pleased by Nora's decision.

16. When Nora says that she was Torvald's *little skylark* and *doll*, she is suggesting that he

    (1) treated her like an equal.

    (2) was mean to her.

    (3) treated her like a pet or a toy.

    (4) acted like her brother.

    (5) had been the perfect husband.

"This is James T. Kirk, of the starship *Enterprise*, on a mission of peace. Please respond."

The speakers remained silent.

"Nothing, sir," Uhura said. "Complete silence."

"Go to visual," Jim said. "Simplest protocol. Black and white bit map, one bit per pixel. Give them the horizontal and vertical primes so they'll have a chance of deciphering the transmission before next Tuesday."

"Aye, sir. You're on visual . . . now."

"Everybody look peaceful," Jim said. Trying to appear relaxed, he gazed into the sensor. He rested his hands on his knees, palms up and open. The other people on the bridge faced the sensor and opened their hands. Aware of the irony of proving his peaceful intentions by opening his hands to beings who perhaps did not even have hands, Jim thought, You do what you can with what you've got.

"Sir, I'm getting a transmission!"

This was it; this was a first contact.

"Let's see it." Jim tried to keep his voice as matter-of-fact as Commander Spock's, but he failed. His pulse raced. He took a deep breath.

Picture elements formed lines; lines built up to form a two-dimensional surface.

Jim whistled softly.

"My mother's magnolias," McCoy whispered.

A being gazed at Jim from the slightly blurred image on the viewscreen.

He had no way to estimate its size, but it possessed a humanoid shape of delicate proportions.

Its face was less humanoid, though it had two eyes, a mouth, a nose. At least Jim assumed the organs to be analogous. The being's jaw and nose projected forward, and its huge, luminous eyes glowed in its dark face. A structure like a mustache surrounded the nostrils and bracketed the mouth, but it was neither hair nor a longer outgrowth of the being's short, sleek pelt. The structure was flesh, dark-pigmented and glistening. The being extended its tongue and delicately brushed the tip across the structure. What color it was he could not tell, for the transmission, like the one he had sent, arrived in black and white.

Outwardly calm, Jim struggled to maintain inner control. What he wanted to do was leap up and shout with glee.

To learn more about this passage, turn to page 239.

Items 17–22 refer to the passage on page 6.

Fill in the blanks with the word or words that best complete the statements.

17. The setting of the passage is on the _____ of a

    _____.

18. The captain and crew show that they come in friendship by

    _____ their hands.

19. This scene is about people who are making the _____

    _____ with an alien being.

Circle the number of the best answer to each question.

20. The being on the viewscreen is described as having *luminous eyes.* The best meaning for *luminous* is

    (1) dark.

    (2) glowing.

    (3) blind.

    (4) closed.

    (5) open.

21. Seeing the image of the being has what effect on Jim?

    (1) It makes him feel sick.

    (2) It frightens him.

    (3) He faints.

    (4) He relaxes.

    (5) He gets excited inside.

22. Why does the author have Jim say, *Black and white bit map, one bit per pixel*? The author wants to

    (1) suggest an advanced technology.

    (2) explain what *visual* means.

    (3) show how simple communication is.

    (4) suggest that Jim is not a human being.

    (5) make the reader laugh.

Jazz life on dream street: days of drizzly twilight, long spiky nights of taking a nick off Nirvana with a piano run or a horn solo, walking arm in arm into a rainy dawn with your next sad love affair. Meanwhile, real life on Lawrence Street: a two-story frame house in a working-class neighborhood of Washington. The den extension and the enlarged kitchen were not built by the man of the house, Shep Deering, but by his wife, who is handy with a hammer and saw. Her husband of 35 years still works as a mechanic for the Metropolitan Transit Authority. But, says Mrs. Deering, "I'd never marry a musician. I've seen so many bad marriages with musicians."

Mrs. Shep Deering has a night job herself—as a musician. She plays a fine jazz piano and sings a supernal jazz ballad. People like Miles Davis, Wynton and Branford Marsalis and Toots Thielemans play along with her. She also has a brand-new album that is hovering near the top of the *Billboard* jazz chart. *You Won't Forget Me* is the title. It may also be read as an unconditional guarantee: Shirley Horn is indelible.

"It's been written that Shirley Horn is back on the scene," Horn reflects. "Well, I haven't been anywhere. And I've been busy." All that busyness hasn't got her the kind of wide attention she deserves, until this moment. She's had a career for some 40 of her 55 years, but recognition, while often fervid, has been . . . well, say, finely focused. Sales on three of her albums in the early '80s were so slender that a persistent record company still bills her for production costs. If *You Won't Forget Me* keeps on sailing, she may actually see her first royalty check after about 30 years of recordmaking. "My secret is out of the closet now," she laughs.

More precisely, Horn is front and center, but her secret—her jazz essence—is still intact. It's what draws you first when you hear the smoky timber of her voice, the leisured elegance of her phrasing. And it's what holds you, wondering about the magic she brings to tunes as varied as *Don't Let the Sun Catch You Crying* and *You Won't Forget Me*. Says jazz critic Martin Williams: "She's not only good and tasteful, but she also has that wonderful sense of drama that can turn any little song into a three-minute one-act play." Horn concedes, "Well, I'm a good actress. I've never had a lot of pain."

Items 23–27 refer to the passage on page 8.

Write your answers in the space provided.

23. Shirley Horn is known for what kind of music?

_____

24. Why hasn't Shirley Horn received a royalty check for her recordings?

_____

_____

Circle the number of the best answer for each question.

25. Which statement is a fact about Shirley Horn's recent success?

   (1) Her new album is near the top of the *Billboard* jazz chart.

   (2) Recognition of her talent is overdue.

   (3) Her success is due to the popularity of jazz singing.

   (4) The secret of her jazz style has not changed.

   (5) She has a wonderful sense of drama.

26. What do you think Shirley Horn will do if *You Won't Forget Me* doesn't make a lot of money? She will

   (1) give up music altogether.

   (2) ask the record company for an advance.

   (3) go back to being a carpenter.

   (4) continue to play her music.

   (5) blame the critics.

27. Which statement best expresses the reviewer's opinion of Shirley Horn as a musician?

   (1) She is unforgettable.

   (2) She has been too busy to play well.

   (3) She is handy with a hammer.

   (4) She would be better off if she weren't married to a mechanic.

   (5) Her singing is not as good as her piano playing.

INVENTORY
Correlation Chart

Literature

The chart below will help you determine your strengths and weaknesses in interpreting literature and the arts.

Directions

Circle the number of each item that you answered correctly on the Inventory. Count the number of items you answered correctly in each row. Write the amount in the Total Correct space in each row. (For example, in the Popular Literature row, write the number correct in the blank before *out of 11*). Complete this process for the remaining rows. Then add the 3 totals to get your Total Correct for the whole 27-item Inventory.

Content Areas	Items	Total Correct	Pages
Popular Literature (Pages 12–105)	7, 8, 9, 10, 11 17, 18, 19, 20 21, 22	_____ out of 11	Pages 56–61, 93–95 Pages 20–25
Classical Literature (Pages 106–163)	1, 2, 3, 4, 5, 6 12, 13, 14, 15, 16	_____ out of 11	Pages 120–125 Pages 126–131
Commentary (Pages 164–201)	23, 24, 25, 26, 27	_____ out of 5	Pages 181–186, 192–195
TOTAL CORRECT FOR INVENTORY _____ out of 27			

If you answered fewer than 24 items correctly, look more closely at the three areas of literature covered. In which areas do you need more practice? Page numbers to refer to for practice are given in the right-hand column above.

Tips for Interpreting Literature

■ When the main idea is not directly stated, it is probably implied in the details and examples. To understand the unstated main idea, ask yourself the following questions: Who is doing something? What is being done? When is it happening? Where is it happening? Why is it being done? These questions will help you find the details that add up to the main idea.

■ Remember that restating an idea does not mean just repeating it. Each time the author adds another detail or example, the central idea of the passage is made clearer. Each supporting detail helps you to understand the author's purpose. The details help to bring the ideas to life.

■ When you are trying to draw a conclusion from the reading passage, you will have to use reasoning skills as well as comprehension skills. Identify the main idea and study the meanings of unfamiliar words from the context. Then come to a conclusion.

■ When you are reading to determine the mood of a passage, try to imagine yourself in the scene or situation. How would you feel? Imagine yourself as several of the characters. How would you feel as each one?

■ When you read a poem, pay attention to the details in the same way you would if you were reading a passage from a novel or a short story.

■ When you read a passage from a play, pay attention to the stage directions. The stage directions can give you information about the characters and the situation.

Study Skills

These are some things you can do to improve your study skills while reading this book.

■ Organize your time by making a schedule.

■ Find a quiet place to study.

■ Organize your study materials. Make sure you have pencils, pens, a notebook, and a dictionary.

■ Ask for help when you need it.

Unit 1

POPULAR LITERATURE

During the 1968 Olympics, Tommie Smith (center) and John Carlos (right) made their silent protest against racial injustice in the United States. Peter Norman from Australia is at the left.

Literature takes many forms. **Popular literature** includes several types of recently written works. The topics in popular literature may be the ordinary things people do in their day-to-day lives. The topics also may be ideas that people can only imagine.

Reading popular literature is not like reading a bus schedule or a weather report. You may read popular literature to entertain yourself or to relax after a hard day. You may read to find out more about a topic that interests you. Or you may read to find out more about other people or yourself. Whatever your reason for reading popular literature, the choice is yours. You can choose what to read, when to read, and how much time to spend reading.

Authors of popular literature have many ways to tell you about what people are thinking today. If you want to learn people's opinions or get information about a famous person's life, read popular nonfiction. Nonfiction is writing that is about real people and events. Essays, biographies, and autobiographies are examples of popular nonfiction. Essays give an author's opinion about a particular topic. Biographies and autobiographies tell the story of a person's life.

On the other hand, if you want to read a story that comes from a writer's imagination, try popular fiction. You might choose to curl up with a romantic novel or follow along as a detective solves a mystery.

Popular fiction includes short stories, novels, plays, and poems. Short stories tell about only one event or part of life. Novels are much longer. They can include many events, people, and experiences. Some popular novels even trace the history of families through several generations. Plays are unlike short stories or novels because they are meant to be acted out on a stage. Plays are written as conversations among the characters. Poets use words in a special way. The language in poetry is meant to show feelings and create images. Poetry can make you think about love, joy, loneliness, or the loss of something special.

Popular literature isn't hard to find. Many magazines carry short stories and poems as regular features. A local bookstore will have a special display of recent best-sellers and shelves of popular books ranging from westerns to romances.

Another way to find books is to go to a used-book store. Many people buy a book for a dollar and trade it in later for another book. The best way to find good popular literature is free. Go to the local public library. Some libraries have special sections for new books. If you need help, ask a librarian.

You can enjoy popular literature more when you know how it is written. Understanding difficult ideas and relationships gets easier as you read more.

This unit presents passages from all types of popular literature such as the following.

- The novels and the short story take a look at the variety of people and ideas that make up American culture.

- The plays deal with living with a disability and handling family relationships.

- The biographical passages look closely at the early lives of two well-known people.

- The essays offer opinions about the issues of government spending and giving directions.

Mystery Novel

Setting the Stage

Mystery novels are stories about solving a puzzle. The main character is often a detective who has to figure out who committed a crime. The detective has to find clues or collect facts about how and why a crime happened. Detecting often involves figuring out if people are lying or telling the truth. Most of the fun of reading mysteries is putting all the clues together to solve the puzzle.

Past: What you already know

You may have read a mystery story or seen a TV program about a mystery. If so, describe the puzzle the detective had to solve.

1. _____

_____

Present: What you learn by previewing

You can get a good idea of what you will be reading by looking at the title and reading the first few sentences. Read the first two **paragraphs. Name** the two characters.

2. _____

Future: What you predict

The passage on pages 15–17 is from a mystery novel called *The Ghostway*. Based on the title, what do you think the passage will be about?

3. _____

_____

Now reread the first two paragraphs. What do you predict will happen in the rest of the passage? Read on to find out if you are correct.

4. _____

_____

_____

Check your answers on page 214.

The Ghostway by Tony Hillerman

As you read each section, circle the words you don't know. Look up the meanings.

The night breeze was beginning now as it often did with twilight on the east slope of mountains. Nothing like the morning's dry gusts, but enough to ruffle the mare's ragged mane and replace the dead silence with a thousand little wind sounds among the ponderosas. Under cover of these whispers, Chee moved along the arroyo rim, looking for the horse thief.

He checked up the arroyo. Down the arroyo. Along the ponderosa timber covering the slopes. He stared back at the talus slope, where he had been when he'd heard the horse. But no one could have gotten there without Chee seeing him. There was only the death hogan and the holding pen for goats and the brush arbor, none of which seemed plausible. The thief must have tied his horse and then climbed directly up the slope across the arroyo. But why?

Just behind him, Chee heard a cough.

He spun, fumbling for his pistol. No one. Where had the sound come from?

He heard it again. A cough. A sniffling. The sound came from inside Hosteen Begay's hogan.

Chee stared at the corpse hole, a black gap broken through the north wall. He had cocked his pistol without knowing he'd done it. It was incredible. People do not go into a death hogan. People do not step through the hole into darkness. White men, yes. As Sharkey had done. And Deputy Sheriff Bales. As Chee himself, who had come to terms with the ghosts of his people, might do if the reason was powerful enough. But certainly most Navajos would not. So the horse thief was a white. A white with a cold and a runny nose.

Finding the Stated Main Idea.   The main idea of a paragraph or passage is the most important idea. The stated main idea of a paragraph tells you clearly what the important point of that paragraph is. For example, in the first paragraph of the passage, the stated main idea is "Under cover of these whispers, Chee moved along the arroyo rim, looking for the horse thief."

Applying Your Skills and Strategies

In the second paragraph, Chee thinks he knows something about the horse thief. Write the sentence that gives the stated main idea about what Chee thinks.

_____

_____

_____

Check your answer on page 214.

Chee moved quietly to his left, away from the field of vision of anyone who might be looking through the hole. Then he moved silently to the wall and along it. He stood beside the hole, back pressed to the planking. Pistol raised. Listening.

Something moved. Something sniffled. Moved again. Chee breathed as lightly as he could. And waited. He heard sounds and long silences. The sun was below the horizon now, and the light had shifted far down the range of colors to the darkest red. Over the ridge to the west he could see Venus, bright against the dark sky. Soon it would be night.

There was the sound of feet on earth, of cloth scraping, and a form emerged through the hole. First a stocking cap, black. Then the shoulders of a navy pea coat, then a boot and a leg—a form crouching to make its way through the low hole.

"Hold it," Chee said. "Don't move."

A startled yell. The figure jumped through the hole, stumbled. Chee grabbed.

He realized almost instantly he had caught a child. The arm he gripped through the cloth of the coat was small, thin. The struggle was only momentary, the product of panic quickly controlled. A girl, Chee saw. A Navajo. But when she spoke, it was in English.

"Turn me loose," she said, in a breathless, frightened voice. "I've got to go now."

Chee found he was shaking. The girl had handled this startling encounter better than he had. "Need to know some things first," Chee said. "I'm a policeman."

"I've got to go," she said. She pulled tentatively against his grip and relaxed, waiting.

Identifying Details. The details of a paragraph or passage support the main idea. Details are facts about a person, place, thing, event, or time. Details answer the questions *who, what, when, where, why,* and *how.* For example, the passage above gives several details about the time during which this part of the story takes place, such as: the sun is below the horizon, the light is dark and red, and the planet Venus is visible in the dark sky.

Applying Your Skills and Strategies

Reread the passage above. As you read, write three details that tell more about the person Chee finds.

_____

_____

"Your horse," Chee said. "You took her last night from over at Two Gray Hills."

"Borrowed it," the girl said. "I've got to go now and take her back."

"What are you doing here?" Chee asked. "In the hogan?"

"It's my hogan," she said. "I live here."

Check your answer on page 214.

"It is the hogan of Hosteen Ashie Begay," Chee said. "Or it was. Now it is a *chindi* hogan. Didn't you notice that?"

It was a foolish question. After all, he'd just caught her coming out of the corpse hole. She didn't bother to answer. She said nothing at all, simply standing slumped and motionless.

"It was stupid going in there," Chee said. "What were you doing?"

"He was my grandfather," the girl said. For the first time she lapsed into Navajo, using the noun that means the father of my mother. "I was just sitting in there. Remembering things." It took her a moment to say it because now tears were streaming down her cheeks. "My grandfather would leave no *chindi* behind him. He was a holy man. There was nothing in him bad that would make a *chindi*."

"It wasn't your grandfather who died in there," Chee said. "It was a man named Albert Gorman. A nephew of Ashie Begay." Chee paused a moment, trying to sort out the Begay family. "An uncle of yours, I think."

The girl's face had been as forlorn as a child's face can be. Now it was radiant. "Grandfather's alive? He's really alive? Where is he?"

"I don't know," Chee said. "Gone to live with some relatives, I guess. We came up here last week to get Gorman, and we found Gorman had died. And that." Chee pointed at the corpse hole. "Hosteen Begay buried Gorman out there, and packed up his horses, and sealed up his hogan, and went away."

The girl looked thoughtful.

"Where would he go?" Chee asked. The girl would be Margaret Sosi. No question about that. Two birds with one stone. One stolen pinto mare and the horse thief, plus one missing St. Catherine's student. "Hosteen Begay is your mother's father. Would he . . . ?" He remembered then that the mother of Margaret Billy Sosi was dead.

"No," Margaret said.

"Somebody else then?"

"Almost everybody went to California. A long time ago. My mother's sisters. My great-grandmother. Some people live over on the Cañoncito Reservation, but . . . " Her voice trailed off, became suddenly suspicious. "Why do you want to find him?"

To find out more about this passage, turn to page 238.

Identifying Details. The details of a passage can give more information about how the characters feel. In the part of the passage that begins at the bottom of page 16, several details are given that help show how the young girl feels, such as: she stood slumped and motionless and tears streamed down her face.

Applying Your Skills and Strategies

Reread the part of the passage that begins at the bottom of page 16. Then write three more details that describe how Margaret feels.

_____

_____

_____

Check your answer on page 214.   Section 1: Mystery Novel   17

Thinking About the Story

Find the words listed below in the passage and underline them. Read the words and other sentences that surround each of these words. Then complete the following sentences by writing the correct words in the blanks.

gusts	hogan	*chindi*	arroyo
ponderosa	tentatively	forlorn	plausible

1. A Navajo home is called a _____ .

2. A _____ is the bad spirit or ghost left behind when a person dies.

3. In autumn, _____ of wind blow the leaves around.

4. If you believe a story could be true, you think it is

   _____ .

5. The man stood _____ on his sprained ankle and found it hurt too much to walk.

6. The sad news made the woman feel _____ .

7. An _____ is a deep channel caused by a flood.

8. The _____ pine is a kind of tree.

Write your answers in the space provided.

9. Review your predictions on page 14. Were you right about what happened? If you said *yes*, write what you correctly predicted. If not, write two or three things that you didn't expect to happen.

   _____

   _____

10. What are Chee's first clues to the horse thief's hiding place?

    _____

11. How do Chee and the girl meet?

    _____

12. To whom does the hogan belong?

    _____

Check your answers on page 214.

Circle the number of the best answer.

13. What did Margaret Sosi think had happened to her grandfather?

    (1) He had gone on vacation.

    (2) He had killed Albert Gorman.

    (3) He had been arrested by the police officer.

    (4) He had died in the hogan.

    (5) He had stolen the horse.

Write your answers in the space provided.

14. Why does Chee first think the horse thief cannot be a Navajo?

    _____

    _____

15. Now that Chee has found the horse thief, what other crime do you think he is trying to solve?

    _____

16. Hosteen Begay is a Navajo like Chee and Margaret. Why do you think he left his home?

    _____

    _____

17. Do you think Chee was right to have his pistol ready when he went up to the corpse hole? Why or why not?

    _____

    _____

18. If you were the detective, what would you do next? Why?

    _____

19. Have you ever been involved in a real-life mystery or puzzle? For example, you may have misplaced your keys or your wallet. If so, what did you do to figure out what happened? If not, what do you think you might do to solve the puzzle?

    _____

    _____

    _____

Section 2

Science Fiction

Setting the Stage

Science fiction is fiction that shows us what life and people might be like in another time or place. Science fiction is often set in the future, in outer space or on other planets. It is called science fiction because the stories are based on the possibilities found through science. Examples are space travel, communication with other species, or human beings who develop new and wonderful powers. Much science fiction is adventurous and scary, while some is very hopeful.

Past: What you already know

You may have read science fiction or seen movies based on this kind of writing. If so, describe a problem the main character had to solve.

1. _____

_____

Present: What you learn by previewing

You can get a good idea of what you will be reading by looking at the title and reading the first few sentences. Read enough of the passage to list three of the characters below.

2. _____

_____

Future: What you predict

The passages on pages 21–23 are from a science fiction story called "I, Robot." Based on the title, what do you think the passage will be about?

3. _____

_____

Now read the first few sentences. What do you predict the passage will be about? Read on to find out if you are correct.

4. _____

_____

I, Robot by Isaac Asimov

*As you read each
section, circle the
words you don't
know. Look up the
meanings.*

Alfred Lanning met Dr. Calvin just outside his office. He lit a nervous cigar and motioned her in.

He said, "Well, Susan, we've come pretty far, and Robertson's getting jumpy. What are you doing with The Brain?"

Susan Calvin spread her hands, "It's no use getting impatient. The Brain is worth more than anything we forfeit on this deal."

"But you've been questioning it for two months."

The psychologist's voice was flat, but somehow dangerous, "You would rather run this yourself?"

"Now you know what I meant."

"Oh, I suppose I do," Dr. Calvin rubbed her hands nervously. "It isn't easy. I've been pampering it and probing it gently, and I haven't gotten anywhere yet. Its reactions aren't normal. Its answers—they're queer, somehow. But nothing I can put my finger on yet. And you see, until we know what's wrong, we must just tiptoe our way through. I can never tell what simple question or remark will just . . . push him over . . . and then— Well, and then we'll have on our hands a completely useless Brain. Do you want to face that?"

"Well, it can't break the First Law."

"I would have thought so, but—"

"You're not even sure of that?" Lanning was profoundly shocked.

"Oh, I can't be sure of anything, Alfred—"

The alarm system raised its fearful clangor with a horrifying suddenness. Lanning clicked on communications with an almost paralytic spasm. The breathless words froze him.

He said, "Susan . . . you heard that . . . the ship's gone. I sent those two field men inside half an hour ago. You'll have to see The Brain again."

Identifying the Implied Main Idea.   The main idea is the most important idea of a paragraph or a passage. In fiction the main idea is often not stated, but is only suggested or implied by the author. This means you must figure out or infer the main idea yourself. To do this read the entire passage and think about what is going on. What are the characters saying or thinking or doing? Read between the lines. What do the stated facts seem to show? What is the author hinting?

*Applying
Your Skills
and
Strategies*

In the passage so far, Dr. Calvin and Dr. Lanning are talking about a third character, The Brain. Reread the passage and write the implied main idea.

_____

_____

_____

Susan Calvin said with enforced calm, "Brain, what happened to the ship?"

The Brain said happily, "The ship I built, Miss Susan?"

"That's right. What has happened to it?"

"Why, nothing at all. The two men that were supposed to test it were inside, and we were all set. So I sent it off."

"Oh—Well, that's nice." The psychologist felt some difficulty in breathing. "Do you think they'll be all right?"

"Right as anything, Miss Susan. I've taken care of it all. It's a bee-yoo-tiful ship."

"Yes, Brain, it *is* beautiful, but you think they have enough food, don't you? They'll be comfortable?"

"Plenty of food."

"This business might be a shock to them, Brain. Unexpected, you know."

The Brain tossed it off, "They'll be all right. It ought to be interesting for them."

"Interesting? How?"

"Just interesting," said The Brain, slyly.

"Susan," whispered Lanning in a fuming whisper, "ask him if death comes into it. Ask him what the dangers are."

Susan Calvin's expression contorted with fury, "Keep quiet!" In a shaken voice, she said to The Brain, "We can communicate with the ship, can't we, Brain?"

"Oh, they can hear you if you call by radio. I've taken care of that."

"Thanks. That's all for now."

Once outside, Lanning lashed out ragingly, "Great Galaxy, Susan, if this gets out, it will ruin all of us. We've got to get those men back. Why didn't you ask if there was danger of death—straight out?"

"Because," said Calvin, with a weary frustration, "that's just what I can't mention. If it's got a case of dilemma, it's about death. Anything that would bring it up badly might knock it completely out. Will we be better off then? Now, look, it said we could communicate with them. Let's do so, get their location, and bring them back. They probably can't use the controls themselves; The Brain is probably handling them remotely. Come!"

Identifying the Implied Main Idea. Reread the dialogue between Dr. Calvin and the Brain in this second passage. What is the implied main idea? The stated facts give you some clues. Can The Brain answer the questions Dr. Calvin asks? (yes) This is a clue about The Brain's abilities. Can The Brain answer in more than one way—happily or slyly for instance? (yes) This is another clue about what The Brain is capable of doing.

Applying Your Skills and Strategies

Put these clues together and read between the lines. Write the implied main idea.

_____

_____

It was quite a while before Powell shook himself together.

"Mike," he said out of cold lips, "did you feel any acceleration?"

Donovan's eyes were blank, "Huh? No . . . no."

And then the redhead's fists clenched and he was out of his seat with sudden frenzied energy and up against the cold, wide-curving glass. There was nothing to see—but stars.

He turned, "Greg, they must have started the machine while we were inside. Greg, it's a put-up job; they fixed it up with the robot to jerry us into being the try-out boys, in case we were thinking of backing out."

Powell said, "What are you talking about? What's the good of sending us out if we don't know how to run the machine? How are we supposed to bring it back? No, this ship left by itself, and without any apparent acceleration." He rose, and walked the floor slowly. The metal walls dinned back the clangor of his steps.

He said tonelessly, "Mike, this is the most confusing situation we've ever been up against."

"That," said Donovan, bitterly, "is news to me. I was just beginning to have a very swell time, when you told me."

Powell ignored that. "No acceleration—which means the ship works on a principle different from any known."

"Different from any we know, anyway."

"Different from *any* known. There are no engines within reach of manual control. Maybe they're built into the walls. Maybe that's why they're thick as they are."

"What are you mumbling about?" demanded Donovan.

"Why not listen? I'm saying whatever powers this ship is enclosed, and evidently not meant to be handled. The ship is running by remote control."

"The Brain's control?"

"Why not?"

To find out more about this passage, turn to page 237.

"Then you think we'll stay out here till The Brain brings us back."

"It could be. If so, let's wait quietly. The Brain is a robot. It's got to follow the First Law. It can't hurt a human being."

Recognizing Supporting Details.

In the last passage The Brain sent two men and a space ship into space. In this passage the implied main idea is this: The men in the ship are smart enough to figure out what has happened to them.

Applying Your Skills and Strategies

On the lines below, write three facts or details the men said that support this implied main idea. What facts have the men figured out?

_____

_____

_____

_____

Thinking About the Story

Find the numbered words below and underline them in the passage. Read the words and other sentences that surround each of these words. Then match each word with its meaning. Write the letter of the meaning by each word.

_____ 1. pampering

_____ 2. clangor

_____ 3. contorted

_____ 4. dilemma

_____ 5. acceleration

_____ 6. manual

_____ 7. remote control

_____ 8. paralytic

a. unable to move

b. moving, or speeding up

c. twisted

d. a problem

e. a harsh, ringing noise

f. by hand

g. spoiling, or taking special care of

h. control from a distance

Write your answers in the space provided.

9. Review your prediction on page 20. Were you right about what happened? If you said *yes*, write what you correctly predicted. If not, write two or three things that you didn't expect to happen.

_____

_____

10. Who is The Brain?

_____

11. What is the First Law?

_____

12. What do the two doctors fear will happen to the men in the ship?

_____

13. Why does Dr. Calvin have to be so careful about what she says to The Brain?

_____

Circle the number of the best answer.

14. Which statement best expresses the implied main idea of the entire passage?

    (1) Robots can be a problem if they act on their own.

    (2) Robots are angry about being used by human beings.

    (3) Robots are always smarter than human beings.

    (4) Robots make life easier for human beings.

    (5) Robots are able to build things.

15. Which of the following statements does not support the implied main idea of the entire passage?

    (1) The Brain is worth a great deal of money.

    (2) The Brain has sent two men into outer space without being told to do so.

    (3) The Brain answers Susan's questions in a sly unhelpful manner.

    (4) The Brain has provided food for the men in the ship.

    (5) The Brain has set up only one-way contact with the men in the ship.

Write your answers in the space provided.

16. Which of the two doctors do you think has more power? Why?

    _____

    _____

17. Do you think the men will be safe? Why or why not?

    _____

    _____

18. If you were Mike and Greg, what other steps would you take to figure out what is going on and to protect yourselves?

    _____

    _____

    _____

    _____

Section 3

Biography

Setting the Stage

A **biography** is a true story about the life of a real person. The author of a biography is called a *biographer*. Some biographers meet and talk to the people they write about. Other biographers have to rely on diaries, letters, and other records to write the story. These authors try to find out as much as they can about the time and place in which the person lived. Biographies tell about the important events, people, and decisions that affected a person's life. Biographies often explain reasons why a person is successful or famous.

Past: What you already know

You may have read a biography of a well-known person or watched a TV program based on someone's life. If so, name the person and problem the person faced.

1. _____

_____

Present: What you learn by previewing

You can get a good idea of what you will be reading by looking at the title and reading the first few sentences. Read the title and the first paragraph of the passage. What is going on in the life of Langston Hughes at this point?

2. _____

Read enough of the passage to find out where the action begins. What is the name of the place?

3. _____

Future: What you predict

The passage on pages 27–29 is from a biography of Langston Hughes. Read the first two paragraphs. What do you predict you will learn about this man's life? Read on to find out if you are correct.

4. _____

_____

Check your answers on page 215.

<u>Langston Hughes: A Biography</u> by Milton Meltzer

As you read each section, circle the words you don't know. Look up the meanings.

Heading for Harlem he took his first subway ride. The train rushed madly through the tunnel, green lights punctuating the dark and stations suddenly glaring whitely and then blacking out. He counted off the numbered signs till 135th Street and got off. The platform was jammed with people—colored people—on their way to work. Lugging his heavy bags up the steps, he came out breathless on the corner of Lenox Avenue. The September morning was clear and bright. He stood there, feeling good. It was a crazy feeling—as though he had been homesick for this place he had never been to.

He walked down the block to register at the YMCA, the first place young Negroes stayed when they hit Harlem. That afternoon he crossed the street to visit the Harlem Branch Library. All newcomers were swiftly made at home there by Miss Ernestine Rose, the white librarian, and her *café-au-lait* assistant, Catherine Latimer, who had charge of the Schomburg Collection. Here you could drown in thousands and thousands of books by and about black folks. That night, dazzled by the electric signs on the marquee, he went into the Lincoln Theatre to hear a blues singer.

Identifying Point of View. A point of view is a way of looking at a situation. In a biography, the author is telling someone else's story. Biographers can tell the story through the eyes of an outsider, telling facts but not telling how the person feels. Biographers can also tell the story from the person's own point of view, telling both the facts and how the person feels.

Applying Your Skills and Strategies

In the passage above, Langston Hughes has been experiencing many new things. The author doesn't just watch the young man. He tries to make the reader understand how Hughes feels. Write three words or phrases that describe how Hughes is feeling.

_____

_____

_____

He had a week to himself before classes began at Columbia, and he spent every moment mapping Harlem with his feet. The great dark expanse of this island within an island fascinated him. In 1921 it ran from 127th Street north to 145th, and from Madison Avenue west to Eighth Avenue. Eighty thousand black people (it would be three times that number within ten years) were packed into the long rows of once private homes as the flood of Southern Negroes continued to roll North. It was a new black colony in the midst of the Empire City, the biggest of the many "Bronzevilles" and "Black Bottoms" beginning to appear across the nation.

Check your answer on page 215.

The high rents charged Negroes and the low wages paid them made Harlem a profitable colony for landlords and merchants, but a swollen, aching slum for the people who lived there. To the boy from the Midwest, however, this was not yet its meaning. He had been in love with Harlem long before he got there, and his dream was to become its poet. That first week of wonderful new insights and sounds passed swiftly. He loved the variety of faces—black, brown, peach, and beige—the richest range of types any place on earth. He hated to move out of Harlem, but his tuition was paid at Columbia and he felt he had to go. At the dormitory office they looked startled when he showed up for his room key. There must be some mistake, they told him; no room was left. He did not know it but Columbia did not allow Negroes to live in the dormitories. There was a big flurry when he insisted he had made a reservation long ago, by mail. He got the room finally, but it was a token of what was to come.

The university was too big, too cold. It was like being in a factory. Physics, math, French—he had trouble with all of them and the instructors were too busy or too indifferent to help. His only friend was Chun, a Chinese boy who didn't like Columbia either. Nobody asked the yellow man or the black man to join a fraternity and none of the girls would dance with them. Not being used to this, Chun expected them to. Langston didn't.

Nothing went right at school. Langston stopped studying, spent very little time on campus and all the time he could in Harlem or downtown. He made the city his school, read a lot of books, and dented his allowance badly buying tickets night after night for the all-Negro musical hit *Shuffle Along*, whose songs were written by Noble Sissle and Eubie Blake. His mother, separated again from Homer Clarke, showed up in New York and he had to help her with money while she looked for work.

Drawing Conclusions. When you draw a conclusion, you make a decision or form an opinion based on facts and details. To draw a conclusion from something you have read, find two or more stated ideas that lead to a decision or an opinion that is not directly stated.

Applying Your Skills and Strategies

Reread the passage above. What can you conclude about how Langston Hughes felt about Columbia University and about Harlem?

_____

_____

_____

_____

All the time, feeling out of place at Columbia, he kept writing poems. That winter he sent several to *The Crisis*, and in January his "Negro" appeared, with these lines, which open and close the poem:

I am a Negro:
Black as the night is black,
Black like the depths of my Africa.

The editors of *The Crisis* awoke to the fact that the boy who had been sending them poems from Toluca was now in New York. They invited him to lunch. Langston panicked, imagining they were all so rich or remote that he wouldn't know what to say. Much as he admired Dr. Du Bois, he was afraid to show the great man how dumb he was. He went, anyhow, taking along his mother for anchorage. Although they tried to put him at ease, telling him how much the readers liked his work, he was too scared to see any more of them.

Despite the little amount of time he said he spent on the campus, he did not do badly at Columbia. His final grades show three Bs, a C, and a failing F in physical education. He was given no grade at all in mathematics because he was absent so often. He made no honors, but he didn't care, perhaps because it was honor enough to see his poems printed in *The Crisis* month after month. One of the staff even arranged for him to read his poems at the Community Church. These were signs that he was not standing still. But neither was he moving in the direction his father wanted him to go. So he wrote and said he was quitting college and going to work. He wouldn't ask for money any more.

His father never answered.

Langston was on his own. His mother had gone back to Cleveland. He took a room by himself in Harlem, and began to hunt for a job. It was June 1922, and business was booming. At least it looked like it from the number of help-wanted ads in the papers. Langston wasn't trained for much, so he followed up the unskilled jobs. But no matter what he applied for—office boy, busboy, clerk, waiter—the employer would always say he wasn't looking for a colored boy.

He turned to the employment agencies. It was no use here, either. Where was the job for a black man who wanted to work? Everyone was trying to prove Langston's father was right: the color line wouldn't let you live.

To find out more about this passage, turn to page 239.

Drawing Conclusions. Reread the last two paragraphs of the passage above. What can you conclude about the situation of African-American men in 1921?

Applying Your Skills and Strategies

_____

_____

_____

_____

Check your answer on page 215.

Thinking About the Story

Find the numbered words below and underline them in the passage. Read the words and other sentences that surround each of these words. Then match each word with its meaning. Write the letter of the meaning by each word.

_____ 1. *café-au-lait*

_____ 2. dazzled

_____ 3. marquee

_____ 4. flurry

_____ 5. fraternity

_____ 6. anchorage

a. a men's club on campus

b. a large, lighted sign

c. a means of being secure

d. the color of coffee with milk

e. a rush of activity

f. impressed by something shiny

Write your answers in the space provided.

7. Review your predictions on page 26. Were your predictions correct? If you said *yes*, write what you learned. If not, write two things you had not expected to learn.

_____

_____

_____

8. How did Hughes spend his first days in New York?

_____

_____

9. What details support the conclusion that Hughes did not do badly at Columbia?

_____

_____

10. What are two reasons Hughes had trouble finding a job?

_____

_____

Check your answers on page 216.

Circle the number of the best answer for each question.

11. Which of the following is the best meaning for the phrase *mapping Harlem with his feet*?

   (1) taking a course in map making

   (2) walking all over Harlem

   (3) counting his footsteps

   (4) finding directions by reading a map

   (5) wasting time in Harlem

12. Hughes went to lunch with the editors of *The Crisis*. Based on what you read in the passage, what can you conclude about *The Crisis*? It is

   (1) part of Columbia University.

   (2) a Negro musical hit.

   (3) the group that published his poetry.

   (4) a division of the public library.

   (5) a New York restaurant.

Write your answers in the space provided.

13. In what way was the housing situation in Harlem like the dorms at Columbia?

   _____

   _____

14. Why do you think Langston's father didn't answer Langston's letter about leaving school?

   _____

   _____

15. What do you think Langston will do next?

   _____

16. Imagine that you have just arrived in a large city you have never been in before. What city would you like to go to? What places and events would you want to see first?

   _____

   _____

Section
4

Drama

Setting the Stage

Plays are stories written to be acted out on a stage. Reading a play is different from reading a novel or a short story. This is because the action in a play is not described in paragraphs. Instead, plays are made up of conversations, called dialogue. Each time a person speaks, the name of that person is given. The lines of dialogue follow. Understanding what a play is about means figuring out what is happening between the speakers, or characters. Popular plays are often about the problems people have.

Past: What you already know

You may have seen a play at a local theater or at a school. If so, what was the main idea of the play or what problem was it about?

1. _____

_____

_____

Present: What you learn by previewing

You can get a good idea of what you will be reading by looking at some of the dialogue. Read the first few lines of the play. Write the names of the two characters having a conversation.

2. _____

_____

Future: What you predict

The passage on pages 33–35 is from a play called *Butterflies Are Free*. Read the rest of the dialogue on page 33. What do you predict the characters will talk about in the rest of the passage? Read on to find out if you are correct.

3. _____

_____

_____

Check your answers on page 216.

Butterflies Are Free by Leonard Gershe

As you read each section, circle the words you don't know. Look up the meanings.

DON: Right. And I don't meet a stranger and say, "Hi, Don Baker—blind as a bat."

JILL: I think you should've told me. I would've told you.

DON: Well . . . I wanted to see how long it would take for you to catch on. Now you know. Do you want to run screaming out into the night or just faint?

JILL: How can you make jokes?

DON: Listen, the one thing that drives me up the wall is pity. I don't want it and I don't need it. Please—don't feel sorry for me. I don't feel sorry for me, so why should you?

JILL: You're so . . . adjusted.

DON: No, I'm not. I never *had* to adjust. I was born blind. It might be different if I'd been able to see and then went blind. For me, blindness is normal. I was six years old before I found out everyone else wasn't blind. By that time it didn't make much difference. So, let's relax about it. Okay? And if we can have a few laughs, so much the better.

JILL: A few laughs? About *blindness*?

DON: No, not about blindness. Can't you just forget that?

JILL: I don't know. You're the first blind person I've ever met.

DON: Congratulations. Too bad they don't give out prizes for that.

JILL: I've seen blind men on the street—you know, with dogs. Why don't you have a dog?

DON: They attract too much attention. I'd rather do it myself.

Drawing Conclusions About Characters in Drama. The characters in a play usually are not described directly. You have to figure out what the people are like. Sometimes the characters say or suggest how they feel about themselves and the world around them. Characters may also state their opinions about other people in the play. The dialogue in a play gives you clues about why the characters act the way they do. A character might joke at one time and be serious at another. Keep in mind that a character might not always be telling the truth. As you read the passage, draw conclusions about the characters.

Applying Your Skills and Strategies

In the passage so far, Don and Jill have been talking about Don's blindness. What conclusion can you draw about Jill's attitude toward Don?

_____

_____

_____

_____

Check your answer on page 216.

JILL: But isn't it rough getting around New York? It is for me!

DON: Not at all. I manage very well with my cane. I've got so I know exactly how many steps to take to the grocery . . . the laundry . . . the drugstore.

JILL: Where's a laundry? I need one.

DON: Next to the delicatessen. Forty-four steps from the front door.

JILL: I didn't see it.

DON: I'll show it to you.

JILL: What about here in the apartment? Aren't you afraid of bumping into everything? You could hurt yourself.

DON: I've memorized the room. (*Moves around the room with grace and confidence, calling off each item as he touches it or points to it*) Bed . . . bathroom . . . bookcase . . . guitar . . . my cane. (*He holds up the white aluminum walking stick, then puts it back on the shelf*)

JILL: What are those books?

DON: Braille . . . Front door . . . tape recorder. (*Moving on*) Dining table . . . bathtub. (*Walks quickly to the chest of drawers against the door to* JILL'S *apartment*) Chest of drawers. (*Touching the things on top*) Wine . . . more wine . . . glasses. (*He opens the top drawer*) Linens. (*Closes the drawer; opens the front door and shuts it; moves on to the kitchen*) Kitchen . . . (*He opens the cabinet over the sink*) Dishes . . . cups . . . glasses. (*He opens the next cabinet*) Coffee . . . sugar . . . salt and pepper . . . corn flakes . . . ketchup . . . etcetera. (*Returning to* JILL) Now, if you'll put the ashtray back. (*She replaces the ashtray on the table, and* DON *stamps out his cigarette in it. He sits on the sofa and holds out his arms with bravura*) Voilà! If you don't move anything, I'm as good as anyone else.

Understanding Setting in Drama. The setting of a play tells where and when the action takes place. You can find out about the setting in two ways. The dialogue may give clues about where the characters are. For example, a person might describe the furniture in a room. Or a character might talk about the time of day. The stage directions may also give clues about the setting. Stage directions are the words in parentheses that tell the actors what to do. Stage directions also describe what things look like and where they are on the stage.

Applying Your Skills and Strategies

Reread the passage above. Where are Don and Jill? What helped you figure this out?

_____

_____

_____

_____

JILL: Better . . . I can't find anything in my place. The ketchup usually winds up in my stocking drawer and my stockings are in the oven. If you really want to see chaos, come and look at . . . (*She catches herself, self-consciously*) I mean . . . I meant . . .

DON: I know what you mean. Relax. I'm no different from anyone else except that I don't see. The blindness is nothing. The thing I find hard to live with is other people's reactions to my blindness. If they'd only behave naturally. Some people want to assume guilt—which they can't because my mother has that market cornered—or they treat me as though I were living in some Greek tragedy, which I assure you I'm not. Just be yourself.

JILL: I'll try . . . but I've never met a blind person before.

DON: That's because we're a small, very select group—like Eskimos. How many Eskimos do you know?

JILL: I never thought blind people would be like you.

DON: They're not all like me. We're all different.

JILL: I mean . . . I always thought blind people were kind of . . . you know . . . spooky.

DON: (*In a mock-sinister voice*) But, of course. We sleep all day hanging upside-down from the shower rod. As soon as it's dark, we wake up and fly into people's windows. That's why they say, "Blind as a bat."

JILL: No, seriously . . . don't blind people have a sixth sense?

DON: No. If I had six senses, I'd still have five, wouldn't I? My other senses—hearing, touch, smell—maybe they're a little more developed than yours, but that's only because I use them more. I have to.

Identifying Conflict in Drama.

A play is often based on a conflict or problem between the characters. The conflict can come from different opinions or ways of life. The dialogue gives clues about what the conflict is. As the play goes along, the characters may try to work out a solution. They may agree and start to understand one another. Or they may never be able to solve their differences.

Applying Your Skills and Strategies

Reread the passage. What is Don and Jill's conflict?

_____

_____

_____

JILL: Boy, I think it's just so great that you aren't bitter. You don't seem to have any bitterness at all. (*She shifts to sitting on the sofa, burying her feet under a cushion*) I've moved. I'm sitting on the sofa now.

DON: I know.

JILL: How did you know?

DON: I heard you—and your voice is coming from a different spot.

JILL: Wow! How do you do it?

To find out more about this passage, turn to page 237.

Thinking About the Play

Find the words below and underline them in the passage. Read the words and other sentences that surround each of these words. Try to figure out the meaning of each word. Then complete the following sentences by writing the correct words in the blanks provided.

delicatessen	self-consciously	bravura
braille	sinister	

1. Blind people can read special books written in _____ .

2. When someone speaks in a _____ voice, that person may seem to be evil.

3. A _____ is a type of store that sells food.

4. Making a move with _____ means doing it in a bold way.

5. The man looked around _____ when he realized that everyone was looking at him.

Write your answers in the space provided.

6. Review your prediction on page 32. Was your prediction correct? If you said *yes*, write what they said. If not, write two subjects you did not expect them to talk about.

_____

_____

_____

7. When did Don realize that most other people are not blind?

_____

8. From the stage directions, what can you conclude about where Jill lives?

_____

9. What does Don mean by "my mother has that market cornered"?

_____

_____

Check your answers on page 216.

10. What conclusion can you draw about Don's character?

    (1) He is bitter about being blind.

    (2) He is independent and funny.

    (3) He enjoys being taken care of.

    (4) He doesn't know how to laugh at himself.

    (5) He enjoys making people feel uncomfortable.

11. How does Don react to the conflict between Jill and himself?

    (1) He ignores the problem.

    (2) He gets angry at Jill for asking questions.

    (3) He admits that Jill's opinion is right.

    (4) He explains how he feels about being blind.

    (5) He decides he should develop a sixth sense.

Write your answers in the space provided.

12. Whose attitude about blindness do you think is more positive? Why?

    _____

    _____

    _____

13. Why do you think Don objects to other people's attitudes about his blindness?

    _____

    _____

    _____

14. Imagine that you have a physical disability like Don. How would you want other people to act around you?

    _____

    _____

    _____

    _____

Section 5

Poetry

Setting the Stage

Poetry uses language in a special way. In a poem the writer tries to help the reader both see and experience the scene. Poets usually use fewer words than other writers do. They do not just give facts or information. Often they use words that show emotion. Some words may bring a picture, or an image, to the reader's mind. Many poems are about feelings or experiences that everyone has had. When you read a poem, ask yourself, "How does this make me feel?"

Past: What you already know

You may have read a poem in a book or magazine. Describe how the poem made you feel.

1. _____

_____

Present: What you learn by previewing

You can get an idea of what you will be reading by looking at the title and the first few lines. In poetry, when the word *I* is used, the main character is the speaker, not the poet. Read the first few lines of the first poem. Describe the main character.

2. _____

_____

Future: What you predict

The poem on pages 39–40 is titled "The Thirty Eighth Year of My Life." Based on the title, what do you think the poem will be about? Read on to find out if you are correct.

3. _____

The poem on page 41 is called "The Picture on the Mantel." Read the first few lines of the poem. What do you predict this poem will be about? Then read on to find out if you are correct.

4. _____

The Thirty Eighth Year of My Life
by Lucille Clifton

As you read each section, circle the words you don't know. Look up the meanings.

the thirty eighth year
of my life,
plain as bread
round as a cake
an ordinary woman.

an ordinary woman.

i had expected to be
smaller than this,
more beautiful
wiser in Afrikan ways,
more confident,
i had expected
more than this.

i will be forty soon.
my mother once was forty.

my mother died at forty four,
a woman of sad countenance
leaving behind a girl
awkward as a stork.
my mother was thick,
her hair was a jungle and
she was very wise
and beautiful
and sad.

Identifying Figurative Language. Instead of using words and phrases as they normally are used, figurative language uses words in a special way to make a point. Some figurative language compares two things that are very different. In the passage above, the poet compares her mother's hair to a jungle. By using figurative language, she forcefully makes the point that her mother's hair is hard to control (wild).

In this passage the poet compares herself to both bread and cake. What two points is she making about herself?

Applying Your Skills and Strategies

_____

_____

_____

Check your answer on page 217.

i have dreamed dreams
for you mama
more than once.
i have wrapped me
in your skin
and made you live again
more than once.
i have taken the bones you hardened
and built daughters
and they blossom and promise fruit
like Afrikan trees.
i am a woman now.
an ordinary woman.

in the thirty eighth
year of my life,
surrounded by life,
a perfect picture of
blackness blessed.
i had not expected this
loneliness.

if it is western,
if it is the final
Europe in my mind,
if in the middle of my life
i am turning the final turn
into the shining dark
let me come to it whole
and holy
not afraid
not lonely

out of my mother's life
into my own
into my own.

*To find out more
about this poem,
turn to page 237.*

i had expected more than this.
i had not expected to be
an ordinary woman.

*Applying
Your Skills
and
Strategies*

Summarizing. Like other forms of writing, poetry can be summarized.
A **summary** is a short statement of the main idea and the most important
supporting details.

Reread the whole poem. Write a short summary of it.

_____

_____

Check your answer on page 217.

A Picture on the Mantel
by James Lafayette Walker

All he knew about his mom
Was the picture of her face
That always seemed to have been on
The mantel by a vase.
He didn't have the love that every
Child of five should know
That only mothers can extend
Mixed with a warming glow.
One day while shopping with his dad
He stopped and gave a stare
"Look, Dad, look, can't you see
That's mother over there?"
"That isn't mother," said the dad
"Your mother's now with God."
"Are you sure, Dad, are you sure?"
Dad gave a knowing nod.
The dad said "Please excuse my son"
As tears welled in his eyes
"He's too young to understand
when someone precious dies."
The child said to the lady,
"But you have my mother's face."
He longed for her to hold him
In a mother's fond embrace.
"Are you a mother?" He then asked
"Why yes," she sadly smiled
"Will you hold me close?", he begged
The mother held the child.

To find out more about this poem, turn to page 240.

Identifying Details. Details are facts that tell you more about the main idea. Some details help you understand how the characters are thinking and feeling.

The little boy in this poem is unsure about what happened to his mother. The father understands how confused his son feels. He explains this to the woman in the store. The father shows his understanding in two ways. Find two details that show how the father feels.

Applying Your Skills and Strategies

_____

_____

_____

_____

Check your answer on page 217.

Thinking About the Poems

Find the numbered words below in the poems and underline them. Read the words and other sentences that surround each of these words. Then match each word with its meaning. Write the letter of the meaning by each word.

_____ 1. countenance	a. a hug
_____ 2. awkward	b. the shelf above a fireplace
_____ 3. mantel	c. very valuable
_____ 4. extend	d. offer
_____ 5. precious	e. clumsy
_____ 6. embrace	f. face

Write your answers in the space provided.

7. Review your predictions on page 38. Were your predictions correct? If you said *yes*, write two things you were right about. If not, write two things you did not expect to find out.

_____

_____

_____

8. What four things had the speaker in "The Thirty Eighth Year of My Life" expected to be at the age of 38?

_____

_____

9. "A Picture on the Mantel" is like a story. Summarize the story in three or four sentences.

_____

_____

_____

_____

Check your answers on page 217.

Circle the number of the best answer for each question.

10. The speaker in "The Thirty Eighth Year of My Life" speaks about her mother and her own daughters. From these lines you can conclude that the speaker

    (1) disliked her mother.

    (2) wishes she had sons instead of daughters.

    (3) was trying to be like her mother.

    (4) dreams too much.

    (5) wants to go back to Africa.

11. The speaker in "The Thirty Eighth Year of My Life" realizes that she is unhappy with her life. What does she want to do?

    (1) accept her own life as it is

    (2) be more ordinary

    (3) die at forty-four like her mother

    (4) go to Europe

    (5) have more children

Write your answers in the space provided.

12. In what way are the speaker in "The Thirty Eighth Year of My Life" and the boy in "A Picture on the Mantel" alike? Why do you think this is important in each poem?

    _____

    _____

    _____

13. What is the boy in "A Picture on the Mantel" looking for? Do you think meeting the woman in the store will give the boy what he needs?

    _____

    _____

14. Both poems are about people who have lost someone close to them. Have you ever lost someone you felt very close to? What do you miss most about that person?

    _____

    _____

Thriller Novel

Setting the Stage

Thriller novels are scary stories. Thrillers may be about witches or vampires or ghosts. They are about the unknown. Reading a thriller novel can make you shiver, cause chills to run up your spine, or make the hair on the back of your neck stand up. Even so, a thriller usually makes readers want to keep reading. This is because they need to find out what will happen. For many people, the scarier a thriller story is, the better.

Past: What you already know

You may have seen a movie or TV show that was a thriller. If so, what was it about? Were you scared? Why?

1. _____

_____

_____

Present: What you learn by previewing

You can get a good idea of what you will be reading by looking at the title and reading the first few sentences of a story. Read the first few sentences of the passage to find out about the main character. What is the name of the main character? How old is he?

2. _____

Future: What you predict

The passage on pages 45–47 is from a novel called *'Salem's Lot*. Read the first four paragraphs. What do you predict the passage will be about? Read on to find out if you are correct.

3. _____

_____

_____

Check your answers on page 218.

'Salem's Lot by Stephen King

As you read each section, circle the words you don't know. Look up the meanings.

When he first heard the distant snapping of twigs, he crept behind the trunk of a large spruce and stood there, waiting to see who would show up. *They* couldn't come out in the daytime, but that didn't mean *they* couldn't get people who could; giving them money was one way, but it wasn't the only way. Mark had seen that guy Straker in town, and his eyes were like the eyes of a toad sunning itself on a rock. He looked like he could break a baby's arm and smile while he did it.

He touched the heavy shape of his father's target pistol in his jacket pocket. Bullets were no good against *them*—except maybe silver ones—but a shot between the eyes would punch that Straker's ticket, all right.

His eyes shifted downward momentarily to the roughly cylindrical shape propped against the tree, wrapped in an old piece of toweling. There was a woodpile behind his house, half a cord of yellow ash stove lengths which he and his father had cut with the McCulloch chain saw in July and August. Henry Petrie was methodical, and each length, Mark knew, would be within an inch of three feet, one way or the other. His father knew the proper length just as he knew that winter followed fall, and that yellow ash would burn longer and cleaner in the living room fireplace.

His son, who knew other things, knew that ash was for men—things—like *him*. This morning, while his mother and father were out on their Sunday bird walk, he had taken one of the lengths and whacked one end into a rough point with his Boy Scout hatchet. It was rough, but it would serve.

Identifying Point of View in Fiction.

Applying Your Skills and Strategies

An author can write about characters from several different points of view. From one point of view, the author seems to know everything each character is thinking or feeling. From another point of view, the author tells the story as if it were seen through the eyes of only one character. The character telling the story is called the narrator.

From what point of view is this passage written? Who is the narrator?

_____

_____

He saw a flash of color and shrank back against the tree, peering around the rough bark with one eye. A moment later he got his first clear glimpse of the person climbing the hill. It was a girl. He felt a sense of relief mingled with disappointment. No henchman of the devil there; that was Mr. Norton's daughter.

Check your answers on page 218.

His gaze sharpened again. She was carrying a stake of her own! As she drew closer, he felt an urge to laugh bitterly—a piece of snow fence, that's what she had. Two swings with an ordinary tool box hammer would split it right in two.

She was going to pass his tree on the right. As she drew closer, he began to slide carefully around his tree to the left, avoiding any small twigs that might pop and give him away. At last the synchronized little movement was done; her back was to him as she went on up the hill toward the break in the trees. She was going very carefully, he noted with approval. That was good. In spite of the silly snow fence stake, she apparently had some idea of what she was getting into. Still, if she went much further, she was going to be in trouble. Straker was at home. Mark had been here since twelve-thirty, and he had seen Straker go out to the driveway and look down the road and then go back into the house. Mark had been trying to make up his mind on what to do himself when this girl had entered things, upsetting the equation.

Perhaps she was going to be all right. She had stopped behind a screen of bushes and was crouching there, just looking at the house. Mark turned it over in his mind. Obviously she knew. How didn't matter, but she would not have had even that pitiful stake with her if she didn't know. He supposed he would have to go up and warn her that Straker was still around, and on guard. She probably didn't have a gun, not even a little one like his.

Understanding the Setting.   Setting tells where and when the action takes place. Look for clues to find out what the setting is. For example, look for words that describe objects that are near the characters.

Applying Your Skills and Strategies

Describe the setting of the passage so far.

_____

_____

_____

He was pondering how to make his presence known to her without having her scream her head off when the motor of Straker's car roared into life. She jumped visibly, and at first he was afraid she was going to break and run, crashing through the woods and advertising her presence for a hundred miles. But then she hunkered down again, holding on to the ground like she was afraid it would fly away from her. She's got guts even if she is stupid, he thought approvingly.

Straker's car backed down the driveway—she would have a much better view from where she was; he could only see the Packard's black roof—hesitated for a moment, and then went off down the road toward town.

He decided they had to team up. Anything would be better than going up to that house alone. He had already sampled the poison atmosphere that enveloped it. He had felt it from a half a mile away, and it thickened as you got closer.

Now he ran lightly up the carpeted incline and put his hand on her shoulder. He felt her body tense, knew she was going to scream, and said, "Don't yell. It's all right. It's me."

She didn't scream. What escaped was a terrified exhalation of air. She turned around and looked at him, her face white. "W-Who's me?"

He sat down beside her. "My name is Mark Petrie. I know you; you're Sue Norton. My dad knows your dad."

"Petrie . . . ? Henry Petrie?"

"Yes, that's my father."

"What are you doing here?" Her eyes were moving continually over him, as if she hadn't been able to take in his actuality yet.

"The same thing you are. Only that stake won't work. It's too . . ." He groped for a word that had checked into his vocabulary through sight and definition but not by use. "It's too flimsy."

She looked down at her piece of snow fence and actually blushed. "Oh, that. Well, I found that in the woods and . . . and thought someone might fall over it, so I just—"

To find out more about this passage, turn to page 238.

He cut her adult temporizing short impatiently: "You came to kill the vampire, didn't you?"

Identifying Supporting Details. The main idea of a passage is supported by details. The main idea of this part of the passage is that Mark and Sue have something in common in a scary situation. Mark thinks they need to team up.

Mark points out two things he and Sue have in common. What are they?

_____

_____

_____

_____

Thinking About the Story

Find the words below in the passage and underline them. Read the words and other sentences that surround each of these words. Try to figure out the meanings of the words. Then complete the following sentences by writing the correct words in the blanks provided.

momentarily	cylindrical	pondering
methodical	glimpse	incline
synchronized	hunkered	

1. When you look briefly at a tree, you get only a _____ of it.

2. Alan is very _____ ; he always works in a very careful and precise way.

3. Mark spent several days _____ the problem, trying to think of a solution.

4. She _____ down, kneeling on her hands and knees, close to the ground.

5. It took him only a short time to ride his bike up the

   _____ to the top of the hill.

6. Something that has the shape of a tube is _____ .

7. Ellen stopped watching the road _____ , and in that moment she had the accident.

8. Figure skating pairs must always be _____ , carefully making their movements at the same time.

Write your answers in the space provided.

9. Review your prediction on page 44. Were you right? If you said *yes*, write what you correctly predicted. If not, write two things you didn't expect to happen.

   _____

   _____

10. What two things does Sue do that make Mark approve of her?

   _____

    Check your answers on page 218.

Circle the best answer for each question.

11. Who do you think *They* are?

    (1) other kids

    (2) men from town

    (3) girls

    (4) vampires

    (5) Mark and Sue's fathers

12. How do you think Mark and Sue are planning to kill the vampire?

    (1) by shooting him

    (2) with a wooden stake

    (3) with a knife

    (4) by running him down with a car

    (5) by burning him

Write your answers in the space provided.

13. How did Sue feel when Mark put his hand on her shoulder?

    _____

14. Mark's father knows practical facts about good wood. Mark thinks he knows about "other things." What kinds of things does Mark think he knows about?

    _____

    _____

15. Stephen King creates suspense by not telling us right away why Mark and Sue are there. Did he make you wonder what was going to happen? Why or why not?

    _____

    _____

16. Have you ever worried that someone else's actions might upset your own plans? If so, what did you do? If not, write what you would do if you were in Mark's situation.

    _____

    _____

    _____

Section 7

Popular Novel

Setting the Stage

Popular novels are recently written books about people and events that are not real. Popular fiction, such as *I, Robot,* may be about ideas that the reader can only imagine. However, popular novels often are about ordinary people in their daily lives. The central idea of this type of popular novel might be families, love, marriage, or work. These novels entertain, but they also show that people have many things in common with each other. We can learn more about ourselves by reading about people who have problems similar to ours.

Past: What you already know

You may have read a novel or seen a movie about people in an everyday situation. If so, what was the situation?

1. _____

_____

Present: What you learn by previewing

You can get a good idea of what you will be reading by looking at the title and reading a few sentences. Read the first few sentences of the passage and list the three characters below.

2. _____

Future: What you predict

The passage on pages 51–53 is from a novel called *The Women of Brewster Place.* Based on the title, what do you think the passage will be about?

3. _____

_____

Read the first few paragraphs. Now what do you predict the passage will be about? Read on to find out if you are correct.

4. _____

_____

Check your answers on page 218.

The Women of Brewster Place by Gloria Naylor

As you read each section, circle the words you don't know. Look up the meanings.

"Miss Johnson, you wanna dance?" A handsome teenager posed himself in a seductive dare before Etta. She ran her hand down the side of her hair and took off her apron.

"Don't mind if I do." And she pranced around the table.

"Woman, come back here and act your age." Mattie speared a rib off the grill.

"I am acting it—thirty-five!"

"Umph, you got *regrets* older than that."

The boy spun Etta around under his arms. "Careful, now, honey. It's still in working order, but I gotta keep it running in a little lower gear." She winked at Mattie and danced toward the center of the street.

Mattie shook her head. "Lord keep her safe, since you can't keep her sane." She smiled and patted her foot under the table to the beat of the music while she looked down the street and inhaled the hope that was bouncing off swinging hips, sauce-covered fingers, and grinning mouths.

*Applying
Your Skills
and
Strategies*

Using Context Clues. Sometimes you will see an unfamiliar word in a passage. Pay attention to the words and sentences around the unfamiliar word. This is the context of the word. Details are one type of context clue that can help you guess the meaning of a word.

The first paragraph states, "a teenager posed himself in a seductive dare." *Seductive* may be a new word for you. In this sentence, the word means "to behave in a flirting way." One clue to the meaning is that the boy has asked the woman to dance. What details in the next few sentences also help you figure out what the word means?

_____

_____

_____

A thin brown-skinned woman, carrying a trench coat and overnight case, was making her way slowly up the block. She stopped at intervals to turn and answer the people who called to her—"Hey, Ciel! Good to see you, girl!"

Ciel—a knot formed at the base of Mattie's heart, and she caught her breath. "No."

Ciel came up to Mattie and stood in front of her timidly. "Hi, Mattie. It's been a long time."

"No." Mattie shook her head slowly.

"I know you're probably mad at me. I should have written or at least called before now."

"Child." Mattie placed a hand gently on Ciel's face.

"But I thought about you all the time, really, Mattie."

"Child." Both of Mattie's hands cupped Ciel's face.

"I had to get away; you know that. I needed to leave Brewster Place as far behind me as I could. I just kept going and going until the highway ran out. And when I looked up, I was in San Francisco and there was nothing but an ocean in front of me, and since I couldn't swim, I stayed."

"Child. Child." Mattie pulled Ciel toward her.

"It was awful not to write—I know that." Ciel was starting to cry. "But I kept saying one day when I've gotten rid of the scars, when I'm really well and over all that's happened so that she can be proud of me, then I'll write and let her know."

"Child. Child. Child." Mattie pressed Ciel into her full bosom and rocked her slowly.

"But that day never came, Mattie." Ciel's tears fell on Mattie's chest as she hugged the woman. "And I stopped believing that it ever would."

"Thank God you found that out." Mattie released Ciel and squeezed her shoulders. "Or I woulda had to wait till the Judgment Day for this here joy."

She gave Ciel a paper napkin to blow her nose. "San Francisco, you said? My, that's a long way. Bet you ain't had none of this out there." She cut Ciel a huge slice of angel food cake on her table.

"Oh, Mattie, this looks good." She took a bite. "Tastes just like the kind my grandmother used to make."

"It should—it's her recipe. The first night I came to Miss Eva's house she gave me a piece of that cake. I never knew till then why they called it angel food—took one bite and thought I had died and gone to heaven."

Ciel laughed. "Yeah, Grandma could cook. We really had some good times in that house. I remember how Basil and I used to fight. I would go to bed and pray, God please bless Grandma and Mattie, but only bless Basil if he stops breaking my crayons. Do you ever hear from him, Mattie?"

Mattie frowned and turned to baste her ribs. "Naw, Ciel. Guess he ain't been as lucky as you yet. Ain't run out of highway to stop and make him think."

Drawing Conclusions.
To draw a conclusion, use two or more stated ideas to come up with an idea that was not directly stated in the text.

Give two facts from the passage above that support the conclusion that Ciel and Mattie have known each other for a very long time.

Applying Your Skills and Strategies

_____

_____

Check your answer on page 218.

Etta came back to the table out of breath. "Well, looka you!" She grabbed Ciel and kissed her. "Gal, you looking good. Where you been hiding yourself?"

"I live in San Francisco now, Miss Etta, and I'm working in an insurance company."

"Frisco, yeah, that's a nice city—been through there once. But don't tell me it's salt water putting a shine on that face." She patted Ciel on the cheeks. "Bet you got a new fella."

Ciel blushed. "Well, I have met someone and we're sort of thinking about marriage." She looked up at Mattie. "I'm ready to start another family now."

. . . Mattie beamed.

"But he's not black." She glanced hesitantly between Etta and Mattie.

"And I bet he's *not* eight feet tall, and he's *not* as pretty as Billy Dee Williams, and he's *not* president of Yugoslavia, either," Etta said. "You know, we get so caught up with what a man *isn't*. It's what he is that counts. Is he good to you, child?"

"And is he good for you?" Mattie added gently.

"Very much so." Ciel smiled.

"Then, I'm baking your wedding cake." Mattie grinned.

"And I'll come dance at your reception." Etta popped her fingers.

Mattie turned to Etta. "Woman, ain't you done enough dancing today for a lifetime?"

"Aw, hush your mouth. Ciel, will you tell this woman that this here is a party and you supposed to be having a good time."

To find out more about this passage, turn to page 239.

"And will you tell that woman," Mattie said, "that hip-shaking is for young folks, and old bags like us is supposed to be behind these tables selling food."

"You two will never change." Ciel laughed.

Visualizing Characters. Sometimes characters in fiction are described in detail. Sometimes we learn very little about a character. Either way, the characters become more alive if you can form mental pictures of them. To visualize a character, use all the details you can find about how the character looks. What the person does and says also helps create a mental picture. Based on the passage, describe what you think Etta looks like.

Applying Your Skills and Strategies

_____

_____

_____

_____

Check your answer on page 218.

Thinking About the Story

Find the numbered words below in the passage and underline them. Read the words and other sentences that surround each of these words. Then match each word with its meaning. Write the letter of the meaning by each word.

_____ 1. posed	a. breathed in
_____ 2. pranced	b. spaces in time between events
_____ 3. inhaled	c. brush liquid on roasting meat
_____ 4. intervals	d. in an unsure way
_____ 5. baste	e. stood in a way intended to impress
_____ 6. hesitantly	f. walked in a proud, happy way

Write your answers in the space provided.

7. Review your prediction on page 50. Were you right about what happened? If you said *yes,* write what you correctly predicted. If not, write two things you did not expect to happen.

_____

_____

8. Where has Ciel been?

_____

9. You have already found the meaning of the word *intervals*. What two clues in the surrounding words and sentences helped you figure out the meaning?

_____

_____

10. Etta and Mattie are different in personality. Review your description of Etta. Now, how do you visualize Mattie?

_____

_____

_____

Check your answers on page 218.

Circle the number of the best answer for each question.

11. What do the details in the passage tell you about the setting? These people are at

    (1) a family reunion.

    (2) Etta's birthday party.

    (3) an outdoor neighborhood party.

    (4) a San Francisco restaurant.

    (5) a wedding reception.

12. What can you conclude about why Ciel had left Brewster Place?

    (1) She had had some kind of personal trouble.

    (2) She had left to go to college.

    (3) She wanted to see the ocean.

    (4) Her grandma had died.

    (5) Her friend Mattie had sent her away.

Write your answers in the space provided.

13. How do the two women feel about Ciel's new boyfriend?

_____

_____

14. Do you think Ciel will feel comfortable being back at Brewster Place? Why?

_____

_____

_____

15. Do you know of a person who returned home after being away for a long time? Why had the person left? How was that person greeted?

_____

_____

_____

_____

Section
8

<u>Autobiography</u>

Setting the Stage

Autobiographies are books in which people tell their own life stories. The story is told from the point of view of the subject. Like biographies, autobiographies describe the important events, people, and decisions that affect a person's life. Autobiographies are different because we learn about the person's thoughts and feelings in a very personal way. The author does not need to find out about what happened in the person's life. Instead, the author is the one who actually has had the experiences.

Past: What you already know

You may have read an autobiography of a famous person or seen a TV show in which someone told his or her own life story. Who was the autobiography about? Why was the person famous?

1. _____

_____

Present: What you learn by previewing

You can get a good idea of what you will be reading by looking at the title and reading a few sentences. Read the first few sentences of the passage. Who is this autobiography about? What is going on in the life of this person at this time?

2. _____

_____

Future: What you predict

The passage on pages 57–59 is from an autobiography called *Say Hey*. Now read the first paragraph. What do you predict the passage will be about? Read on to find out if you are correct.

3. _____

_____

_____

Say Hey by Willie Mays with Lou Sahadi

As you read each section, circle the words you don't know. Look up the meanings.

I reported to Fort Eustis, Virginia. They discovered pretty quickly that I was a ball player. I went through the regular basic training, which didn't bother me, since I was in good shape. We played games against some other Army camps and colleges, and I came across other major-leaguers: Johnny Antonelli of the Braves, Vernon Law of the Pirates, and Lou Skizas of the Yankees. Although there were plenty of photographs showing me marching, they didn't take many of me playing ball, which is how the Army really used me most of the time. Of course, I enjoyed it. I was raised to say "Yes, sir," and I always respected authority, so the Army and I got along very well.

Meanwhile, Leo was looking after me even while I was in the service. Somehow, he would find out things that would disturb him. Once he found out that I sprained an ankle while I was playing basketball. He told me, "No more basketball, Willie." Another time he called me over an unnecessary chance I had taken—I tried to steal a base with my team leading. Leo couldn't stand dumb plays, even if he was a few hundred miles away and it wasn't even his team. When he got excited he would scream and talk so fast he sounded like Donald Duck. Leo used to send me a little money now and then, I think just to let me know he still cared.

Besides playing, I was also an instructor—not in how to use a hand grenade, but how to throw and catch and hit. One of the soldiers I was talking to suddenly said to me, "Try it my way," and he held his glove in front of his stomach, but with the palm up. I tried it and it felt more comfortable. My body was aligned correctly. I adopted that style. It came to be called my "basket" catch. What it allowed me to do was have my hands in the correct position to make a throw instantly. What's wrong with it, though, is that you tend to take your eyes off the ball at the last second. Still, I dropped only a couple of flies in my career that way.

Understanding Cause and Effect.

Applying Your Skills and Strategies

When something happens as the result of something else, the two events have a cause-and-effect relationship. The cause is what makes something happen. The effect is what happens. In the passage above, Willie Mays sprains his ankle playing basketball. Playing basketball is the cause, and a sprained ankle is the effect. To find cause and effect when you read, first ask yourself what has happened. Then find out what made it happen.

What happened as a result of the army finding out Mays was a baseball player?

_____

_____

_____

My worst time in the service came the day I heard my mother had died while giving birth to her eleventh child. I now had ten brothers and sisters, the oldest only eighteen. So there were a lot of younger ones to look after. I had always thought of them as my brothers and sisters. Now, certainly, the Army would let me out to be with them and take care of them. I always have believed that if a lesser-known soldier had gone through that ordeal, he would have been free to leave. I don't know whether the Army was concerned because the public thought it would be playing favorites, or whether there was just some technicality. All I knew then was that I was very sad. Even though my aunts had raised me, I had remained close to my mother and her new family. Now, although I wasn't much older than some of my brothers and sisters, I felt responsible for taking care of them. It didn't help my final months in the Army.

It was a cold late-winter day when I was discharged from Fort Eustis on March 1, 1954, and left immediately for the Giants' spring-training site in Phoenix. The Giants sent Frank Forbes from New York to meet me and send me off to Arizona. I didn't have an overcoat, so Frank took his off and gave it to me. It was two sizes too big, but I put it on anyway, probably looking like a scarecrow, or a panhandler. Frank stuffed some newspapers under his sports jacket for insulation. We must have been a sight when we arrived in Washington to catch a train for Phoenix. We had some time to kill, so naturally I suggested we go to the movies. When we got out, we were stopped by two F.B.I. agents. They must have thought they were arresting Dillinger, the way they grabbed us when we left the theater! . . . it turned out to be a case of mistaken identity. It turned out that they had been tipped off that two guys they were looking for might be in the same movie theater. I guess we did look sort of suspicious, after all.

I finally made my train, but I didn't stay on it for long. It made a stop in New Orleans, and I got off to get a sandwich and a soda. I didn't do it quickly enough, though, and when I got back to the track, the train had gone. I had to call Leo and tell him I was going to be late.

Understanding Cause and Effect. Certain words and phrases can help you identify cause-and-effect relationships. Look for expressions such as *because*, *so*, *the reason for*, and *as a result*. These words are clues that lead to information about why something happened.

Applying Your Skills and Strategies

In the passage above, Willie arrives in New York in March without an overcoat. What is the effect of this action? What clue word did you recognize?

_____

_____

"Didn't they teach you about trains in the Army?" he said. He sounded exasperated, but I could tell he probably was laughing about the whole thing.

Check your answers on page 219.

I couldn't wait to see all the guys, to be in the old locker room, to be on the same field again. I had heard that things hadn't been the same. There wasn't much joking around the clubhouse anymore. I guess when you finish fifth and aren't even playing .500 ball, there's not much to laugh about, especially when Leo is there every day kicking and screaming when things don't go the way he likes. I hoped that my return would make a difference in terms of morale. I always tried to keep things light, and I know the guys used to enjoy making fun of me and my squeaky voice. Even though I had played part of two seasons with the Giants, I was still three years younger than anyone else on the club.

I finally got to the ballpark. When I went into the clubhouse, Eddie Logan, the equipment manager, was the first person I saw. He didn't say anything to me. I thought maybe he didn't recognize me. I found my locker and changed into my uniform. I was alone. The players were already on the field when I walked onto the Arizona diamond for the first time in two years. Nobody said anything to me, and I was beginning to wonder what was going on. Then I remembered: the silent treatment. It's a way that ball players have of not showing emotion, of doing just the opposite of how they feel. We'd do that after someone hit a home run, say, a player who normally wasn't a long-ball hitter. He'd come back to the bench all excited, and we'd just sit there, yawning, or just looking out into space, and it would drive him crazy because he'd be looking for someone to say something nice, a pat on the back, anything at all.

Just when I was starting to get a little annoyed, someone yelled out, "Hey, Leo, here comes your pennant!" Leo turned around and with a big grin he rushed at me and grabbed me in a bear hug that took the wind out of me. The last time I had seen him do that to someone was when Thomson's homer won the pennant for us against Brooklyn. I couldn't even grab a bat and take some swings, though. Leo explained that I had to sign a contract first.

"Hey, give me the pen," I told him.

"Don't you even want to know how much we're paying you?" he asked.

"I'll sign for whatever they're offering me," I told him.

I trusted Leo, but I also loved playing baseball so much that I hardly cared what my salary was. I guess that always showed through. When I was in the Army, I once saw a tap dancer at a nightclub. He could make his feet fly, he was having so much fun. He'd laugh and say, "It's a shame to take the money." He said it for a laugh, but somehow I could tell that he really meant it. That's just how I always felt about baseball.

To find out more about this passage, turn to page 239.

Understanding the Author's Purpose. Sometimes authors tell the reader directly why they included certain details to make a point. In the passage above, Mays tells the reader why he included the example of the tap dancer. What was Mays' purpose?

*Applying
Your Skills
and
Strategies*

Check your answer on page 219.

Thinking About the Story

Find the words below in the passage and underline them. Study the context in which the words appear. Then complete the following sentences by writing the correct words in the blanks provided.

authority   ordeal   suspicious

technicality   morale

1. A team that feels good about itself has good _____ .

2. The people in charge have _____ over the others.

3. A small detail that has meaning to only a certain group is called a

   _____ .

4. You might be _____ if you noticed someone waiting around for several hours on a street corner late at night.

5. Getting through the _____ of the fire took courage and patience.

Write your answers in the space provided.

6. Review your prediction on page 56. Were you right? If you said *yes*, write what you correctly predicted. If not, write two things that you didn't expect to find out.

   _____

   _____

   _____

7. How did Mays feel about being in the army after he found out his mother had died?

   _____

   _____

   _____

8. What is the baseball player's version of *the silent treatment*?

   _____

   _____

Check your answers on page 219.

9. What made the FBI agents mistake Frank and Willie for criminals? Frank and Willie

   (1) had tipped off the FBI.

   (2) had sneaked into the movie without paying.

   (3) were dressed in odd-looking clothes.

   (4) were acting in an odd manner.

   (5) had been meeting with the criminal Dillinger.

10. What caused Willie Mays to be late getting to spring training?

    (1) The FBI agents had delayed him.

    (2) He didn't know what train to take.

    (3) He took too long getting his snack in New Orleans.

    (4) Leo made him feel he wasn't wanted.

    (5) The army discharged him too late in the day.

Write your answers in the space provided.

11. What kind of person do you think Willie Mays is?

    _____

    _____

12. What does Mays want the reader to understand about his relationship with Leo?

    _____

    _____

13. If you were one of the New York Giants, how would you feel about having Willie Mays back on the team?

    _____

    _____

14. Is there something you feel as strongly about as Mays does about baseball? Would you do it even if you didn't get paid?

    _____

    _____

    _____

Check your answers on page 219.

Drama

Setting the Stage

Many plays are about the funny side of life. A play that is meant to be funny is called a **comedy**. Even though the characters may have serious problems, the author wants to make the audience laugh. The conflict may not be funny, but the way the characters behave is. People in a comedy may act foolishly, but most comedies have happy endings.

Past: What you already know

You may have seen a comedy at a theater or on TV. What was the comedy about?

1. _____

_____

Present: What you learn by previewing

You can get a good idea of what you will be reading by looking at the title and reading a few lines of the play. Read the first few lines of the play. What are the names of the characters?

2. _____

_____

Future: What you predict

The passage on pages 63–65 is from a play called *Crimes of the Heart*. Based on the title, what do you think the passage will be about?

3. _____

_____

Read the rest of the passage on page 63. Now what do you predict the passage will be about? Read on to find out if you are correct.

4. _____

_____

_____

Check your answers on page 220.

Crimes of the Heart by Beth Henley

As you read each section, circle the words you don't know. Look up the meanings.

MEG: But, Babe, we've just got to learn how to get through these real bad days here. I mean, it's getting to be a thing in our family. *Slight pause as she looks at Babe:*   Come on, now. Look, we've got Lenny's cake right here. I mean, don't you wanna be around to give her her cake, watch her blow out the candles?

BABE, *realizing how much she wants to be here:*   Yeah, I do, I do. 'Cause she always loves to make her birthday wishes on those candles.

MEG: Well, then we'll give her her cake and maybe you won't be so miserable.

BABE: Okay.

MEG: Good. Go on and take it out of the box.

BABE: Okay. *She takes the cake out of the box. It is a magical moment.* Gosh, it's a pretty cake.

MEG, *handing her some matches:*   Here now. You can go on and light up the candles.

BABE: All right. *She starts to light the candles.* I love to light up candles. And there are so many here. Thirty pink ones in all, plus one green one to grow on.

MEG, *watching her light the candles:*   They're pretty.

BABE: They are. *She stops lighting the candles.* And I'm not like Mama. I'm not so all alone.

MEG: You're not.

BABE, *as she goes back to lighting candles:*   Well, you'd better keep an eye out for Lenny. She's supposed to be surprised.

Making Inferences.

Making Inferences.   When you make an inference, you are figuring out something the author is suggesting but not stating directly. To make an inference, use the facts that are given and what you already know to find out what the author is suggesting.

Applying Your Skills and Strategies

In the first few lines of this passage, Meg asks whether Babe wants to be around to give Lenny the cake. Babe says that she does. What inference can you make about what Babe had been planning to do instead?

_____

_____

MEG: All right. Do you know where she's gone?

BABE: Well, she's not here inside—so she must have gone on outside.

MEG: Oh, well, then I'd better run and find her.

BABE: Okay; 'cause these candles are gonna melt down.
   Meg starts out the door.

MEG: Wait—there she is coming. Lenny! Oh, Lenny! Come on! Hurry up!

Check your answer on page 220.

BABE, *overlapping and improvising as she finishes lighting the candles:*
Oh, no! No! Well, yes—Yes! No, wait! Wait! Okay! Hurry up!
Lenny enters. Meg covers Lenny's eyes with her hands.

LENNY, *terrified:* What? What is it? What?

MEG AND BABE: Surprise! Happy birthday! Happy birthday to Lenny!

LENNY: Oh, no! Oh, me! What a surprise! I could just cry! Oh, look: *Happy birthday, Lenny—A Day Late!* How cute! My! Will you look at all those candles—it's absolutely frightening.

BABE, *a spontaneous thought:* Oh, no, Lenny, it's good! 'Cause—'cause the more candles you have on your cake, the stronger your wish is.

LENNY: Really?

BABE: Sure!

LENNY: Mercy! *Meg and Babe start to sing.*

LENNY, *interrupting the song:* Oh, but wait! I—can't think of my wish! My body's gone all nervous inside.

MEG: . . . Lenny—Come on!

BABE: The wax is all melting!

LENNY: My mind is just a blank, a total blank!

MEG: Will you please just—

BABE, *overlapping:* Lenny, hurry! Come on!

LENNY: Okay! Okay! Just go!

Meg and Babe burst into the "Happy Birthday" song. As it ends, Lenny blows out all the candles on the cake. Meg and Babe applaud loudly.

MEG: Oh, you made it!

BABE: Hurray!

Identifying Conflict in Drama.

Applying Your Skills and Strategies

Sometimes a conflict between characters comes from the situation. This type of conflict may last for only a short time before it is quickly resolved. A brief conflict can create a feeling of suspense or excitement.

In the passage above, a minor conflict happens when Lenny is supposed to blow out the candles on the cake. What is the conflict?

How does it create suspense?

_____

_____

_____

LENNY: Oh, me! Oh, me! I hope that wish comes true! I hope it does!

BABE: Why? What did you wish for?

LENNY, *as she removes the candles from the cake:* Why, I can't tell you that.

BABE: Oh, sure you can—

LENNY: Oh, no! Then it won't come true.

Check your answer on page 220.

BABE: Why, that's just superstition! Of course it will, if you made it deep enough.

MEG: Really? I didn't know that.

LENNY: Well, Babe's the regular expert on birthday wishes.

BABE: It's just I get these feelings. Now, come on and tell us. What was it you wished for?

MEG: Yes, tell us. What was it?

LENNY: Well, I guess it wasn't really a specific wish. This—this vision just sort of came into my mind.

BABE: A vision? What was it of?

LENNY: I don't know exactly. It was something about the three of us smiling and laughing together.

BABE: Well, when was it? Was it far away or near?

LENNY: I'm not sure; but it wasn't forever; it wasn't for every minute. Just this one moment and we were all laughing.

BABE: Then, what were we laughing about?

LENNY: I don't know. Just nothing, I guess.

MEG: Well, that's a nice wish to make.

Lenny and Meg look at each other a moment.

MEG: Here, now, I'll get a knife so we can go ahead and cut the cake in celebration of Lenny being born!

BABE: Oh, yes! And give each one of us a rose. A whole rose apiece!

LENNY, *cutting the cake nervously:*   Well, I'll try—I'll try!

MEG, *licking the icing off a candle:*   Mmmm—this icing is delicious! Here, try some.

BABE: Mmmm! It's wonderful! Here, Lenny!

LENNY, *laughing joyously as she licks icing from her fingers and cuts huge pieces of cake that her sisters bite into ravenously:*   Oh, how I do love having birthday cake for breakfast! How I do!

The sisters freeze for a moment laughing and catching cake. The lights change and frame them in a magical, golden, sparkling glimmer; saxophone music is heard. The lights dim to blackout, and the saxophone continues to play.

To find out more about this passage, turn to page 238.

Determining Plot.   The plot of a story or drama is the series of events that create the action. The events of a plot can be described in the order in which they happen. A scene in a play has a plot. Reread the scene on pages 63–65. The first event of the plot is Meg and Babe planning a birthday surprise for Lenny. Describe the rest of the plot of this scene.

Applying Your Skills and Strategies

_____

_____

_____

_____

_____

Check your answer on page 220.

Section 9: Drama   65

Thinking About the Play

Find the numbered words below and underline them in the play. Study the context in which the words appear. Then match each word with its meaning. Write the letter of the meaning by each word.

_____ 1. improvising   a. hungrily

_____ 2. absolutely   b. a soft light

_____ 3. superstition   c. completely

_____ 4. vision   d. making up a story as you go along

_____ 5. ravenously   e. a belief in luck or magic

_____ 6. glimmer   f. something you imagine

Write your answers in the space provided.

7. Review your predictions on page 62. Were you right? If you said *yes*, write what you correctly predicted. If not, write two things you did not expect to read about.

_____

_____

_____

8. How are Meg, Babe, and Lenny related?

_____

9. What is Lenny's wish?

_____

10. What does Babe mean when she says "keep an eye out for Lenny"?

_____

11. You can conclude from the scene that Babe seems to make up "facts" as she goes along. What two details support this conclusion?

_____

_____

_____

Circle the number of the best answer for each question.

12. What does Lenny do to annoy Meg and Babe?

    (1) She takes a long time to make up her mind.

    (2) She complains that her cake has too many candles.

    (3) She complains that she is getting old.

    (4) She makes a bad wish.

    (5) She gives them too much cake.

13. Based on the information in the passage, what do you think might have happened earlier in the plot?

    (1) The family has always gotten along well.

    (2) Meg was causing problems in the family.

    (3) Lenny said she hated birthday celebrations.

    (4) Babe was taking saxophone lessons.

    (5) All the sisters were having problems.

Write your answers in the space provided.

14. Why do you think Babe makes up beliefs about birthday traditions?

_____

_____

_____

15. Do you think Lenny's wish has been granted? Why or why not?

_____

_____

_____

16. You have probably made a wish at some time. What was it? Did it come true? Did you do anything that helped it come true?

_____

_____

_____

_____

Check your answers on page 220.

Folk Novel

Setting the Stage

Some novels include stories from the far-distant past. People have been telling certain tales over and over for centuries. These stories are called folktales. **Folktales** often teach a lesson or explain how people believe things began. Folktales also include ideas that are important to a group of people or culture. By using a folktale as part of a longer story, an author can show how events today are connected to the past.

Past: What you already know

You may have read a novel or seen a movie based on a folktale. If so, what was the story about?

1. _____

   _____

   _____

Present: What you learn by previewing

You can learn a lot about what you will be reading by looking at the title and reading a few sentences. Read the first few sentences of the passage. What are the two characters doing?

2. _____

Future: What you predict

The passage on pages 69–71 is from a novel called *Bless Me, Ultima*. Based on the title, what do you think the passage will be about?

3. _____

   _____

Read a few more sentences. Now what do you predict the passage will be about?

4. _____

   _____

Check your answers on page 220.

<u>Bless Me, Ultima</u> by Rudolfo A. Anaya

As you read each section, circle the words you don't know. Look up the meanings.

"You fish a lot?" I asked.

"I have always been a fisherman," he answered, "as long as I can remember—"

"You fish," he said.

"Yes. I learned to fish with my brothers when I was very little. Then they went to war and I couldn't fish anymore. Then Ultima came—" I paused.

"I know," he said.

"So last summer I fished. Sometimes with Jasón."

"You have a lot to learn—"

"Yes," I answered.

The afternoon sun was warm on the sand. The muddy waters after-the-flood churned listlessly south, and out of the deep hole by the rock in front of us the catfish came. They were biting good for the first fishing of summer. We caught plenty of channel catfish and a few small yellow-bellies.

"Have you ever fished for the carp of the river?"

The river was full of big, brown carp. It was called the River of the Carp. Everybody knew it was bad luck to fish for the big carp that the summer floods washed downstream. After every flood, when the swirling angry waters of the river subsided, the big fish could be seen fighting their way back upstream. It had always been so.

Identifying Figurative Language (Personification).

Applying Your Skills and Strategies

Authors sometimes use figurative language in a special way called personification. In personification, something that is not human is given human qualities. For example, an author might say that the wind whistled sadly through the trees. People can feel the emotion of sadness, but wind cannot. The author has used the word *sadly* to make the reader think of a low, soft sound.

In the last paragraph above, find the description of rapidly moving water. What word does the author use to give the water human qualities?

_____

What does that word suggest to you?

_____

_____

The waters would subside very fast and in places the water would be so low that, as the carp swam back upstream, the backs of the fish would raise a furrow in the water. Sometimes the townspeople came to stand on the bridge and watch the struggle as the carp splashed their way back to the pools from which the flood had uprooted them. Some of the town kids, not knowing it was bad luck to catch the carp, would scoop them out of the low waters and toss the fish upon the sand bars.

There the poor carp would flop until they dried out and died, then later the crows would swoop down and eat them.

Some people in town would even buy the carp for a nickel and eat the fish! That was very bad. Why, I did not know.

It was a beautiful sight to behold, the struggle of the carp to regain his abode before the river dried to a trickle and trapped him in strange pools of water. What was beautiful about it was that you knew that against all the odds some of the carp made it back and raised their families, because every year the drama was repeated.

"No," I answered, "I do not fish for carp. It is bad luck."

"Do you know why?" he asked and raised an eyebrow.

"No," I said and held my breath. I felt I sat on the banks of an undiscovered river whose churning, muddied waters carried many secrets.

"I will tell you a story," Samuel said after a long silence, "a story that was told to my father by Jasón's Indian—"

I listened breathlessly. The lapping of the water was like the tide of time sounding on my soul.

Applying Your Skills and Strategies

Identifying Point of View.
Point of view in fiction is the way the action is seen. A story can be told as if it were seen through the eyes of only one character, the narrator. A clue word for identifying the narrator is *I*. Using this point of view makes the action in a story seem very real.

Who is the narrator in this passage?

_____

How does the narrator make the action in the story seem real?

_____

_____

"A long time ago, when the earth was young and only wandering tribes touched the virgin grasslands and drank from the pure streams, a strange people came to this land. They were sent to this valley by their gods. They had wandered lost for many years but never had they given up faith in their gods, and so they were finally rewarded. This fertile valley was to be their home. There were plenty of animals to eat, strange trees that bore sweet fruit, sweet water to drink and for their fields of maíz [corn]—"

"Were they Indians?" I asked when he paused.

"They were *the people*," he answered simply and went on. "There was only one thing that was withheld from them, and that was the fish called the carp. This fish made his home in the waters of the river, and he was sacred to the gods. For a long time the people were happy. Then came the forty years of the sun-without-rain, and crops withered and died, the game was killed, and the people went hungry. To stay alive they finally caught the carp of the river and ate them."

I shivered. I had never heard a story like this one. It was getting late and I thought of my mother.

"The gods were very angry. They were going to kill all of the people for their sin. But one kind god who truly loved the people argued against it, and the other gods were so moved by his love that they relented from killing the people. Instead, they turned the people into carp and made them live forever in the waters of the river—"

The setting sun glistened on the brown waters of the river and turned them to bronze.

"It is a sin to catch them," Samuel said, "it is a worse offense to eat them. They are a part of *the people*." He pointed towards the middle of the river where two huge back fins rose out of the water and splashed upstream.

"And if you eat one," I whispered, "you might be punished like they were punished."

"I don't know," Samuel said. He rose and took my fishing line.

"Is that all the story?" I asked.

He divided the catfish we had caught and gave me my share on a small string. "No, there is more," he said. He glanced around as if to make sure we were alone. "Do you know about the golden carp?" he asked in a whisper.

"No," I shook my head.

"When the gods had turned the people into carp, the one kind god who loved the people grew very sad. The river was full of dangers to the new fish. So he went to the other gods and told them that he chose to be turned into a carp and swim in the river where he could take care of his people. The gods agreed. But because he was a god they made him very big and colored him the color of gold. And they made him the lord of all the waters of the valley."

To find out more about this passage, turn to page 237.

Applying Your Skills and Strategies

Understanding Sequence. One way an author can organize a story is by using sequence. Events organized by sequence are written in the order in which they occur. To find out the sequence in a story, look for the way things happen in time. Look for clue words such as *first, second, later, then, while, before, after, during,* and *since.*

In Samuel's story, what happened after the forty years of sun-without-rain?

_____

What clue words help you follow the sequence of Samuel's story?

_____

_____

Thinking About the Story

Find the words below in the passage and underline them. Study the context in which the words appear. Then complete the following sentences by writing the correct words in the blanks provided.

churned   furrow   relent

listlessly   abode   subsided

1. The path left in the ground by a plow is called a _____ .

2. The boiling water _____ in the pot on the hot stove.

3. Samuel had no energy, so he lay _____ on his bed.

4. The woman knew she could change the run-down apartment into a

   cozy _____ .

5. We waited until the flood _____ before we cleaned up the mess.

6. Fathers sometimes _____ on their strict rules when their children give good reasons for breaking them.

Write your answers in the space provided.

7. Review your predictions on page 68. Were you right? If you said *yes*, write what you correctly predicted. If not, write two things you did not expect to find out.

_____

_____

_____

8. When does the narrator learn about the golden carp?

_____

_____

9. What is the main idea of Samuel's story?

_____

_____

Check your answers on page 220.

Circle the number of the best answer for each question.

10. How does the narrator feel about the first part of Samuel's story?

    (1) bored

    (2) uncomfortable

    (3) happy

    (4) angry

    (5) contented

11. Why was the kind god turned into a fish?

    (1) The other gods were angry with him.

    (2) His people had broken the rules.

    (3) He wanted to take care of the carp people.

    (4) He looked like the huge golden carp.

    (5) He had caught one of the sacred carp.

Write your answers in the space provided.

12. What does the author mean when he says, "I sat on the banks of an undiscovered river whose churning, muddied waters carried many secrets"?

    _____

    _____

13. Do you believe Samuel's story? Does the narrator? Why or why not?

    _____

    _____

    _____

14. Have you ever heard an old story that explains why people act in a certain way? What was the action and what was the reason?

    _____

    _____

    _____

    _____

Essays

Setting the Stage

Essays are short works of nonfiction. An essayist expresses an opinion about a specific topic. An essay can be about any topic, from everyday problems to major global issues. To get readers interested, the author appeals to our common sense and our emotion. The author's approach in an essay can be serious or humorous. Either way, the author's purpose is to get the reader to agree with a certain point of view.

Past: What you already know

You may have read an essay in a magazine or newspaper. What was the topic of the essay? Did you agree or disagree with the author's point of view?

1. _____

Present: What you learn by previewing

You can get a good idea of what you will be reading by looking at the title. Read the titles of the two essays. What do you think the general topic of each essay is?

2. _____

_____

Future: What you predict

Read the first few sentences of "Street Directions." Based on these sentences, what point do you think the author will make about the topic?

3. _____

_____

Read the first few sentences of "Back When a Dollar Was a Dollar." Based on these sentences, what point do you think the author will make about the topic?

4. _____

_____

Check your answers on page 221.

Street Directions by Andy Rooney

As you read each section, circle the words you don't know. Look up the meanings.

Where do streets go in a strange city and where do they come from?

If America wants to save gas, it ought to start over with its street signs and give everyone directions on how to give directions. It would not do this country any harm at all if there were college courses on the subject of direction giving.

Someone will say, "Go down here and turn left at the third traffic light. Keep going until you run into a dead end at Sixteenth Street, then bear right."

Those are simple enough, so you set out to follow directions. Within ten minutes you're at the corner of Broad and 4th streets, hopelessly lost. You never saw a Sixteenth Street. You feel either stupid and frustrated for not being able to follow simple directions or you feel outraged at the person who gave them to you.

I've often wanted to go back, find the guy and grab him by the throat. "All right, fella. You told me to turn left at the third traffic light and then keep going until I hit a dead end at Sixteenth. You were trying to get me lost, weren't you? Confess!"

It wouldn't be any use though. I know what he'd say. He'd say, "That's not counting this light right here. If you count this light, it's four."

Or he'd say, "Maybe it's Eighteenth Street where the dead end is . . . " or "You see, Sixteenth Street turns into Terwilliger Avenue after you cross Summit Boulevard."

Whatever his answer is, it's hopeless. He didn't mean to mislead you and you didn't mean to get lost, but that's what usually happens.

You can't lay all the blame on the people giving directions. People don't *take* them any better than they give them.

My own ability to retain directions in my head ends after the first two turns I'm given. Then I usually say to whomever I'm with, "Did he say right or left at the church on the right?" If there are seven or eight turns, including a couple of "bear rights" and a "jog left" or two, I might as well find a motel room and get a fresh start in the morning.

Understanding the Author's Tone.   When people speak, they may use a serious or humorous tone of voice to show how they feel. Authors do the same. The tone of a passage reflects the author's attitude or feelings about the topic. An author's tone may be angry, humorous, sad, happy, or serious.

Applying Your Skills and Strategies

Reread the passage above. What tone does the author use?

_____

_____

_____

The superhighways that bisect and trisect our cities now aren't any help at all in finding your way around. Streets that used to lead across town in a direct fashion now end abruptly where the highway cut through. Finding the nearest entrance to the superhighway, so you can drive two miles to the next exit in order to get a block and a half from where you are, is the new way to go.

If they do start college courses in direction giving, I hope they devote a semester to arrow drawing for signmakers. It seems like a simple enough matter, but it is often not clear to a stranger whether an arrow is telling you to veer off to the right or to keep going straight.

Different towns and cities have different systems for identifying their streets with the signs they erect. Some have the name of the street you are crossing facing you as you drive past. Others identify the street with a sign that is parallel to it. This is more accurate, but you can't see it. And if you don't know which system they're using, it's further trouble.

There are cities in America so hard to find your way around that, unless you're going to live there for several years, it isn't worth figuring them out.

Many cities, like Washington, pretend to be better organized than they are. They have numbers and they use the alphabet just as though everything was laid out in an orderly fashion.

New York City, for example, has numbered avenues that run longitudinally up and down the island. What the stranger would never know is that in midtown the names go from Third Avenue to Lexington, to Park, and then to Madison before the numbers start again with Fifth Avenue. Where did Fourth Avenue go? Sorry about that, that's what we call "Park."

And then "Sixth Avenue" is next? Well, not actually. New Yorkers call it "Sixth," but the official name and the name on the signs is "Avenue of the Americas." No one calls it that but the post office.

To find out more about this passage, turn to page 240.

I have long since given up asking for directions or reading maps. I am one of that large number of lost souls who finds that, in the long run, it's better simply to blunder on until you find where you're going on your own.

Understanding the Author's Tone. One way an author can include a humorous tone is to use exaggeration. When authors exaggerate, they make a situation sound better or worse than it really is. Authors can also exaggerate by offering unlikely solutions to problems. On page 75, the author exaggerates the problem of giving directions by suggesting that colleges should offer courses on how to give directions.

Applying Your Skills and Strategies

Reread the passage above. Give an example of the use of exaggeration in this passage.

_____

_____

_____

Back When a Dollar Was a Dollar
by Diane C. Arkins

I remember dollars. When I was growing up in the not-so-distant '50s and '60s, dollars used to be wonderful things.

Just one of them could fund a month's worth of kindergarten milk-money obligations—with change to spare. You could buy 10 newspapers. You could mail a hundred post cards. You could easily top off the tank when you borrowed Dad's car. Why, even Malcolm Forbes used to throw himself a birthday bash for $49.95.

Yessir. Back then, with a shine on your shoes and a buck in your pocket, you could really go places. Yet Mom and Dad made certain that we understood the clear connection between the Work Ethic and spending those hard-earned $$$.

The American Way also meant a careful look prior to leaping with your signature on a dotted line of double-digit interest payments.

But somehow, some time, some*where* along the way, it happened. When we weren't looking, the feds managed to redefine the currency in which . . . we trusted. They seem far too eager to pencil in a few extra zeros on their growing mountains of red ink. And from Jane Taxpayer's point of view, Washington's current juggling—debt ceilings, capital gains, wage floorings—looks like a shotgun marriage between *Let's Make a Deal* and the old "new math."

It's time for Washington's creative accounting to be accountable. Perhaps instead of promoting a policy of dreaming up new prefixes to add to the word "million," the feds could benefit from a refresher course on the value of a buck. Here are some suggestions to help Washington realign its outlook and put a "punch" back into middle America's pocketbook.

Welcome to Money Management 101.

- Require all members of Congress to redecorate their homes by shopping at the Pentagon Specials Hardware Store, where toilet seats are always on sale for $795.
- Arrange for the Washington hierarchy to get back to basics and collect their vacation pay at minimum wage.
- Reorganize frequent-flier discounts. Whenever Donald Trump flies, 200 working stiffs fly free.
- Help Congress understand the true meaning of those extra budgetary zeros—make them collect a million-billion-zillion bottle caps just to see what that number actually represents before they agree to spend it.

To find out more about this passage, turn to page 237.

Comparing and Contrasting.   Comparing two things means finding the ways they are alike. Contrasting means finding the ways they are different. You can contrast the two essays because the subject of one (money) is serious, while the subject of the other (directions) is not serious. Compare the tone and point of view of the two essays.

Applying Your Skills and Strategies

Thinking About the Essays

Find the numbered words below in the passage and underline them. Study the context in which the words appear. Then match each word with its meaning. Write the letter of the meaning by each word.

_____ 1. retain

_____ 2. bisect

_____ 3. abruptly

_____ 4. veer

_____ 5. obligations

_____ 6. prior

_____ 7. realign

_____ 8. hierarchy

a. before

b. suddenly

c. people in authority

d. keep

e. straighten out again

f. cut in two

g. duties; things that are owed

h. change direction

Write your answers in the space provided.

9. Review your predictions on page 74. Were you right? If you said *yes*, write what you correctly predicted. If not, for each question write two points you did not expect the author to make.

_____

_____

10. The word *longitudinally* refers to direction. What context clue from the first essay helps you understand the meaning of the word?

_____

_____

11. What important point is the author making in "Back When a Dollar Was a Dollar"?

_____

_____

12. After reading the first essay, what can you conclude about getting around in New York City?

_____

Check your answers on page 221.

Circle the number of the best answer for each question.

13. Which of the following is the best example of the humorous tone of "Street Directions"?

    (1) "You were trying to get me lost, weren't you?"

    (2) "Different towns and cities have different systems for identifying their streets. . . . "

    (3) "New York City, for example, has numbered avenues that run longitudinally. . . . "

    (4) "Those are simple enough, so you set out to follow directions."

    (5) "I hope they devote a semester to arrow drawing for signmakers."

14. What can you infer the author of "When a Dollar Was a Dollar" thinks the value of a dollar should be? It should be

    (1) whatever the federal government thinks is right.

    (2) of some real value to the average American.

    (3) used for getting better airfares.

    (4) enough to pay for Donald Trump's airfare.

    (5) enough to buy 100 postcards.

Write your answers in the space provided.

15. Do you agree with the first author's view about street directions? Why or why not?

    _____

    _____

16. Do you think the second author's suggestions about money management would make any difference in how the government spends tax dollars? Why or why not?

    _____

    _____

17. These two essayists wrote about things that annoy them. Is there something that often annoys you? Write a brief suggestion about how to solve the problem.

    _____

    _____

    _____

Check your answers on page 221.

12

Popular Novel

Setting the Stage

Some fiction deals with problems between parents and children. A special kind of problem comes up when the parents come to the United States from a different country. The immigrant parents sometimes want to keep many of their traditional cultural values. The American-born children have to choose between the old ways and the new ways. A number of young authors have described the personal conflict that results. They often look at the problem from both sides. In this way, both the authors and the readers can learn more about themselves and their values.

Past: What you already know

You may have read a story or seen a movie about someone living in a new culture. What did the person have to learn about that culture?

1. _____

_____

Present: What you learn by previewing

You can get a good idea of what you will be reading by looking at the title and reading a few sentences. Read the first few sentences of the passage. List the two main characters below.

2. _____

_____

Future: What you predict

The passage on pages 81–83 is from a novel called *The Joy Luck Club*. Based on the title and the first few sentences, what do you think the two cultures in the novel are?

3. _____

Based on the first few sentences, what do you predict will happen in the passage? Now read on to find out if you are correct.

4. _____

_____

The Joy Luck Club by Amy Tan

As you read each section, circle the words you don't know. Look up the meanings.

My daughter wanted to go to China for her second honeymoon, but now she is afraid.

"What if I blend in so well they think I'm one of them?" Waverly asked me. "What if they don't let me come back to the United States?"

"When you go to China," I told her, "you don't even need to open your mouth. They already know you are an outsider."

"What are you talking about?" she asked. My daughter likes to speak back. She likes to question what I say.

"Aii-ya," I said. "Even if you put on their clothes, even if you take off your makeup and hide your fancy jewelry, they know. They know just watching the way you walk, the way you carry your face. They know you do not belong."

My daughter did not look pleased when I told her this, that she didn't look Chinese. She had a sour American look on her face. Oh, maybe ten years ago, she would have clapped her hands—hurray!—as if this were good news. But now she wants to be Chinese, it is so fashionable. And I know it is too late. All those years I tried to teach her! She followed my Chinese ways only until she learned how to walk out the door by herself and go to school. So now the only Chinese words she can say are *sh-sh*, *houche*, *chr fan*, and *gwan deng shweijyau*. How can she talk to people in China with these words? . . . , choo-choo train, eat, close light sleep. How can she think she can blend in? Only her skin and her hair are Chinese. Inside—she is all American-made.

Comparing and Contrasting.

Applying Your Skills and Strategies

Comparing shows how things are alike. Contrasting shows how things are different. In the passage, the mother describes Waverly as having Chinese hair and skin. But her mother also says that in some ways Waverly looks different from the people in China.

In what ways is Waverly different from the people in China?

_____

_____

It's my fault she is this way. I wanted my children to have the best combination: American circumstances and Chinese character. How could I know these two things do not mix?

I taught her how American circumstances work. If you are born poor here, it's no lasting shame. You are first in line for a scholarship. If the roof crashes on your head, no need to cry over this bad luck. You can sue anybody, make the landlord fix it. You do not have to sit like a Buddha under a tree letting pigeons drop their dirty business on your head. You can buy an umbrella. Or go inside a Catholic church. In America, nobody says you have to keep the circumstances somebody else gives you.

Check your answer on page 221.

She learned these things, but I couldn't teach her about Chinese character. How to obey parents and listen to your mother's mind. How not to show your own thoughts, to put your feelings behind your face so you can take advantage of hidden opportunities. Why easy things are not worth pursuing. How to know your own worth and polish it, never flashing it around like a cheap ring. Why Chinese thinking is best.

No, this kind of thinking didn't stick to her. She was too busy chewing gum, blowing bubbles bigger than her cheeks. Only that kind of thinking stuck.

"Finish your coffee," I told her yesterday. "Don't throw your blessings away."

"Don't be so old-fashioned, Ma," she told me, finishing her coffee down the sink. "I'm my own person."

And I think, How can she be her own person? When did I give her up?

Making Inferences.   When you make an inference, you figure out something that is suggested or implied by an author. There may not be direct evidence to support your inference. Combine the facts you have with your own knowledge and experiences. In this passage, the mother gives examples of how American circumstances work. You can infer from these examples that she believes Americans have many choices in life.

Applying Your Skills and Strategies

What can you infer about Chinese values from the mother's saying *Don't throw your blessings away*?

_____

_____

My daughter is getting married a second time. So she asked me to go to her beauty parlor, her famous Mr. Rory. I know her meaning. She is ashamed of my looks. What will her husband's parents and his important lawyer friends think of this backward old Chinese woman?

"Auntie An-mei can cut me," I say.

"Rory is famous," says my daughter, as if she had no ears. "He does fabulous work."

So I sit in Mr. Rory's chair. He pumps me up and down until I am the right height. Then my daughter criticizes me as if I were not there. "See how it's flat on one side," she accuses my head. "She needs a cut and a perm. And this purple tint in her hair, she's been doing it at home. She's never had anything professionally done."

She is looking at Mr. Rory in the mirror. He is looking at me in the mirror. I have seen this professional look before. Americans don't really look at one another when talking. They talk to their reflections. They look at others or themselves only when they think nobody is watching. So they never see how they really look. They see themselves smiling without their mouth open, or turned to the side where they cannot see their faults.

                Check your answer on page 221.

"How does she want it?" asked Mr. Rory. He thinks I do not understand English. He is floating his fingers through my hair. He is showing how his magic can make my hair thicker and longer.

"Ma, how do you want it?" Why does my daughter think she is translating English for me? Before I can even speak, she explains my thoughts: "She wants a soft wave. We probably shouldn't cut it too short. Otherwise it'll be too tight for the wedding. She doesn't want it to look kinky or weird."

And now she says to me in a loud voice, as if I had lost my hearing, "Isn't that right, Ma? Not too tight?"

I smile. I use my American face. That's the face Americans think is Chinese, the one they cannot understand. But inside I am becoming ashamed. I am ashamed she is ashamed. Because she is my daughter and I am proud of her, and I am her mother but she is not proud of me.

Mr. Rory pats my hair more. He looks at me. He looks at my daughter. Then he says something to my daughter that really displeases her: "It's uncanny how much you two look alike!"

I smile, this time with my Chinese face. But my daughter's eyes and her smile become very narrow, the way a cat pulls itself small just before it bites. Now Mr. Rory goes away so we can think about this. I hear him snap his fingers. "Wash! Mrs. Jong is next!"

So my daughter and I are alone in this crowded beauty parlor. She is frowning at herself in the mirror. She sees me looking at her.

"The same cheeks," she says. She points to mine and then pokes her cheeks. She sucks them outside in to look like a starved person. She puts her face next to mine, side by side, and we look at each other in the mirror.

"You can see your character in your face," I say to my daughter without thinking. "You can see your future."

"What do you mean?" she says.

And now I have to fight back my feelings. These two faces, I think, so much the same! The same happiness, the same sadness, the same good fortune, the same faults.

I am seeing myself and my mother, back in China, when I was a young girl.

To find out more about this passage, turn to page 240.

Identifying Conflict in Fiction. Fiction is often based on a conflict between characters. The conflict can come from cultural differences, different opinions, or different ways of life. This passage is based on the conflict between Waverly and her mother. What is the conflict between these two characters?

Applying Your Skills and Strategies

_____

_____

_____

_____

Check your answer on page 222.   *Section 12: Popular Novel* **83**

Thinking About the Story

Find the words below in the passage and underline them. Study the context in which each word appears. Try to figure out the meaning of each word. Then complete the following sentences by writing the correct words in the blanks provided.

blend	opportunities	fabulous
circumstances	pursuing	advantage

1. I have not given up my goals. I am still _____ them.

2. The more education you have, the more _____ you will have.

3. If things are mixed together enough, they will _____ .

4. She thought it would be _____ if she won the state lottery.

5. The scholarships for Chinese Americans gave Waverly a financial

   _____ .

6. The bad _____ Mrs. Jong grew up in did not stop her from trying to improve herself.

Write your answers in the space provided.

7. Review your predictions on page 80. Were you right? If you said *yes*, write what you correctly predicted. If not, what were you wrong about?

   _____

   _____

   _____

8. What does the mother realize is a bad combination?

   _____

9. What is the difference between the mother's Chinese and American faces?

   _____

   _____

Check your answers on page 222.

Circle the number of the best answer for each question.

10. From the mother's thoughts about Americans, what can you infer about the way the Chinese talk to each other?

    (1) They always look away from each other.

    (2) They look directly at each other.

    (3) They do not smile when talking.

    (4) They do not talk in public.

    (5) They prefer translators.

11. Why does Waverly act as though her mother cannot speak for herself?

    (1) She doesn't believe her mother understands American ways.

    (2) The mother is hard-of-hearing.

    (3) Mr. Rory does not understand Chinese.

    (4) The mother is not sure of what she wants.

    (5) The mother has poor taste in fashion.

12. The mother thinks some of her daughter's ideas are silly. She shows this attitude in her tone. Which of the following shows how the mother feels?

    (1) "Now she is afraid."

    (2) "Don't be so old-fashioned."

    (3) " . . . her famous Mr. Rory . . . "

    (4) "She is not proud of me."

    (5) "You can see your character in your face."

Write your answers in the space provided.

13. Do you think that Waverly will understand what she has in common with her mother? Why or why not?

    _____

    _____

14. Are your feelings or attitudes different from those of your parents or your children? In what ways?

    _____

    _____

    _____

Magazine Article

Setting the Stage

At the 1968 ●lympics in Mexico City, two athletes made a silent protest against racial injustice in the United States. The protest was made on television for all the world to see. The picture on page 12 shows the two Olympic athletes with their fists raised in the air. This gesture represented African-American unity and power. The men stood in their stocking feet as a symbol of the poverty of many African Americans. The scarf worn by one man and the beads worn by the other were reminders of the senseless killings of some African Americans. Only months before the Olympic Games, civil rights leader Martin Luther King, Jr., had been killed. Many African-American athletes wanted to boycott the 1968 Olympics. But a few athletes found another way to make their feelings known.

Past: What you already know

You may have read an article or seen a TV program about a civil rights protest. Give an example of one way people have protested to protect their civil rights.

1. _____

_____

Present: What you learn by previewing

You can get a good idea of what you will be reading by looking at the title and reading a few sentences. Read the first three paragraphs of the passage. What are the names of the two athletes in the article?

2. _____

_____

Future: What you predict

The passage on pages 87–89 is from a magazine article called "A Courageous Stand." Reread the first paragraph. Now what do you predict the passage will be about? Read on to find out if you are correct.

3. _____

_____

Check your answers on page 222.

A Courageous Stand by Kenny Moore

As you read each section, circle the words you don't know. Look up the meanings.

As the Olympics began, Smith was a man in search of a gesture. "It had to be silent—to solve the language problem—strong, prayerful and imposing," he says. "It kind of makes me want to cry when I think about it now. I cherish life so much that what I did couldn't be militant, not violent. I'll argue with you, but I won't pick up a gun.

"We had to be heard, forcefully heard, because we represented what others didn't want to believe. I thought of how my sisters cringed because they didn't want me to embarrass the family by describing how poor we were, when we *were* poor. No one likes to admit flaws, even though it's the first step to fixing them."

Symbols began to present themselves to him. He asked Denise [Smith's wife] to buy a pair of black gloves. A few days before his race, Smith knew what he would do. He did not tell Carlos. Until the race was over, Carlos was a competitor. . . .

After the semifinals of the 200 two days later, it appeared that Smith would not stand on any victory platform. Carlos won the first semi in 20.11, unbothered by running in the tight inside lane. Smith took the second semi in 20.13, but as he slowed, he felt a jab high in his left thigh. "It was like a dart in my leg. I went down, not knowing where the next bullet was coming from."

Using Context Clues for Special Terms. Looking at the context can provide clues to the meaning of unfamiliar terms. Special terms used in sports may not be familiar to you. In the passage, the word *race* helps you figure out that *200* is probably the distance of the race. Find the numbers *20.11* and *20.13* in the passage. They refer to races won by Carlos and Smith. What do you think these numbers stand for?

Applying Your Skills and Strategies

_____

Find the word *semi*. What do you think this word means?

_____

As he crouched on the track, he knew he had strained or torn an adductor muscle. All the work, he thought, was now useless. He raised his head and saw before him a familiar pair of hunting boots. They belonged to his San Jose State coach, Winter, who got him up, walked him to ice, packed his groin and then wrapped it.

The final was two hours later. "Thirty minutes before it, I went to the practice field," Smith says. "I jogged a straightaway, then did one at 30 percent. It was holding. I did one at 60 percent, then one at 90. It held. . . . Don't let there be any delays, I thought."

Check your answers on page 222.

As the eight finalists were led into the stadium, Carlos remembers saying to Smith, "I'm going to do something on the stand to let those in power know they're wrong. I want you with me."

Smith, Carlos recalls, said, "I'm with you."

"That made me feel good," says Carlos. "And it made the medal mean nothing. Why should I have to prove my ability when they'd just take it away somehow? I made up my mind. Tommie Smith gets a gift."

They were placed on their marks. "I took no practice starts," says Smith. John was in Lane 4. I was in 3. I calculated it this way: Come out hard but keep power off my inside leg on the turn with a short, quick stride. Then in the straightaway I'd maintain for four strides and attack for eight."

At the gun, Carlos was away perfectly. Smith ran lightly and with building emotion. He felt no pain. Carlos came out of the turn with a 1½-meter lead. Then, a man unto himself, he swiveled his head to his left and, he says, told Smith, "If you want the gold, . . . come on." Smith didn't hear him. Eighty thousand people were roaring as Smith struck with his eight long, lifting strides. They swept him past Carlos.

"I pulled back on the reins," Carlos says now. "America deprived our society of seeing what the world record would have been."

"If Carlos wants to say that," Smith says, "I applaud him for his benevolence."

"The medal meant more to Tommie," says Carlos. "Everyone got what he wanted, even Peter Norman." Carlos slowed so much that Norman, an Australian sprinter, caught him at the line for second.

When Smith knew he had won, he threw out his arms. He still had 15 meters to go. "I guess if I'd calculated a 12-stride attack, the time would have been 19.6," Smith says now. That record would have stood to this day.

Understanding Cause and Effect.   Remember that a cause is what makes something happen. The effect is what happens. Smith showed that he supported Carlos when he said, "I'm with you." Because of Smith's support, Carlos felt that winning the medal was no longer important. During the race, Carlos slowed down. What two effects did that action have?

Applying Your Skills and Strategies

_____

_____

_____

He crossed the line with his arms outflung at the angle of a crucifix. His smile was of joy, relief and vindication. When he came to a stop, he felt resolve cool and strong in him.

The medalists were guided through a warren of stone tunnels under the stadium to a room that held their sweatsuits and bags. "It was a dungeon under there," says Smith.

Check your answer on page 222.

He went to Carlos. "John, this is it, man," he said. "All those years of fear, all the suffering. This is it. I'll tell you what I'm going to do. You can decide whether you want to."

"Yeah, man," said Carlos. "Right."

"I got gloves here. I'm going to wear the right. You can have the left." Carlos slipped it on.

Smith explained the symbolism of the gloves, the scarf, the stocking feet and the posture. "The national anthem is a sacred song to me," Smith said. "This can't be sloppy. It has to be clean and abrupt."

"Tommie, if anyone cocks a rifle," said Carlos, "you know the sound. Be ready to move."

Silver medalist Norman, who is white, overheard these preparations, and Carlos asked him if he would participate in the protest. Norman agreed, and Carlos gave him a large Olympic Project for Human Rights button. Norman pinned it to his Australian sweatsuit.

"I thought, In the '50s, blacks couldn't even *live* in Australia," says Smith. "And now he's going back there after doing this." (Norman would be severely reprimanded by Australian sports authorities.)

Smith, Norman and Carlos were placed behind three young Mexican women in embroidered native dress, each of whom carried a velvet pillow. Upon each pillow lay a medal. IOC vice-president Lord Killanin of Ireland, who would succeed Brundage [the president of the International Olympic Committee who had been accused of ignoring the civil rights issue] in four years, and the president of the International Amateur Athletic Federation, the Marquess of Exeter, led them to the ceremony.

"As Killanin hung the medal around my neck and shook my hand," says Smith, "his smile was so warm that I was surprised. I smiled back. I saw peace in his eyes. That gave me a two- or three-second relaxation there, to gather myself."

Along with his gold medal, Smith received a box with an olive tree sapling inside, an emblem of peace. He held the box in his left hand, accepting it into his own symbolism.

To find out more about this article, turn to page 239.
Then the three athletes turned to the right, to face the flags. *The Star-Spangled Banner* began. Smith bowed his head as if in prayer and freed his young face of expression. Then he tensed the muscles of his right shoulder and began the irrevocable lifting of his fist.

Predicting Outcomes.

Applying Your Skills and Strategies

Use the information given in the passage and what you already know to predict the final outcome of the story. The passage above does not say what happened to Carlos and Smith after the Olympic Games. It does say that Peter Norman was severely reprimanded by Australian sports authorities. What do you predict may have happened to Carlos and Smith after the Olympic Games?

_____

_____

_____

Thinking About the Article

Find the numbered words below in the passage and underline them. Study the context in which each word appears. Then match each word with its meaning. Write the letter of the meaning by each word.

_____ 1.	symbols	a. kindness
_____ 2.	calculated	b. figured, estimated
_____ 3.	benevolence	c. unable to be changed
_____ 4.	vindication	d. severely scolded
_____ 5.	reprimanded	e. things that stand for something
_____ 6.	irrevocable	f. the act of being proved right
_____ 7.	abrupt	g. sudden

Write your answers in the space provided.

8. Review your prediction on page 86. Were you right? If you said *yes*, write what you correctly predicted. If not, write two things you didn't expect to find out.

_____

_____

_____

9. What does Smith mean by *the language problem*?

_____

_____

10. How did Norman, the Australian sprinter, share in the protest?

_____

11. Why wasn't Smith expected to win the final race?

_____

12. What does Carlos think would have happened if he had not slowed down?

_____

Circle the number of the best answer for each question.

13. Smith held the olive tree box in his left hand because

    (1) the left hand is a symbol for peace.

    (2) he objected to its symbolism.

    (3) his left hand was stronger than his right.

    (4) he didn't know what to do with it.

    (5) he was going to raise his gloved right hand.

14. What did Carlos mean by saying that he *pulled back on the reins*?

    (1) He was riding a horse in the race.

    (2) He slowed down.

    (3) He grabbed Smith's shoelaces.

    (4) He started to run faster.

    (5) He realized he couldn't win the race.

15. What can you infer that Smith and Carlos represented that some others didn't want to believe?

    (1) the excellence of African-American athletes

    (2) the flaws of African-American athletes

    (3) poor people who become rich

    (4) people with speech problems

    (5) the strength of American athletes

Write your answers in the space provided.

16. How do you think Smith and Carlos feel today about their protest?

    _____

    _____

17. Is there something you would like to make a strong protest about? Describe a manner of protest that might make your point.

    _____

    _____

    _____

    _____

Biography

Setting the Stage

Many biographies are about people who have helped to change the world. These people may be inventors, explorers, scientists, or others who have accomplished great things. The reader may not learn much about the person's private life. Instead, the author explains why this person is famous. To do this, the author gives information about the important things the person did. With this type of biography, readers can find out about the inventions and discoveries that have changed the way we live.

Past: What you already know

You may have read a biography about a famous inventor or scientist. Who was the biography about and what was the person famous for?

1. _____

_____

Present: What you learn by previewing

You can get a good idea of what you will be reading by looking at the title and reading a few sentences. Read the first few lines of the passage. Who is the biography about and what kind of work did this person do?

2. _____

Future: What you predict

The passage on pages 93–95 is from a biography called *Luis W. Alvarez*. Read the first three paragraphs. What do you predict the passage will tell about Luis Alvarez? Now read on to find out if you are correct.

3. _____

_____

    Check your answers on page 223.

Luis W. Alvarez by Corinn Codye

As you read each section, circle the words you don't know. Look up the meanings.

In 1939, World War II broke out in Europe. In 1940, [Luis] Alvarez joined a group of scientists who were designing a way to guide airplanes through fog or darkness.

Alvarez and his group built a radar system called Ground-Controlled Approach, or GCA. In this system, a radio signal bounces off a lost plane and back to the sender of the signal. Then a flight controller on the ground can guide the plane safely to the ground.

Later during the war, Alvarez worked in Los Alamos, New Mexico, on a secret project for the government. Nuclear scientists there were searching for a way to make a powerful new weapon, the atom bomb.

It was a tricky job. The radiation given off by the atoms in such a bomb is deadly to living things. Also, an accidental explosion would cause a terrible disaster. The project to build the bomb was a top-secret race, because the first country to build an atom bomb would have the power to win the war.

Recognizing Supporting Details.   Supporting details help explain the main idea of a paragraph. The stated main idea of the last paragraph above is that making the bomb was *a tricky job*. One detail that explains why the job was tricky is the fact that radiation is deadly to living things. What other detail supports the main idea of the paragraph?

Applying Your Skills and Strategies

_____

_____

Finally, in July 1945, the atom bomb, which the scientists called the "Little Boy," was ready. The government planned to drop the bomb on Japan. Alvarez had the job of measuring the energy released by the bomb that would be dropped from the plane. Alvarez, the atom bomb, and a handful of others were taken to a tiny island in the Pacific Ocean.

On August 6, 1945, three planes took off toward Japan. One carried the bomb, and another carried photographers to film the blast. The third held Alvarez and his team with their blast-measuring instruments. They watched out of the window as the plane flew high over Japan, heading for the city of Hiroshima.

Suddenly they heard the "ready" signal from the plane that held the atom bomb. Alvarez and his team hurried to launch their measuring equipment. The bomb fell 30,000 feet (about 9,000 meters) in 45 seconds, while Alvarez's equipment, attached to parachutes, floated gently above

Check your answer on page 223.

it. The planes made a hard turn and sped away. As Alvarez and his team flew away from the bomb, a bright flash hit the airplane. On their electronic screens, they saw the blast being recorded by their measuring instruments. The screens showed two shock waves—one from the blast itself, then a second wave after the shock hit the ground and bounced back into the air.

A few seconds later, two sharp shocks jolted their plane, hard. A giant mushroom-shaped cloud filled the sky, from the ground all the way to where they flew at 30,000 feet.

They flew around the mushroom cloud once before returning to their tiny island base. Since Alvarez could see nothing but green forests below, he thought they had missed the target. The pilot explained that the city had been *entirely* destroyed.

Alvarez felt sad when he thought of all the people who had lost their lives. He later wrote a letter to his four-year-old son. In it he said that he hoped the powerful and destructive atom bomb would inspire people to prevent future wars.

After the war, Alvarez worked again at the Radiation Laboratory at Berkeley. There he built a device called a hydrogen bubble chamber. With this device, Alvarez discovered that atoms and other particles, when driven through liquid hydrogen, leave a track of bubbles. The larger the chamber, the easier it is to see particle tracks. Using bubble chambers, Alvarez's team discovered many new atomic particles.

In 1968, Alvarez received the Nobel prize, which recognizes the highest achievements in the world. The Nobel description of his important work and discoveries in physics was the longest in the prize's history.

Understanding Cause and Effect. A cause is a situation or an event that makes something happen. The effect is what happens as a result of the cause. Words such as *since* and *because* can help you recognize a cause-and-effect relationship that is directly stated. In the sentence *Since Alvarez could see nothing but green forests below, he thought they had missed the target*, the cause comes first. In this statement, the cause is that Alvarez could see nothing but green forests. The effect, or result, is that Alvarez thought they had missed the target.

Applying Your Skills and Strategies

Cause-and-effect relationships are not always directly stated. Why was there a second shock wave after the bomb was dropped? State your answer as a cause-and-effect relationship using the word *since* or *because*.

_____

_____

_____

Check your answer on page 223.

Circle the number of the best answer for each question.

12. According to the passage, Luis Alvarez may be best known for which of the following?

   (1) building the atom bomb

   (2) bombing Hiroshima

   (3) his work as a geologist

   (4) receiving the Nobel prize

   (5) finding the first dinosaur fossil

13. Luis and Walter Alvarez concluded that early animals died of starvation or froze to death during a short period in Earth's history. Which detail supports this conclusion?

   (1) A large black cloud blocked off all sunlight.

   (2) A clay layer formed on Earth.

   (3) Fossil shells were found in both layers of the rock.

   (4) The rock held a mystery about Earth.

   (5) Dinosaurs are no longer around.

14. What did Luis Alvarez hope would be the effect of dropping "Little Boy" on Japan?

   (1) America would win the war.

   (2) Future wars would be avoided.

   (3) His son would be inspired to become a scientist.

   (4) He would become famous.

   (5) Scientists would stop nuclear research.

Write your answer in the space provided.

15. If you could be known for an important discovery, invention, or accomplishment, what would it be? Why? How would it affect the way people live?

_____

_____

_____

_____

Unit 1 Review:
Popular Literature

Read the following passage from the novel _Mutation_ by Robin Cook.

"But he's not crying?" questioned Victor. Doubt clouded his euphoria.

The resident lightly slapped the soles of Victor Jr.'s feet, then rubbed his back. Still the infant stayed quiet. "But he's breathing fine."

The resident picked up the bulb syringe and tried to suction Victor Jr.'s nose once again. To the doctor's astonishment, the newborn's hand came up and yanked the bulb away from the fingers of the resident and dropped it over the side of the infant care unit.

"Well that settles that," said the resident with a chuckle. "He just doesn't want to cry."

"Can I?" asked Victor, motioning toward the baby.

"As long as he doesn't get cold."

Gingerly, Victor reached into the unit and scooped up Victor Jr. He held the infant in front of him with both hands around his torso. He was a beautiful baby with strikingly blond hair. His chubby, rosy cheeks gave his face a picturesquely cherubic quality, but by far the most distinctive aspect of his appearance was his bright blue eyes. As Victor gazed into their depths he realized with a shock that the baby was looking back at him.

"Beautiful, isn't he?" said Marsha over Victor's shoulder.

"Gorgeous," Victor agreed. "But where did the blond hair come from? Ours is brown."

"I was blond until I was five," Marsha said, reaching up to touch the baby's pink skin.

Victor glanced at his wife as she lovingly gazed at the child. She had dark brown hair peppered with just a few strands of gray. Her eyes were a sultry gray-blue; her features quite sculptured: they contrasted with the rounded, full features of the infant.

"Look at his eyes," Marsha said.

Victor turned his attention back to the baby. "They are incredible, aren't they? A minute ago I'd have sworn they were looking right back at me."

"They are like jewels," Marsha said.

To find out more about this passage, turn to page 237.

Victor turned the baby to face Marsha. As he did so he noticed the baby's eyes remained locked on his! Their turquoise depths were as cold and bright as ice. Unbidden, Victor felt a thrill of fear.

Items 1–6 refer to the passage on page 98.

Find the numbered words in the passage. Study the context in which each word appears. Match each word with its meaning. Write the letter of the meaning by each word.

_____ 1. euphoria   a. carefully

_____ 2. gingerly   b. angel-like

                c. extreme happiness

_____ 3. cherubic

Circle the number of the best answer for each question.

4. What can you conclude about how Marsha feels about her child? Marsha feels

   (1)   proud.

   (2)   puzzled.

   (3)   worried.

   (4)   uninterested.

   (5)   surprised.

5. Newborn babies cannot focus their eyes. What can you infer from Victor's noticing _the baby's eyes remained locked on his_?

   (1)   The baby is not a newborn infant.

   (2)   Victor has poor eyesight.

   (3)   The baby is not normal.

   (4)   The baby is not Victor's son.

   (5)   Victor knows a lot about babies.

6. Which of the following pairs of words does the author use to show how Victor feels about the baby's eyes?

   (1)   chuckle and gazed

   (2)   beautiful and brown

   (3)   jewels and bright

   (4)   turquoise and locked

   (5)   shock and fear

Read the following poem, "Getting Out," by Cleopatra Mathis.

That year we hardly slept, waking like inmates
who beat the walls. Every night
another refusal, the silent work
of tightening the heart.
Exhausted, we gave up; escaped
to the apartment pool, swimming those laps
until the first light relieved us.

Days were different: FM and full-blast
blues, hours of guitar "you gonna miss me
when I'm gone." Think how you tried
to pack up and go, for weeks stumbling
over piles of clothing, the unstrung tennis rackets.
Finally locked into blame, we paced
that short hall, heaving words like furniture.

I have the last unshredded pictures
of our matching eyes and hair. We've kept
to separate sides of the map,
still I'm startled by men who look like you.
And in the yearly letter, you're sure to say
you're happy now. Yet I think of the lawyer's bewilderment
when we cried, the last day. Taking hands
we walked apart, until our arms stretched
between us. We held on tight, and let go.

To find out more about this passage, turn to page 239.

Items 7–13 refer to the poem on page 100.

Fill in the blanks with the word or words that best complete the statements.

7. The poem describes how the couple acted during the year before they

    were _____ .

8. The first thing the speaker talks about is how the couple spent their

    _____ .

9. The phrase *men like you* suggests that the speaker is a

    _____ .

10. You can conclude that the speaker has _____ most of
    the couple's photographs.

Circle the number of the best answer for each question.

11. What does the figurative phrase *heaving words like furniture* suggest
    the couple was doing?

    (1) arguing bitterly

    (2) throwing chairs at each other

    (3) rearranging the furniture

    (4) moving out of the apartment at the same time

    (5) throwing books at each other

12. What is the best meaning of the phrase *kept to separate sides of the
    map*?

    (1) The couple kept a map in the middle of the apartment.

    (2) Both people need maps to find their way around.

    (3) The man and woman now live in different parts of the country.

    (4) The apartment was laid out like a city street.

    (5) The couple was always arguing about where to live.

13. The speaker seems sad but sure that the divorce was right. Which of
    the following phrases from the poem best expresses this feeling?

    (1) tightening the heart

    (2) relieved us

    (3) you gonna miss me

    (4) paced that short hall

    (5) held on tight, and let go

When I stepped inside the door, I saw a small-framed man with light brown hair, leaning back in a big leather chair with his feet propped up on his desk. He looked to be in his late twenties, not much older than me. He had on ordinary clothes—an open-collared shirt, casual pants and loafers—and he didn't appear very prosperous. He just sat there looking at me in a disinterested way, waiting for me to say something. He made me feel very uncomfortable; he seemed so cool and detached.

In my nervousness I blurted out, "My name is Wynette Byrd and I've recently moved here from Birmingham."

He said, "Well, I'm from Alabama myself, but you probably never heard of the place. It's a little town called Haleyville."

I said, "Yes, I have! That's the town where my father was born, and my grandparents still have a little house down there."

He almost smiled then and I thought, Well, at least the ice has been broken a little bit. He asked, "What can I do for you?"

I stammered, "I want a recording contract."

His expression didn't change at all. He said, "Do you have any tapes?"

I said, "No, but I'll sing for you if you'll loan me a guitar."

He reached over behind him and handed me his, then leaned back in his chair again. I sang a couple of songs I had written with Fred Lehner in Birmingham. Then I did a Skeeter Davis song and a George Jones song. His expression still didn't change, and he made no comment whatsoever about my singing. He didn't say anything at all for a minute or two, then spoke in a very matter of fact tone: "I don't have time to look for material for you, but if you can come up with a good song, I'll record you."

Just like that! At first I didn't believe I'd heard right. It couldn't be this easy, this casual, after a year of knocking on doors and facing one rejection after another. He didn't say *when* he would record me and he didn't mention a thing about a contract, but I couldn't have been happier if I had just signed one for a million dollars. Even if this man didn't seem the least bit enthusiastic, someone had at least offered me a chance to record. Billy has never admitted it, but I think the only reason he made the offer was because he felt sorry for me. He once described his first impression of me to a reporter as "a pale, skinny little blond girl who looked like she was at her rope's end." And I guess he was right about that.

*To find out more
about this passage,
turn to page 240.*

Items 14–19 refer to the passage on page 102.

Write your answers in the space provided.

14. Who is the narrator of this story?

_____

15. Why does Tammy Wynette think Billy let her record?

_____

16. State the main idea of the passage.

_____

_____

Circle the number of the best answer for each question.

17. Which of the following is the first event of the plot?

    (1) The woman enters the office and sees the man.

    (2) The woman feels uncomfortable.

    (3) The woman introduces herself.

    (4) The man asks the woman what she wants.

    (5) The man gives the woman a recording contract.

18. The author repeats the fact that Billy had no expression on his face to emphasize that this made her feel

    (1) hopeful.

    (2) nervous.

    (3) calm.

    (4) relaxed.

    (5) disinterested.

19. Wynette was surprised by

    (1) the variety of songs she was able to remember.

    (2) how much she and Billy had in common.

    (3) how enthusiastic Billy was about her singing.

    (4) the casual way Billy offered to record her.

    (5) how much Billy knew about country music.

**Read the following passage from the play *The Tomorrow Radio*,
by Robyn Reeves.**

NARRATOR: Marcos and Adela Perez, a husband-and-wife team of
scientists, are working on a project in their lab at home. For several
years they have been trying to discover evidence of life on other
planets by picking up radio signals from deep outer space. Their work
has been expensive, however, and their money is about to run out. . . .

ADELA: Marcos, wait a minute. . . . I'm not sure. It sounds like—words.

NARRATOR: The sounds become clearer, and Marcos and Adela are able to
make out a voice. . . .

RADIO VOICE: . . . And now, a weather forecast for tomorrow.

ADELA: What next? I never thought we'd be crossing sound waves with an
ordinary radio broadcast. . . .

RADIO VOICE: Today's rain will turn into light showers tonight. Tonight will
be slightly cooler. Sunday will be mostly cloudy. The high will be in the
low fifties. . . .

ADELA: That's odd. It's not raining here. The announcer said "tomorrow's
weather" and then talked about the weather for Sunday. But tomorrow
is Saturday.

RADIO VOICE: Here are today's football scores. Dartmouth beat Yale in New
Haven, 20 to 17. And here's a big upset. Indiana stunned Ohio State,
35 to 7! In the South . . . *(Static)*

ADELA: This is incredible! How could he have these football scores now?
None of these games will be played until tomorrow. . . . This is no
ordinary broadcast. . . .

MARCOS: *(Looking over her shoulder)* What are you doing?

ADELA: I'm writing down the football scores. If this thing is as good as it
seems to be, we may never have to worry about money again!

RADIO VOICE: And that's the last of the football scores. This completes our
broadcast day. Join me tomorrow, Sunday, at 10:00 AM for a sports and
weather update. Until then . . . *(Music plays, then static)*

MARCOS: I still can't believe it. A radio that tells the future! . . . Think of
all the good that people could do if they knew what was going to
happen a day early. . . . And think of all the bad that could be done too.
If this radio ever got into the wrong hands. . . .

NARRATOR: The radio suddenly crackles to life once more.

RADIO VOICE: I've just been handed a special news bulletin. The River
Bridge in Sommerville has just collapsed. So far, one person is known
dead. Stay tuned for more details. *(Static again then silence)*

MARCOS: Did the announcer say River Bridge? Adela, that's just a few
miles from here! . . . Adela, this is important. We can't keep this news
to ourselves. I think we better go to the police.

ADELA: That's fine, Marcos. What are we going to say? That we can predict
the future?

MARCOS: We can tell them anything, just so long as the bridge is cleared
by tomorrow at five o'clock! . . . Let's just tell them about the radio. We
can explain what happened and describe our work.

*To find out more
about this passage,
turn to page 240.*

ADELA: I'm sure they'll believe every word. Let's face it, they'll think we're
a couple of UFO freaks who have gone off the deep end.

MARCOS: We can show them the radio. Then they'll have to believe us.

Items 20–25 refer to the passage on page 104.

Fill in the blanks with the word or words that best complete the statements.

20. This play is about the possibilities found in science. This

    type of fiction is called _____.

21. Adela and Marcos are trying to discover evidence of life on other

    planets by picking up _____.

22. You can conclude from the dialogue that the day on which the action

    of the play takes place is _____ .

Circle the number of the best answer for each question.

23. Why were Adela and Marcos surprised by the broadcast? They

    (1) didn't expect the radio to ever receive anything.

    (2) were trying to contact scientists in other countries.

    (3) were expecting to receive signals from outer space.

    (4) expected to receive ordinary radio broadcasts.

    (5) had turned the radio off.

24. Adela does not want to go to the police to tell them about the bridge
    collapse because

    (1) she wants to keep the radio a secret.

    (2) she doesn't care about the bridge collapse.

    (3) she doesn't believe that the radio can really predict the future.

    (4) she is afraid the police will think she and Marcos are crazy.

    (5) there isn't enough time for them to warn anyone about the
        bridge collapse.

25. After hearing the last broadcast, what do you predict Adela and
    Marcos will do next? They will

    (1) say nothing and continue their research.

    (2) try to sell the radio to make money for their lab.

    (3) wait to see if the bridge collapses before they tell anyone.

    (4) go to the authorities and try to convince them that the bridge
        will collapse.

    (5) try to find out where the broadcast is coming from.

Check your answers on pages 223–224.

CLASSICAL LITERATURE

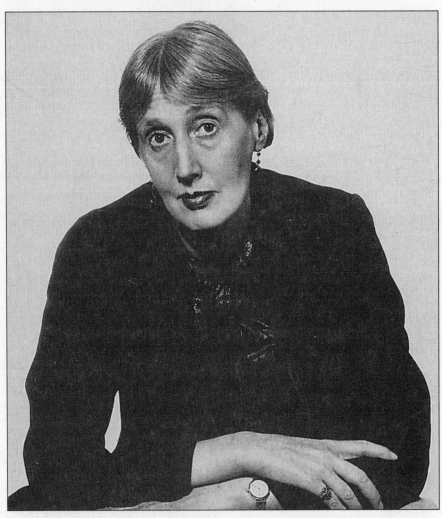

Virginia Woolf (1882–1941) was a critic, novelist, and essayist. She was one of the most highly respected authors of the early twentieth century.

Why is some literature called **classical**? When good popular literature is read by many people over many years, it is said to have stood the test of time. It has become classical.

The word *classical* does not mean old or difficult. Instead, it suggests meeting a standard of excellence. Classical poems, novels, short stories, essays, and plays are read again and again because they are well-written. They are as meaningful to readers now as when they were first published.

Poetry is probably the oldest form of literature. Classical epic poems, which are long poems that tell a story, existed in ancient times. The "Epic of Gilgamesh" is several thousand years old. English poetry written as long ago as the seventh century still is read today. Classical poems show that ancient people had the same concerns that modern people do. Classical poets wrote about love and hate, war and peace, loneliness and friendship. Classical poets such as Geoffrey Chaucer, John Milton, William Wordsworth, Robert Frost, and Emily Dickinson have continued to write about emotions we all understand.

More than two thousand years ago, the Greeks wrote plays that are regarded as classics today. These plays are both comedies and tragedies. The topics of these ancient plays include murder, family relationships, romance, and politics. The same conflicts can be seen in the classical plays of William Shakespeare. In modern classical dramas, these conflicts are treated by such authors as Henrik Ibsen and Arthur Miller.

The first real novels written in English appeared in the eighteenth century. Daniel Defoe's *Robinson Crusoe* and Jonathan Swift's *Gulliver's Travels* are both adventure stories that still have appeal today. Most classical novels are about ordinary people and important social problems.

Short stories first became available to readers in newspapers and magazines. Favorite classical short story writers include Edgar Allan Poe and O. Henry. Early short stories can be read today in books that are collections of stories. These books are called *anthologies*.

The first biographies were written about saints. Later, people wanted to read about the lives of politicians and royalty. In the early days, biographers were less interested in reporting the facts than in flattering the important people they wrote about. However, the best classical biographies tell the truth and help us understand how people lived.

The essay has its roots in moral education. Essays were used as a way to teach students a moral lesson or make a point. The more educated people thought they knew what was best for the general population. Such authors as Virginia Woolf wrote persuasive essays to change opinions about the way things were done. As long as there are differences in opinions, people will write essays on almost every subject imaginable. Essays about ideas that are important to most people will be read over and over.

This unit presents passages from all types of classical literature such as the following.

■ The novels and short stories show a wide range of interests and ideas that have lasted over the years.

■ The poems express universal emotions and experiences.

■ The play deals with a human rights issue that is still important today.

■ The autobiography gives a personal view of an important time in American history.

■ The essay offers a fresh outlook on war and peace.

Section 15

Short Story

Setting the Stage

A **short story** is a piece of fiction that is shorter than a novel but has a full plot and a single theme. A short story usually has only a few characters and takes place over a brief time period. Writers have been publishing scary tales and detective stories in newspapers and magazines for more than a century. One of the first writers to become famous writing scary stories was Edgar Allan Poe. His spine-chilling short stories have been made into movies and TV shows. What makes Poe memorable is his understanding of the dark side of human nature.

Past: What you already know

You may have seen a scary movie or TV show based on one of Poe's stories such as "The Pit and the Pendulum," "The Fall of the House of Usher," or "The Murders in the Rue Morgue." Or you may have seen a movie like one of Poe's stories. How did the movie make you feel?

1. _____

_____

Present: What you learn by previewing

You can get a good idea of what you will be reading by looking at the title and reading the first few sentences. Read the first few sentences of the passage. What is the narrator's state of mind?

2. _____

_____

Future: What you predict

The passage on pages 109–111 is from Poe's story, "The Tell-Tale Heart." Do you think it will be a mystery with a puzzle to solve or a scary thriller?

3. _____

Read the first two paragraphs. What do you think the rest of the passage will be about? Now read on to find out if you are correct.

4. _____

_____

Check your answers on page 224.

The Tell-Tale Heart by Edgar Allan Poe

As you read each section, circle the words you don't know. Look up the meanings.

True!—nervous—very, very dreadfully nervous I had been and am; but why *will* you say that I am mad? The disease had sharpened my senses—not destroyed—not dulled them. Above all was the sense of hearing acute. I heard all things in the heaven and in the earth. . . . How, then, am I mad? Hearken! and observe how healthily—how calmly I can tell you the whole story.

It is impossible to say how first the idea entered my brain; but once conceived, it haunted me day and night. Object there was none. Passion there was none. I loved the old man. He had never wronged me. He had never given me insult. For his gold I had no desire. I think it was his eye! yes, it was this! One of his eyes resembled that of a vulture—a pale blue eye, with a film over it. Whenever it fell upon me, my blood ran cold; and so by degrees—very gradually—I made up my mind to take the life of the old man, and thus rid myself of the eye for ever.

Using Definitions as Context Clues. Sometimes an author defines an unfamiliar word or phrase for the reader. For example, in the passage above, the phrase *sharpened my senses* is used. By saying the opposite, *not destroyed—not dulled them*, the author makes the meaning of the phrase clear. Definition clues usually are found after a word and are set off by commas or dashes.

Applying Your Skills and Strategies

Find the phrase *by degrees* in the passage. Underline it. Write the context clue that tells you the meaning of this phrase.

_____

_____

Now this is the point. You fancy me mad. Madmen know nothing. But you should have seen *me*. You should have seen how wisely I proceeded—with what caution—with what foresight—with what dissimulation I went to work! I was never kinder to the old man than during the whole week before I killed him. And every night, about midnight, I turned the latch of his door and opened it—oh, so gently! And then, when I had made an opening sufficient for my head, I put in a dark lantern, all closed, closed, so that no light shone out, and then I thrust in my head. Oh, you would have laughed to see how cunningly I thrust it in! I moved it slowly—very, very slowly, so that I might not disturb the old man's sleep. It took me an hour to place my whole head within the opening so far that I could see him as he lay upon his bed. Ha!—would a madman have been so wise as this? And then, when my head was well in the room, I undid the lantern cautiously—oh, so cautiously—cautiously (for the hinges creaked)—I undid it just so much that a single thin ray fell upon the vulture eye. And this I did for seven long nights—every night just at midnight—but I found the eye always closed; and so it was impossible to do the work; for it was not the

Check your answer on page 224.

old man who vexed me, but his Evil Eye. And every morning, when the day broke, I went boldly into the chamber, and spoke courageously to him, calling him by name in a hearty tone, and inquiring how he had passed the night. So you see he would have been a very profound old man, indeed, to suspect that every night, just at twelve, I looked in upon him while he slept.

Upon the eighth night I was more than usually cautious in opening the door. A watch's minute hand moves more quickly than did mine. Never before that night had I *felt* the extent of my own powers—of my sagacity. I could scarcely contain my feelings of triumph. To think that there I was, opening the door, little by little, and he not even to dream of my secret deeds or thoughts. I fairly chuckled at the idea; and perhaps he heard me; for he moved on the bed suddenly, as if startled. Now you may think that I drew back—but no. His room was as black as pitch with the thick darkness (for the shutters were close fastened, through fear of robbers), and so I knew he could not see the opening of the door, and I kept pushing it on steadily, steadily.

I had my head in, and was about to open the lantern, when my thumb slipped upon the tin fastening, and the old man sprang up in the bed, crying out—"Who's there?"

I kept quite still and said nothing. For a whole hour I did not move a muscle, and in the meantime I did not hear him lie down. He was still sitting up in the bed listening;—just as I have done, night after night, hearkening to the death watches in the wall.

Understanding Mood.   Mood is how a reader feels about a story. The mood can be anxious, tense, happy, nervous, or satisfied. An author can create a certain mood by using words that express emotion, such as *sad*, *gloomy*, *thrilled*, or *scared*. Another way an author creates mood is by making the action happen quickly or slowly. If the action is slow and repeated, a tense mood is created.

Applying Your Skills and Strategies

What is the mood of this passage?

_____

How does the author create this mood? Give an example.

_____

_____

Presently I heard a slight groan, and I knew it was the groan of mortal terror. It was not a groan of pain or of grief—oh, no!—it was the low stifled sound that arises from the bottom of the soul when overcharged with awe. I knew the sound well. Many a night, just at midnight, when all the world slept, it has welled up from my own bosom, deepening, with its dreadful echo, the terrors that distracted me. I say I knew it well. I knew what the old man felt, and pitied him, although I chuckled at heart. I knew that he had been lying awake ever since the first slight noise, when he had turned in the bed. His fears had been ever since growing upon him. He had been trying to fancy them causeless, but could not. He had been saying to himself—"It is nothing but the wind in the chimney—it is only a mouse crossing the floor," or "it is merely a cricket which has made a single chirp." Yes, he had been trying to comfort himself with these suppositions; but he has found all in vain. *All in vain*; because Death, in approaching him, had stalked with his black shadow before him, and enveloped the victim. And it was the mournful influence of the unperceived shadow that caused him to feel—although he neither saw nor heard—to *feel* the presence of my head within the room.

When I had waited a long time, very patiently, without hearing him lie down, I resolved to open a little—a very, very little crevice in the lantern. So I opened it—you cannot imagine how stealthily, stealthily—until, at length, a single dim ray, like the thread of the spider, shot from out the crevice and full upon the vulture eye.

It was open—wide, wide open—and I grew furious as I gazed upon it. I saw it with perfect distinctness—all a dull blue, with a hideous veil over it that chilled the very marrow in my bones; but I could see nothing else of the old man's face or person: for I had directed the ray as if by instinct, precisely upon the . . . spot.

And now have I not told you that what you mistake for madness is but over-acuteness of the senses?—now, I say, there came to my ears a low, dull, quick sound, such as a watch makes when enveloped in cotton. I knew *that* sound well too. It was the beating of the old man's heart. It increased my fury, as the beating of a drum stimulates the soldier into courage.

To find out more about this passage, turn to page 239.

Predicting Outcomes.

Applying Your Skills and Strategies

Sometimes an author ends a story without telling what finally happened. The reader must figure out the ending. When you do that, you are predicting the outcome. Use the information in the story to predict what will happen.

In the story so far, you have read about how angry the narrator gets because of the old man's *vulture* eye. Now that he has finally seen the eye, what do you think he will do in the next few minutes?

_____

_____

_____

_____

_____

Thinking About the Story

Find the numbered words below and underline them in the passage. Study the context in which each word appears. Then match each word with its meaning. Write the letter of the meaning by each word.

_____ 1. acute

_____ 2. stealthily

_____ 3. sufficient

_____ 4. enveloped

_____ 5. sagacity

_____ 6. stifled

_____ 7. suppositions

_____ 8. unperceived

_____ 9. crevice

_____ 10. dissimulation

a. not seen

b. surrounded

c. enough

d. wisdom

e. small crack

f. secrecy

g. sharp

h. ideas assumed to be correct

i. held in

j. quietly and secretly

Write your answers in the space provided.

11. Review your predictions on page 108. Were you right? If you said *yes*, write what you correctly predicted. If not, what were you wrong about?

_____

_____

_____

12. What about the old man bothered the narrator the most?

_____

13. Find the word *conceived* in the passage and underline it. What is the context clue that defines the meaning of the word?

_____

_____

Check your answers on pages 224–225.

14. Why did it take so long for the narrator to kill the old man?
    The narrator was

    (1) afraid of going to jail.

    (2) hoping to find out where the old man kept his gold.

    (3) waiting for the old man to be fast asleep.

    (4) very fond of the old man.

    (5) waiting to see the vulture eye.

15. Which of the following best describes the narrator's major emotion in the story?

    (1) chilling fear

    (2) constant worry

    (3) deep regret

    (4) quiet happiness

    (5) nervous pride

Write your answers in the space provided. Use complete sentences.

16. The narrator keeps saying that he is not crazy. Do you believe him? Why or why not?

    _____

    _____

    _____

    _____

17. Have you ever known someone who overreacted (reacted too strongly) to something annoying? What annoyed that person? What did the person do?

    _____

    _____

    _____

    _____

Romantic Novel

Setting the Stage

Romantic novels are stories about lovers. Often a couple must overcome obstacles before having a life together. Sometimes the family objects to the romance. At other times social or financial differences get in the way. Whatever the obstacle, stories about the troubles of lovers have always been popular. The reader of a romantic novel can sympathize with the couple as they try to work out their troubles. In most cases, the reader can expect a happy ending.

Past: What you already know

You may have read a novel or seen a movie about romantic problems. What was the main obstacle the couple faced?

1. _____

_____

_____

Present: What you learn by previewing

You can get a good idea of what you will be reading by looking at the title and reading a few sentences. Read the first few sentences of the passage. Write the names of the two main characters.

2. _____

_____

Future: What you predict

The passage on pages 115–117 is from a novel called *Ramona*. Read the first three paragraphs. What do you predict the passage will be about? Now read on to find out if you are correct.

3. _____

_____

_____

          Check your answers on page 225.

Ramona by Helen Hunt Jackson

As you read each
section, circle the
words you don't
know. Look up the
meanings.

Capitan was leaping up, putting his paws on Alessandro's breast, licking his face, yelping, doing all a dog could do, to show welcome and affection.

Alessandro laughed aloud. Ramona had not more than two or three times heard him do this. It frightened her. "Why do you laugh, Alessandro?" she said.

"To think what I have to show you, my Señorita," he said. "Look here;" and turning towards the willows, he gave two or three low whistles, at the first note of which Baba came trotting out of the copse [small group of trees] to the end of his lariat, and began to snort and whinny with delight as soon as he perceived Ramona.

*Applying
Your Skills
and
Strategies*

Making Inferences.   To make an inference, use both the facts you are given and what you already know. Details can be clues that help you make an inference. For example, you are told that Capitan is a dog. But if that fact had not been given, you could have inferred it from the description of his actions. *Leaping up*, *licking*, and *yelping* are details that make you think of a dog.

Reread the sentences describing Baba. What kind of animal can you infer he is?

_____

What details helped you make this inference?

_____

_____

Ramona burst into tears. The surprise was too great.

"Are you not glad, Señorita?" cried Alessandro, aghast. "Is it not your own horse? If you do not wish to take him, I will lead him back. My pony can carry you, if we journey very slowly. But I thought it would be joy to you to have Baba."

"Oh, it is! it is!" sobbed Ramona, with her head on Baba's neck. "It is a miracle,—a miracle. How did he come here? And the saddle too!" she cried, for the first time observing that. "Alessandro," in an awe-struck whisper, "did the saints send him? Did you find him here?" It would have seemed to Ramona's faith no strange thing, had this been so.

"I think the saints helped me to bring him," answered Alessandro, seriously, "or else I had not done it so easily. I did but call, near the corral-fence, and he came to my hand, and leaped over the rails at my word, as quickly as Capitan might have done. He is yours, Señorita. It is no harm to take him?"

"Oh, no!" answered Ramona. "He is more mine than anything else I had; for it was Felipe gave him to me when he could but just stand on his legs; he was only two days old; and I have fed him out of my hand every day till now; and now he is five. Dear Baba, we will never be parted, never!" and she took his head in both her hands, and laid her cheek against it lovingly.

Alessandro was busy, fastening the two nets on either side of the saddle. "Baba will never know he has a load at all; they are not so heavy as my Señorita thought," he said. "It was the weight on the forehead, with nothing to keep the strings from the skin, which gave her pain."

Alessandro was making all haste. His hands trembled. "We must make all the speed we can, dearest Señorita," he said, "for a few hours. Then we will rest. Before light, we will be in a spot where we can hide safely all day. We will journey only by night, lest they pursue us."

"They will not," said Ramona. "There is no danger. The Señora said she should do nothing. 'Nothing!'" she repeated, in a bitter tone. "That is what she made Felipe say, too. Felipe wanted to help us. He would have liked to have you stay with us; but all he could get was, that she would do 'nothing!' But they will not follow us. They will wish never to hear of me again. I mean, the Señora will wish never to hear of me. Felipe will be sorry. Felipe is very good, Alessandro."

They were all ready now,—Ramona on Baba, the two packed nets swinging from her saddle, one on either side. Alessandro, walking, led his tired pony. It was a sad sort of procession for one going to be wed, but Ramona's heart was full of joy.

"I don't know why it is, Alessandro," she said; "I should think I would be afraid, but I have not the least fear,—not the least; not of anything that can come, Alessandro," she reiterated with emphasis. "Is it not strange?"

Using Context Clues to Find Synonyms. Synonyms are words that have the same or nearly the same meaning. You can find synonyms by looking at the context in which the words are used. When two words are used in the same way, you can guess that their meanings are similar. For example, *to repeat* means "to say something again." In the passage above, Ramona repeats the word *nothing*. In the last paragraph Ramona says *not the least* twice. What word in this paragraph is used the same way the word *repeated* is used?

Applying Your Skills and Strategies

"Yes, Señorita," he replied solemnly, laying his hand on hers as he walked close at her side. "It is strange. I am afraid,—afraid for you, my Señorita! But it is done, and we will not go back; and perhaps the saints will help you, and will let me take care of you. They must love you, Señorita; but they do not love me, nor my people."

"Are you never going to call me by my name?" asked Ramona. "I hate your calling me Señorita. That was what the Señora always called me when she was displeased."

"I will never speak the word again!" cried Alessandro. "The saints forbid I should speak to you in the words of that woman!"

"Can't you say Ramona?" she asked.

Alessandro hesitated. He could not have told why it seemed to him difficult to say Ramona.

"What was that other name, you said you always thought of me by?" she continued. "The Indian name,—the name of the dove?"

"Majel," he said. "It is by that name I have oftenest thought of you since the night I watched all night for you, after you had kissed me, and two wood-doves were calling and answering each other in the dark; and I said to myself, that is what my love is like, the wood-dove: the wood-dove's voice is low like hers, and sweeter than any other sound in the earth; and the wood-dove is true to one mate always—" He stopped.

"As I to you, Alessandro," said Ramona, leaning from her horse, and resting her hand on Alessandro's shoulder.

Baba stopped. He was used to knowing by the most trivial signs what his mistress wanted; he did not understand this new situation; no one had ever before, when Ramona was riding him, walked by his side so close that he touched his shoulders, and rested his hand in his mane. If it had been anybody else than Alessandro, Baba would not have permitted it even now. But it must be all right, since Ramona was quiet; and now she had stretched out her hand and rested it on Alessandro's shoulder. Did that mean halt for a moment? Baba thought it might, and acted accordingly; turning his head round to the right, and looking back to see what came of it.

Alessandro's arms around Ramona, her head bent down to his, their lips together,—what could Baba think? As mischievously as if he had been a human being or an elf, Baba bounded to one side and tore the lovers apart. They both laughed, and cantered on,—Alessandro running; the poor Indian pony feeling the contagion, and loping as it had not done for many a day.

"Majel is my name, then," said Ramona, "is it? It is a sweet sound, but I would like it better Majella. Call me Majella."

To find out more about this passage, turn to page 238.

Restating the Main Idea. The main idea of this part of the passage is that Ramona takes on the new name *Majella* to please Alessandro. Reread this part and restate the main idea in your own words.

Applying Your Skills and Strategies

_____

_____

Thinking About the Story

Find the numbered words below and underline them in the passage. Study the context in which each word appears. Then match each word with its meaning. Write the letter of the meaning by each word.

_____ 1. lariat

_____ 2. perceived

_____ 3. aghast

_____ 4. procession

_____ 5. trivial

_____ 6. mischievously

_____ 7. cantered

_____ 8. contagion

a. saw

b. moved at a fast trot

c. not important

d. shocked

e. playfully or teasingly

f. rope

g. group moving in the same direction

h. a feeling of the same influence

Write your answers in the space provided.

9. Review your prediction on page 114. Were you right? If you said _yes_, write what you correctly predicted. If not, write two things you didn't expect to happen.

_____

_____

_____

10. What are Alessandro and Ramona doing?

_____

Circle the number of the best answer.

11. Why do you think Alessandro was in such a hurry?

    (1) He was angry with Ramona.

    (2) The horse and pony couldn't wait.

    (3) Ramona wanted to see her family soon.

    (4) He thought they might be stopped.

    (5) The stores were closing soon.

Check your answers on page 225.

12. What can you infer about the differences between Ramona and Alessandro?

    (1) Ramona is poor and Alessandro is rich.

    (2) Alessandro's parents do not approve of Ramona.

    (3) Ramona's family does not approve of Alessandro.

    (4) Alessandro and Ramona are both from the same kind of family.

    (5) Alessandro is not as sure about their love as Ramona is.

13. Which of the following best states the central idea of this passage?

    (1) Love conquers all problems.

    (2) Look before you leap.

    (3) Time makes all sorrows go away.

    (4) Names are not important.

    (5) Older people always have the right answers.

Write your answers in the space provided.

14. At the end of the passage there is a section describing what Baba thinks. What is the tone of this section? How does this scene help you understand the way the young lovers feel?

_____

_____

_____

15. If Ramona and Alessandro were a young couple today, how would they deal with Ramona's family?

_____

_____

_____

16. Have you or someone you know run into an obstacle in the way of something important? How was the obstacle overcome?

_____

_____

_____

Check your answers on page 225.			*Section 16: Romantic Novel* 119

Poetry

Setting the Stage

Poetry is one of the oldest types of storytelling. Centuries ago, in many cultures poetry was spoken, not written. The form of these poems made them easy for people to remember. They were handed down from one generation to another by word of mouth. In later times, many of these poems were written down. **Classical poems** are poems that are still read and enjoyed today. These poems appeal to people of all ages. They speak about experiences and emotions that are common to everyone.

Past: What you already know

Have you read a poem from long ago? What idea or experience makes you remember the poem?

1. _____

_____

Present: What you learn by previewing

You can get a good idea of what you will be reading by looking at the title and reading a few lines of a poem. Read the first five lines of "The Road Not Taken." What choice is the speaker trying to make?

2. _____

_____

Future: What you predict

Read the first few lines of the poem "Richard Cory." What do you predict the poem will be about? Read on to find out if you are correct.

3. _____

_____

Read the first few lines of the poem "The Minuet." What do you predict the poem will be about? Read on to find out if you are correct.

4. _____

_____

The Road Not Taken by Robert Frost

*As you read each
section, circle the
words you don't
know. Look up the
meanings.*

Two roads diverged in a yellow wood,
And sorry I could not travel both
And be one traveler, long I stood
And looked down one as far as I could
To where it bent in the undergrowth;

Then took the other, just as fair,
And having perhaps the better claim,
Because it was grassy and wanted wear;
Though as for that the passing there
Had worn them really about the same,

And both that morning equally lay
In leaves no step had trodden black.
Oh, I kept the first for another day!
Yet knowing how way leads on to way,
I doubted if I should ever come back.

I shall be telling this with a sigh
Somewhere ages and ages hence:
Two roads diverged in a wood, and I—
I took the one less traveled by,
And that has made all the difference.

*To find out more
about this poem,
turn to page 237.*

Using Context Clues.   Sometimes you will see an unfamiliar word or
phrase in a passage. Study the context in which the word or phrase is used. Look
for clues that might help you guess what it means. For example, the word
undergrowth appears in the fifth line of the poem. The clues *yellow wood*, *grassy*,
and *in leaves* suggest that *undergrowth* means "the plants that grow close to the
ground in a forest."

*Applying
Your Skills
and
Strategies*

Find the phrase *wanted wear*, and underline it in the poem. What do you think
the phrase *wanted wear* means?

_____

_____

What context clues did you use to find the meaning?

_____

_____

_____

Richard Cory by Edwin Arlington Robinson

Whenever Richard Cory went down town,
We people on the pavement looked at him:
He was a gentleman from sole to crown,
Clean favored, and imperially slim.

And he was always quietly arrayed,
And he was always human when he talked;
But still he fluttered pulses when he said,
"Good-morning," and he glittered when he walked.

And he was rich—yes, richer than a king—
And admirably schooled in every grace:
In fine, we thought that he was everything
To make us wish that we were in his place.

So on we worked, and waited for the light,
And went without the meat, and cursed the bread;
And Richard Cory, one calm summer night,
Went home and put a bullet through his head.

To find out more about this poem, turn to page 240.

Recognizing Theme.   A theme is a statement of a general truth about life, or an insight into human nature. A story or poem can have more than one theme. One theme in this poem is that people often want to be something they are not. This can be seen from the lines "We people on the pavement . . ." and " . . . wish that we were in his place." Another theme in this poem could be stated as "Riches don't make a person happy."

Reread the entire poem. How did the people of the town feel about Richard Cory?

_____

_____

How do you think Richard Cory felt about himself?

_____

_____

Based on these ideas, state a theme for the entire poem.

_____

_____

_____

          Check your answers on page 226.

The Minuet by Mary Mapes Dodge

Grandma told me all about it,
Told me so I couldn't doubt it,
How she danced, my grandma danced; long ago—
How she held her pretty head,
How her dainty skirt she spread,
How she slowly leaned and rose—long ago.

Grandma's hair was bright and sunny,
Dimpled cheeks, too, oh, how funny!
Really quite a pretty girl—long ago.
Bless her! why, she wears a cap,
Grandma does, and takes a nap
Every single day: and yet
Grandma danced the minuet—long ago.

"Modern ways are quite alarming,"
Grandma says, "but boys were charming"
(Girls and boys she means, of course) "long ago."
Brave but modest, grandly shy;
She would like to have us try
Just to feel like those who met
In the graceful minuet—long ago.

To find out more about this poem, turn to page 237.

Restating the Main Idea.   A poem, like other forms of literature, has a main idea. The main idea of the first six lines is the way Grandma danced. This idea can be restated in this way: Grandma paid a lot of attention to how she danced.

Reread the last seven lines of the poem. The main idea of this section is that the grandmother would like her grandchildren to experience the things she experienced as a young girl. Restate the main idea in your own words.

_____

_____

_____

_____

Thinking About the Poems

Find the words below and underline them in the poems. Study the context in which each word appears. Try to figure out the meaning of each word. Then complete the following sentences by writing the correct words in the blanks provided.

diverged   arrayed   schooled

claim   trodden   minuet

1. More than a century ago, a popular dance was the _____ .

2. Near the front door, the carpet is worn out because it has been

    _____ on a lot.

3. The road _____ at the fork, and we didn't know which way to go.

4. When people have dressed up for a special occasion, they have

    _____ themselves in nice clothing.

5. Richard Cory was trained, or _____ , in all the social graces.

6. If you say you have a right to something, you are making a

    _____ .

Write your answers in the space provided.

7. Review your prediction on page 120. Were you right? If you said *yes*, write what you correctly predicted. If not, write two things you did not expect to read about.

    _____

    _____

    _____

8. What did the speaker in "The Road Not Taken" do before he chose which road to take?

    _____

9. In "The Minuet," what did Grandma look like when she was young?

    _____

                    Check your answers on page 226.

10. What two words suggest that Richard Cory was like a king?

_____

Circle the number of the best answer for each question.

11. Which of the following from "The Road Not Taken" is the best restatement of the phrase _just as fair_?

   (1) _the better claim_

   (2) _really about the same_

   (3) _the passing there_

   (4) _come back_

   (5) _the one less traveled by_

12. Which of the following sayings best states the theme of "Richard Cory"?

   (1) A bird in the hand is worth two in the bush.

   (2) An apple a day keeps the doctor away.

   (3) You can't judge a book by its cover.

   (4) You can't change a sow's ear into a silk purse.

   (5) Money is the root of all evil.

13. In what way are the poems "A Road Not Taken" and "Richard Cory" similar?

   (1) Both poems discuss individual choice.

   (2) Both speakers are successful.

   (3) Both poems are about failure.

   (4) Both poems are about the future.

   (5) Both poems are about social issues.

Write your answers in the space provided.

14. What important experience in your life would you write a poem about? Why would you share this experience with your readers?

_____

_____

_____

_____

Check your answers on page 226.

Section 18

Social Drama

Setting the Stage

Many classical plays are **social dramas**. These plays, sometimes called *problem plays*, deal with major social issues. Sometimes they are about how society reacts to a certain group. Some plays deal with prejudices against a minority group. Other plays are about individuals who have trouble fitting into society. The conflicts in social drama are not always solved, but the effects of the problem are made clear. Social dramas can be funny, sad, or both.

Past: What you already know

You may have already seen a play that has been performed for many years. Was it a social drama? If so, what social issue was the play about?

1. _____

_____

Present: What you learn by previewing

You can get a good idea of what you will be reading by looking at the title and reading a few lines. Read enough of the play to name the four characters.

2. _____

Future: What you predict

The passage on pages 127–129 is from a play called *A Raisin in the Sun*. The title comes from a protest poem by the African-American poet Langston Hughes. Based on the title, what kind of social problem do you think the play will be about?

3. _____

_____

Read the first few lines of the passage. What do you predict the passage will be about? Read on to see if you are correct.

4. _____

_____

_____

Check your answers on page 226.

A Raisin in the Sun by Lorraine Hansberry

As you read each section, circle the words you don't know. Look up the meanings.

BENEATHA: Sticks and stones may break my bones but . . . words will never hurt me!

(BENEATHA *goes to the door and opens it as* WALTER *and* RUTH *go on with the clowning.* BENEATHA *is somewhat surprised to see a quiet-looking middle-aged white man in a business suit holding his hat and a briefcase in his hand and consulting a small piece of paper*)

MAN: Uh—how do you do, miss. I am looking for a Mrs.— (*He looks at the slip of paper*) Mrs. Lena Younger?

BENEATHA (*Smoothing her hair with slight embarrassment*): Oh—yes, that's my mother. Excuse me. (*She closes the door and turns to quiet the other two*) Ruth! Brother! Somebody's here. (*Then she opens the door. The man casts a curious quick glance at all of them*) Uh—come in please.

MAN (*Coming in*): Thank you.

BENEATHA: My mother isn't here just now. Is it business?

MAN: Yes . . . well, of a sort.

WALTER (*Freely, the Man of the House*): Have a seat. I'm Mrs. Younger's son. I look after most of her business matters.

(RUTH *and* BENEATHA *exchange amused glances*)

MAN (*Regarding* WALTER, *and sitting*): Well—My name is Karl Lindner . . .

WALTER (*Stretching out his hand*): Walter Younger. This is my wife—(RUTH *nods politely*)— and my sister.

LINDNER: How do you do.

WALTER (*Amiably, as he sits himself easily on a chair, leaning with interest forward on his knees and looking expectantly into the newcomer's face*): What can we do for you, Mr. Lindner!

LINDNER (*Some minor shuffling of the hat and briefcase on his knees*): Well—I am a representative of the Clybourne Park Improvement Association—

WALTER (*Pointing*): Why don't you sit your things on the floor?

Drawing Conclusions About Characters. Stage directions and the way characters react to one another give clues about what the characters are like. The stage directions describe Walter's attitude. They also describe the way he greets the guest and how the women react. From these clues, what can you conclude about how Walter sees himself?

Applying Your Skills and Strategies

_____

_____

What can you conclude that Ruth and Beneatha think of Walter's attitude?

_____

_____

_____

LINDNER: Oh—yes. Thank you. (*He slides the briefcase and hat under the chair*)   And as I was saying—I am from the Clybourne Park Improvement Association and we have had it brought to our attention at the last meeting that you people—or at least your mother—has bought a piece of residential property at— (*He digs for the slip of paper again*)—four o six Clybourne Street . . .

WALTER: That's right. Care for something to drink? Ruth, get Mr. Lindner a beer.

LINDNER (*Upset for some reason*):   Oh—no, really. I mean thank you very much, but no thank you.

RUTH (*Innocently*):   Some coffee?

LINDNER: Thank you, nothing at all.

(BENEATHA *is watching the man carefully*)

LINDNER: Well, I don't know how much you folks know about our organization. (*He is a gentle man; thoughtful and somewhat labored in his manner*) It is one of these community organizations set up to look after—oh, you know, things like block upkeep and special projects and we also have what we call our New Neighbors Orientation Committee . . .

BENEATHA (*Drily*):   Yes—and what do they do?

LINDNER (*Turning a little to her and then returning the main force to* WALTER):   Well—it's what you might call a sort of welcoming committee, I guess. I mean they, we, I'm the chairman of the committee—go around and see the new people who move into the neighborhood and sort of give them the lowdown on the way we do things out in Clybourne Park.

BENEATHA (*With appreciation of the two meanings, which escape* RUTH *and* WALTER):   Un-huh.

LINDNER: And we also have the category of what the association calls—(*He looks elsewhere*)—uh—special community problems . . .

Recognizing Theme.   The theme of a story or play is not the same as its plot. A theme is a general truth about life, or human nature, suggested in a story.

In the passage Lindner represents the Clybourne Park Improvement Association. Lindner wants to discuss something with the Youngers and he seems very uncomfortable. Reread the passage, starting at the top of the page. What is the author suggesting about human nature by the way Lindner is acting?

Applying Your Skills and Strategies

_____

_____

_____

_____

_____

Check your answer on page 226.

BENEATHA: Yes—and what are some of those?

WALTER: Girl, let the man talk.

LINDNER (*With understated relief*):   Thank you. I would sort of like to explain this thing in my own way. I mean I want to explain to you in a certain way.

WALTER: Go ahead.

LINDNER: Yes. Well. I'm going to try to get right to the point. I'm sure we'll all appreciate that in the long run.

BENEATHA: Yes.

WALTER: Be still now!

LINDNER: Well—

RUTH (*Still innocently*):   Would you like another chair—you don't look comfortable.

LINDNER (*More frustrated than annoyed*):   No, thank you very much. Please. Well—to get right to the point I—(*A great breath, and he is off at last*) I am sure you people must be aware of some of the incidents which have happened in various parts of the city when colored people have moved into certain areas—(BENEATHA *exhales heavily and starts tossing a piece of fruit up and down in the air*) Well—because we have what I think is going to be a unique type of organization in American community life—not only do we deplore that kind of thing—but we are trying to do something about it. (BENEATHA *stops tossing and turns with a new and quizzical interest to the man*) We feel— (*gaining confidence in his mission because of the interest in the faces of the people he is talking to*)—we feel that most of the trouble in this world, when you come right down to it—(*He hits his knee for emphasis*)—most of the trouble exists because people just don't sit down and talk to each other.

To find out more about this play, turn to page 238.

Summarizing.
Sometimes summarizing a long speech can help you understand what really is being said. When summarizing, include the main idea and most important supporting details.

Reread Lindner's last speech on this page. Summarize it in a few sentences.

Applying Your Skills and Strategies

_____

_____

_____

_____

RUTH (*Nodding as she might in church, pleased with the remark*):   You can say that again, mister.

LINDNER (*More encouraged by such affirmation*):   That we don't try hard enough in this world to understand the other fellow's problem. The other guy's point of view.

Thinking About the Play

Find the numbered words below in the passage and underline them. Study the context in which each word appears. Then match each word with its meaning. Write the letter of the meaning by each word.

_____ 1. consulting

_____ 2. expectantly

_____ 3. affirmation

_____ 4. labored

_____ 5. category

_____ 6. frustrated

_____ 7. deplore

_____ 8. quizzical

a. strongly dislike

b. curious

c. prevented from reaching a goal

d. group

e. looking at to get information

f. had great difficulty

g. a positive statement

h. hopefully

Write your answers in the space provided.

9. Review your predictions on page 126. Were you right? If you said _yes_, write what you correctly predicted. If not, write what you found out the passage was about.

_____

_____

_____

10. What clue in the stage directions first lets you know Lindner is uncomfortable?

_____

11. Lindner is trying to explain what the Clybourne Park Improvement Association does. Summarize what he first tells the Youngers.

_____

_____

12. What can you conclude about the Youngers' race?

_____

Check your answers on pages 226–227.

Circle the number of the best answer for each question.

13. Which of the following best describes Beneatha's attitude toward Lindner?

    (1) very unfriendly

    (2) uninterested

    (3) overly polite

    (4) suspicious

    (5) satisfied

14. The members of the Younger family do not seem to think they have a problem. But their visitor refers twice to neighborhood problems. He also talks about incidents with "colored people." What problem is Lindner suggesting?

    (1) The association does not want an African-American family in the neighborhood.

    (2) The Youngers' house does not meet the building codes.

    (3) They caused race riots in Clybourne Park.

    (4) The association wonders why the Youngers have not joined any local groups.

    (5) The Youngers have protested against African-American people.

15. Based on Lindner's approach to the Younger family, what do you think he probably will do to solve the problem?

    (1) threaten them

    (2) ask them to join the association

    (3) suggest in a nice way that they sell the house

    (4) learn to accept the family

    (5) have them arrested for disturbing the peace

Write your answer in the space provided. Use complete sentences.

16. Have you or someone you know had an experience with some kind of prejudice? Was the prejudice suggested or was it stated directly? Was the problem resolved?

    _____

    _____

    _____

Check your answers on page 227.

Western Novel

Setting the Stage

The **Western novel** began when the frontiers of America were being settled. As the United States grew, the West attracted people who wanted to start a new life. It also drew people who wanted to make a quick fortune, sometimes outside the law. Western novels tell stories about the challenges these people faced. Stories about cowhands and their rugged country were popular even after the West was settled. Readers of today still enjoy exciting tales about taming the "Wild West."

Past: What you already know

You may have read a novel or seen a TV show about the American West. What was the story about?

1. _____

_____

_____

Present: What you learn by previewing

You can get a good idea of what you will be reading by looking at the title and reading a few sentences. Read the first few sentences of the passage. Write the name of the main character.

2. _____

Future: What you predict

The passage on pages 133–135 is from a novel called *Horse Heaven Hill*. Based on the title, what do you think the passage will be about?

3. _____

_____

Reread the first few sentences. Now what do you predict the passage will be about? Read on to find out if you are correct.

4. _____

_____

     Check your answers on page 227.

Horse Heaven Hill by Zane Grey

As you read each section, circle the words you don't know. Look up the meanings.

Chaps found the trail. It was soft and grassy, giving forth no sound under his hoofs. Below, Lark remembered, near the trap she would need to dismount and go very carefully, to avoid making a noise.

As she proceeded, the state of cool pondering alternating with suspense which possessed her gradually underwent a change. It dawned upon her finally what she might expect if she fell into Blanding's hands. But she would have to be caught by his riders first. The possibility seemed remote. Blanding might send a few men to stay all night near the trap, though Lark considered that doubtful. If it did happen, however, these men would undoubtedly camp outside of the gate, and this would put them a quarter of a mile from Lark's objective. In case of a surprise Lark thought grimly that she could shoot her way out. She would not mind taking a shot at Blanding anyhow. Her father had not been a man who ever hesitated to use a firearm. But killing a man, except in defense of her life or honor, was unthinkable. Lark felt extremely dubious about using a gun in the dark upon moving men. Yet she had to go on, risk or no risk, and she did not intend to be caught.

After traveling a couple of miles she drew Chaps to a walk, and soon after that she reached the dark boulder which marked the line for her to descend. It was gray and gloomy down there in the notch. No fires! She had to strain her ears to catch sounds of horses. They were there, apparently resting. Lark, assuring herself that her enterprise was favored by fortune, rode down very slowly.

Understanding Sequence.

Applying Your Skills and Strategies

It is important to understand the sequence of events in a story. After Chaps finds the trail, Lark thinks about what she is about to do. She decides to go on with her plan.

Reread the last paragraph above. What are the next three events in the sequence of the story?

_____

_____

_____

_____

At length she got as far as she needed to go, if she intended to slip down on foot to reconnoiter, and make sure whether or not Blanding had sent a man back. But, after all, what good would it do her to know whether they were there or not? In any case she meant to liberate the horses. She would waive that added work, and proceed under the assumption that Blanding's riders were there.

Check your answer on page 227.

Dismounting, she walked a little apart from Chaps to listen. First she heard the low fall of water, then the light steps and thuds of hoofs of uneasy horses. She was about a hundred yards above the fence, even with the center, where she meant to make the break. Next she heard an owl hoot, and after that the whine of coyotes. They were down in the trap attracted by dead horses.

Lark returned to Chaps and, taking up his bridle, slipped her hand up almost to the bit and led him very cautiously, a few slow steps at a time. Soon she was in the section where it would be easy to crash brush, crack a stick or roll a rock. She bent low, searching the ground, and it was certain that she made no sound which could have been heard many yards away. It took precious time to do this. She realized that, at the last, when she tied the lasso to the trees in order to snake them out and open up the fence. Noise would be unavoidable. Then, however, it would not matter so much, for she could drag three trees out of there in less than three minutes and be gone. But she had forgotten that she must also light the fire.

As she worked down most carefully she turned these things over and over in her mind. And the result was that she elaborated a safer and better plan.

The thicket, which she soon entered, was dark, and the way tortuous. Pine saplings and brush of a leafless variety crowded upon her. The ground was thick with pine needles. This place would burn fiercely; in fact, the whole brushy slope above the fence would go. There was no other plot of timber near, something she had noted before deciding on this hazardous venture. The wild-horse catchers would have to travel far to find more material for a new fence.

Understanding the Setting.   Details that describe the place where the action happens help you to visualize the setting. *The line for her to descend* and *a hundred yards above the fence* are details that suggest that Lark is on a hill.

Applying Your Skills and Strategies

After Lark works her way down the hill, she is in a new setting. Give four details that describe the setting Lark finds.

_____

_____

At last Lark was down, close to the high line of piled trees and brush. A cleared lane, which the riders had cut, offered Lark room to drag out the large bushy treetops she had selected. She made sure that they were the right ones. Then, going beyond them, she gathered armloads of pine needles and dry bits of dead wood, which she piled against the fence.

That done, she was ready. But she waited longer to listen. In that interval she discovered that she was panting; her face was bathed in cold sweat; she felt a tingling and thrilling of nerves. Sounds disturbed her.

The wild horses were restless. They scented her or Chaps. She heard them moving inside the fence. How could she be sure those steps were not made by men?

The moment had come. With firm hands Lark tied one end of the lasso round the first tree she had selected. Then she got on Chaps, and winding the other end round the pommel, she spurred him. He gave a lunge; the rope tightened. The tree rustled loud, branches cracked. Lark's heart leaped high, her tongue clove to the roof of her mouth. She heard wild horses snort inside the fence. They were curious. She saw dark heads pointed up against the background of gray. Chaps appeared to be stuck. She spurred again and beat him with her glove. He plunged, dug down, and straining hard he loosened the tree with a crash and got it moving. Momentarily it caught on the second tree, but this one started too, and presently the sturdy little mustang dragged them both out.

Making Inferences About Characters.

Applying Your Skills and Strategies

To make an inference, use the facts you are given and what you already know. The way a character acts can help you make inferences about that person. For example, you can infer from the way Lark works with Chaps that she is a good rider.

You can also make inferences about how a character feels. Lark piles the brush by the fence and then stops to listen. Read the description of Lark as she stands listening. What can you infer about how Lark feels?

_____

_____

_____

Lark leaped off and flew back. Her hands were not steady now when she untied the rope. A gray aperture broke the solid black outline of the fence. Lark dragged Chaps across this opening to tie on to the third tree. This was wide and bushy, but it came more easily. Its removal left a gateway wide enough to drive through two wagons abreast. It was enough. Just inside wild horses edged close, snorting. Suddenly a gray beast with the whites of his eyes showing broke through the opening.

Lark had to leap to escape him. Then Chaps plunged and dragged her. More horses bolted through. When she got the frightened Chaps under control, a stream of them was pouring out of the break. They did not make a great deal of noise, but even that added to Lark's fright. Nor did they crash the brush, for the reason that the great mass of horses had not yet started. But she heard a quick trampling of hoofs all along the inside of the fence, up to the apex of the trap. They would not rush the break. They were coming steadily, stamping, snorting, but not wild with terror. That sliding, dark stream seemed uncanny.

To find out more about this passage, turn to page 238.

Thinking About the Story

Find the words below and underline them in the passage. Study the context in which each word appears. Try to figure out the meaning of each word. Then complete the following sentences by writing the correct words in the blanks provided.

pondering	liberate	aperture	tortuous
dubious	elaborated	reconnoiter	

1. A small _____ in the roof let a little light into the attic.

2. The scout rode ahead to _____ and find a place for the settlers to camp for the night.

3. We were all _____ that our risky plan would work out.

4. Lark had a plan to _____ the trapped wild horses.

5. She took a long time _____ the problem until she decided what to do.

6. She _____ a new plan, taking into account all of the details.

7. She led the horse down the _____ path, which curved back and forth down the slope.

Write your answers in the space provided.

8. Review your prediction on page 132. Were you right? If you said *yes*, write what you correctly predicted. If not, write two things you didn't expect to find out.

_____

_____

_____

9. What is Lark's goal in this passage?

_____

10. What does the phrase *sliding, dark stream* describe?

_____

11. What can you infer about Blanding's men? They are

    (1) Lark's friends.

    (2) friends of Lark's father.

    (3) the good guys.

    (4) lawmen.

    (5) the wild-horse catchers.

12. Which word best describes Lark?

    (1) cautious

    (2) careless

    (3) shy

    (4) carefree

    (5) timid

13. What do you think will be the result of Lark's burning the fence?

    (1) The horses will be frightened.

    (2) The trap will be ruined.

    (3) Blanding's men will catch Lark.

    (4) Chaps will decide to join the wild horses.

    (5) The nearby timber will have to be used for rebuilding.

Write your answers in the space provided.

14. What do you think Lark would do if she were caught by Blanding's riders?

    _____

    _____

    _____

15. Have you ever taken a risk in order to do something you thought was important? Why did you take the risk?

    _____

    _____

    _____

    _____

Section 20

Autobiography

Some autobiographies give us a look at a world that no longer exists. *Black Elk Speaks* tells about part of a lost America. Over a hundred years ago, the Oglala Sioux followed traditional ways of living. Their lives changed when the "white man," whom they called the *Wasichu*, began to settle on their land. In 1886 Black Elk, a holy man, joined the Wild West Show run by Buffalo Bill. By doing this he hoped to learn more about the *Wasichu*. Black Elk wanted to help his people find a peaceful way of living with the new settlers and a new way of life.

Past: What you already know

You may have read a book or seen a movie about Native Americans. What are some of the problems they faced?

1. _____

   _____

   _____

Present: What you learn by previewing

You can get a good idea of what you will be reading by looking at the title and reading a few sentences. Read the first paragraph. What event is being described?

2. _____

   _____

Future: What you predict

The passage on pages 139–141 is from an autobiography called *Black Elk Speaks*. Based on the title, who do you think will be telling the story?

3. _____

Read the first two paragraphs. What do you predict Black Elk will be learning about? Read on to find out if you are correct.

4. _____

   _____

Black Elk Speaks as told through John G. Neihardt (Flaming Rainbow)

As you read each section, circle the words you don't know. Look up the meanings.

That evening where the big wagons were waiting for us on the iron road, we had a dance. Then we got into the wagons. When we started, it was dark, and thinking of my home and my people made me very sad. I wanted to get off and run back. But we went roaring all night long, and in the morning we ate at Long Pine. Then we started again and went roaring all day and came to a very big town [Omaha, Nebraska] in the evening.

Then we roared along all night again and came to a much bigger town [Chicago]. There we stayed all day and all night; and right there I could compare my people's ways with Wasichu ways, and this made me sadder than before. I wished and wished that I had not gone away from home.

Then we went roaring on again, and afterwhile we came to a still bigger town—a very big town [New York]. We walked through this town to the place where the show was [Madison Square Garden]. Some Pawnees and Omahas were there, and when they saw us they made war-cries and charged, couping us. They were doing this for fun and because they felt glad to see us. I was surprised at the big houses and so many people, and there were bright lights at night, so that you could not see the stars, and some of these lights, I heard, were made with the power of thunder.

We stayed there and made shows for many, many Wasichus all that winter. I liked the part of the show we made, but not the part the Wasichus made. Afterwhile I got used to being there, but I was like a man who had never had a vision. I felt dead and my people seemed lost and I thought I might never find them again. I did not see anything to help my people. I could see that the Wasichus did not care for each other the way our people did before the nation's hoop was broken.

Using Context Clues. Different groups of people use special words and phrases that the rest of us may not always understand. Looking at the context of a word can help you figure out its meaning. For example, find the word *couping* in the passage. Underline it. The context clues, *war-cries* and *charged*, show that *couping* has something to do with war. *Couping* is the act of hitting a defeated enemy to declare victory.

Applying Your Skills and Strategies

Find the phrase *nation's hoop*. Remember that Black Elk is worried about his people and that the *hoop*, or circle, is broken. What do you think Black Elk means by *nation's hoop*?

_____

_____

_____

Check your answer on page 228.

They would take everything from each other if they could, and so there were some who had more of everything than they could use, while crowds of people had nothing at all and maybe were starving. They had forgotten that the earth was their mother. This could not be better than the old ways of my people. There was a prisoner's house on an island where the big water came up to the town, and we saw that one day. Men pointed guns at the prisoners and made them move around like animals in a cage. This made me very sad, because my people too were penned up in islands, and maybe that was the way the Wasichus were going to treat them.

In the spring it got warmer, but the Wasichus had even the grass penned up. We heard then that we were going to cross the big water to strange lands. Some of our people went home and wanted me to go with them, but I had not seen anything good for my people yet; maybe across the big water there was something to see, so I did not go home, although I was sick and in despair.

They put us all on a very big fire-boat, so big that when I first saw, I could hardly believe it; and when it sent forth a voice, I was frightened. There were other big fire-boats sending voices, and little ones too.

Afterwhile I could see nothing but water, water, water, and we did not seem to be going anywhere, just up and down; but we were told that we were going fast. If we were, I thought that we must drop off where the water ended; or maybe we might have to stop where the sky came down to the water. There was nothing but mist where the big town used to be and nothing but water all around.

We were all in despair now and many were feeling so sick that they began to sing their death-songs.

Identifying Point of View. Looking at events through the eyes of another person can help you see the world in a new way. Often, a person from another culture has a different point of view. In the passage so far, Black Elk is describing his experience in the *Wasichus'* world. Describe Black Elk's opinion of what he sees.

*Applying
Your Skills
and
Strategies*

_____

_____

_____

When evening came, a big wind was roaring and the water thundered. We had things that were meant to be hung up while we slept in them. This I learned afterward. We did not know what to do with these, so we spread them out on the floor and lay down on them. The floor tipped in every direction, and this got worse and worse, so that we rolled from one side to the other and could not sleep. We were frightened, and now we were all very sick too. At first the Wasichus laughed at us; but very soon we could see that they were frightened too, because they were running around and were very much excited. Our women were crying and even some of the men cried, because it was terrible and they could do nothing. Afterwhile the Wasichus came and gave us things to tie around us so that we could float. I did not put on the one they gave me. I did not want to float. Instead, I dressed for death, putting on my best clothes that I wore in the show, and then I sang my death song. Others dressed for death too, and sang, because if it was the end of our lives and we could do nothing, we wanted to die brave. We could not fight this that was going to kill us, but we could die so that our spirit relatives would not be ashamed of us. It was harder for us because we were all so sick. Everything we had eaten came right up, and then it kept trying to come up when there was nothing there.

We did not sleep at all, and in the morning the water looked like mountains, but the wind was not so strong. Some of the bison and elk that we had with us for the show died that day, and the Wasichus threw them in the water. When I saw the poor bison thrown over, I felt like crying, because I thought right there they were throwing part of the power of my people away.

After we had been on the fire-boat a long while, we could see many houses and then many other fire-boats tied close together along the bank. We thought now we could get off very soon, but we could not. There was a little fire-boat that had come through the gate of waters and it stopped beside us, and the people on it looked at everything on our fire-boat before we could get off. We went very slowly nearly all day, I think, and afterwhile we came to where there were many, many houses close together, and more fire-boats than could be counted. These houses were different from what we had seen before. The Wasichus kept us on the fire-boat all night and then they unloaded us, and took us to a place where the show was going to be. The name of this very big town was London. We were on land now, but we still felt dizzy as though we were still on water, and at first it was hard to walk.

We stayed in this place six moons; and many, many people came to see the show.

To find out more about this passage, turn to page 239.

Understanding Sequence. Black Elk described the trip from New York to London in sequence. He told the events in the order in which they happened.

Briefly list the sequence of main events that happened on this trip.

Applying Your Skills and Strategies

_____

_____

_____

_____

_____

Thinking About the Story

In this passage, Black Elk talks about some things he does not know the *Wasichu* word for. So he uses words he is familiar with to describe these things. Find the numbered words and phrases below and underline them in the passage. Study the context in which each word appears. Match each word with its meaning. Write the letter of the meaning by each word.

_____ 1. iron road   a. ocean

_____ 2. power of thunder   b. months

     c. electricity

_____ 3. prisoner's house   d. railroad

_____ 4. big water   e. prison

_____ 5. fire-boat   f. steamship

_____ 6. moons

Write your answers in the space provided.

7. Review your predictions on page 138. Were you right about what the narrator learned? If you said *yes*, write what you correctly predicted. If not, write two things the narrator found out.

_____

_____

_____

8. How many times did the train stop before reaching New York?

_____

9. What was the weather like during the ocean voyage?

_____

10. How did Black Elk feel after he had left his people?

_____

11. What can you conclude about what the sailors thought of their Native American passengers?

_____

_____

Circle the number of the best answer for each question.

12. What was Black Elk describing when he talked about the things that he and his people were given to sleep on?

    (1) cotton mattresses

    (2) inflatable life jackets

    (3) cloth hammocks

    (4) silk sheets

    (5) bunk beds

13. Black Elk was a holy man of the Oglala Sioux. But when he was on the voyage, he felt like a man who *never had a vision*. What do you think he meant by *a vision*?

    (1) good eyesight

    (2) a bad dream

    (3) understanding of other cultures

    (4) a spiritual experience

    (5) the strength to face death

14. Black Elk feels like crying when he sees the bison and elk being thrown overboard because

    (1) there will not be enough food for the rest of the trip.

    (2) they will not be able to perform their show without the animals.

    (3) the animals made the passengers sick.

    (4) the animals represented the Native American way of life.

    (5) this means they will have to return to New York.

Write your answer in the space provided.

15. Have you ever been in a place or situation where you seemed to be out of place? How did you feel? What did you decide to do?

    _____

    _____

    _____

    _____

    _____

Check your answers on page 228.

Adventure Story

Setting the Stage

An **adventure story** tells about people facing danger from the unknown. In the late 1800s, journalist Jack London became famous writing adventure stories. His stories described how ordinary people fought to survive in the wilderness of Alaska and Canada. In those times, people could not rely on science and machines to help them. Instead, they had to use their courage, imagination, and knowledge of what to do in the wild. Stories about the bravery of one individual struggling to stay alive are good reading.

Past: What you already know

You may have read a story or seen a movie about surviving in the wild. What was the challenge the people faced?

1. _____

_____

Present: What you learn by previewing

You can get a good idea of what you will be reading by looking at the title and reading a few sentences. Read the first few sentences of the passage and list the two companions.

2. _____

_____

Future: What you predict

The passage on pages 145–147 is from a short story called "To Build a Fire." Based on the title, what do you think the passage will be about?

3. _____

Reread the first few sentences. Now what do you think the passage will be about? Read on to find out if you are correct.

4. _____

_____

To Build a Fire by Jack London

As you read each section, circle the words you don't know. Look up the meanings.

The dog dropped in again at his heels, with a tail drooping discouragement, as the man swung along the creek bed. The furrow of the old sled trail was plainly visible, but a dozen inches of snow covered the marks of the last runners. In a month no man had come up or down that silent creek. The man held steadily on. He was not much given to thinking, and just then particularly he had nothing to think about save that he would eat lunch at the forks and that at six o'clock he would be in camp with the boys. There was nobody to talk to; and, had there been, speech would have been impossible because of the ice muzzle on his mouth. So he continued monotonously to chew tobacco and to increase the length of his amber beard.

Once in a while the thought reiterated itself that it was very cold and that he had never experienced such cold. As he walked along he rubbed his cheekbones and nose with the back of his mittened hand. He did this automatically, now and again changing hands. But, rub as he would, the instant he stopped his cheekbones went numb, and the following instant the end of his nose went numb. He was sure to frost his cheeks; he knew that, and experienced a pang of regret that he had not devised a nose strap of the sort Bud wore in cold snaps. Such a strap passed across the cheeks, as well, and saved them. But it didn't matter much, after all. What were frosted cheeks? A bit painful, that was all; they were never serious.

Understanding Cause and Effect.   A cause is what makes something happen. The effect is what happens as a result of the cause. In the passage above, the man cannot speak. This is the result of his beard being frozen. The author calls the frozen beard the *ice muzzle*.

Applying Your Skills and Strategies

Reread the second paragraph of this section. After the man rubbed his cheeks, they went numb again. What did he think might be the effect of the cold on his cheeks?

_____

_____

_____

Empty as the man's mind was of thoughts, he was keenly observant, and he noticed the changes in the creek, the curves and bends and timber jams, and always he sharply noted where he placed his feet. Once, coming around a bend, he shied abruptly, like a startled horse, curved away from the place where he had been walking, and retreated several paces back along the trail. The creek he knew was frozen clear to the bottom—no creek could contain water in that arctic winter—but he knew also that there were springs that bubbled out from the hillsides and ran along under the snow and on top [of] the ice of the creek. He knew that the coldest snaps never froze these springs, and he knew likewise their danger. They were traps. They hid pools of water under the snow that might be three inches deep, or three feet. Sometimes a skin of ice half an inch thick covered them, and in turn was covered by the snow. Sometimes there were alternate layers of water and ice skin, so that when one broke through he kept on breaking through for a while, sometimes wetting himself to the waist.

That was why he had shied in such panic. He had felt the give under his feet and heard the crackle of a snow-hidden ice skin. And to get his feet wet in such a temperature meant trouble and danger. At the very least it meant delay, for he would be forced to stop and build a fire, and under its protection to bare his feet while he dried his socks and moccasins. He stood and studied the creek bed and its banks, and decided that the flow of water came from the right. He reflected awhile, rubbing his nose and cheeks, then skirted to the left, stepping gingerly and testing the footing for each step. Once clear of the danger, he took a fresh chew of tobacco and swung along at his four-mile gait.

Identifying Figurative Language (Simile).

Applying Your Skills and Strategies

An author may use figurative language to help the reader visualize what is happening. A simile is a figure of speech that compares unlike things. For example, an author might write, "His hair was as white as snow." The author is comparing the unlike objects of snow and hair. A simile always begins with the word *like* or *as*.

Reread the paragraph at the bottom of page 145. Find the simile, and underline it in the passage. To what is the man compared?

In the course of the next two hours he came upon several similar traps. Usually the snow above the hidden pools had a sunken, candied appearance that advertised the danger. Once again, however, he had a close call; and once, suspecting danger, he compelled the dog to go on in front. The dog did not want to go. It hung back until the man shoved it forward, and then it went quickly across the white, unbroken surface. Suddenly it broke through, floundered to one side, and got away to firmer footing. It had wet its forefeet and legs, and almost immediately the water that clung to it turned to ice. It made quick efforts to lick the ice off its legs, then dropped down in the snow and began to bite out the ice that had formed between the toes. This was [a] matter of instinct. To permit the ice to remain would mean sore feet. It did not know this. It merely obeyed the mysterious prompting that arose from the deep crypts of its being. But the man knew, having achieved a judgment on the subject, and he removed the mitten from his right hand and helped tear out the ice particles. He did not expose his fingers more than a minute, and was astonished at the swift numbness that smote them. It certainly was cold. He pulled on the mitten hastily, and beat the hand savagely across his chest.

At twelve o'clock the day was at its brightest. Yet the sun was too far south on its winter journey to clear the horizon. The bulge of the earth intervened between it and Henderson Creek, where the man walked under a clear sky at noon and cast no shadow. At half-past twelve, to the minute, he arrived at the forks of the creek. He was pleased at the speed he had made. If he kept it up, he would certainly be with the boys by six. He unbuttoned his jacket and shirt and drew forth his lunch. The action consumed no more than a quarter of a minute, yet in that brief moment the numbness laid hold of the exposed fingers. He did not put the mitten on, but, instead, struck the fingers a dozen sharp smashes against his leg. Then he sat down on a snow-covered log to eat. The sting that followed upon the striking of his fingers against his leg ceased so quickly that he was startled. He had had no chance to take a bit of biscuit. He struck the fingers repeatedly and returned them to the mitten, baring the other hand for the purpose of eating. He tried to take a mouthful, but the ice muzzle prevented. He had forgotten to build a fire and thaw out. He chuckled at his foolishness, and as he chuckled he noted the numbness creeping into the exposed fingers. Also, he noted that the stinging which had first come to his toes when he sat down was already passing away. He wondered whether the toes were warm or numb. He moved them inside the moccasins and decided that they were numb.

He pulled the mitten on hurriedly and stood up. He was a bit frightened. He stamped up and down until the stinging returned into the feet. It certainly was cold, was his thought. That man from Sulphur Creek had spoken the truth when telling how cold it sometimes got in the country. And he had laughed at him at the time! That showed one must not be too sure of things. There was no mistake about it, it was cold. He strode up and down, stamping his feet and threshing his arms, until reassured by the returning warmth. Then he got out matches and proceeded to make a fire.

To find out more about this passage, turn to page 239.

Applying Ideas in a New Context. When you understand an idea, you can figure out how it might work in another situation. The man in the story prepares himself for his trip across the cold country. For example, he brings food to eat during the trip. In what other ways has the man prepared himself?

Applying Your Skills and Strategies

_____

_____

How would the man prepare if he were taking a trip across the desert?

_____

_____

_____

Thinking About the Story

Find the words below and underline them in the passage. Study the context in which each word appears. Try to figure out the meaning of each word. Then complete the following sentences by writing the correct words in the blanks provided.

automatically	instinct	devised
crypts	floundered	intervened

1. Underground rooms or spaces are called _____.

2. The man _____ in the fight by coming between the two angry dogs.

3. After you have done something over and over, in a while you can do it

    _____ .

4. If you have created a new way of doing something, you have

    _____ a new method.

5. When an animal is in danger, it does not think about what to do, but it

    acts on _____ .

6. When the man started sliding on the ice, he _____ a minute before he was able to walk again.

Write your answers in the spaces provided.

7. Review your prediction on page 144. Were you right? If you said *yes*, write what you were correct about. If not, write two things that you did not expect to read about.

    _____

    _____

    _____

8. Where are the man and dog going?

    _____

9. What is the main threat to the man and dog?

    _____

10. What does the man do right after his fingers get numb from taking out his lunch?

    (1) He puts on his mitten.

    (2) He builds a fire.

    (3) He checks the numbness in his toes.

    (4) He strikes his fingers against his leg.

    (5) He unbuttons his jacket.

11. Which of the following best describes the difference between how the man and dog react to getting wet?

    (1) The dog is more successful in drying off.

    (2) The dog acts on instinct, but the man thinks.

    (3) The dog has no idea what to do, but the man does.

    (4) The dog shakes himself, but the man uses a towel.

    (5) The dog gives up, but the man doesn't.

12. Why does the man in the story become a bit frightened?

    (1) He doesn't have enough water to drink.

    (2) He is afraid the dog will die.

    (3) It is even colder than he thought it would be.

    (4) It is almost dark, and he is not close to the camp.

    (5) He is lost.

Write your answers in the space provided.

13. Do you think the man will reach his goal? Why or why not?

    _____

    _____

    _____

14. Have you ever imagined yourself in a dangerous situation? What do you think you would do to survive?

    _____

    _____

    _____

Section 22

Persuasive Essay

Setting the Stage

Some essayists want readers to do more than just understand a point of view. They also want to persuade the reader. They want to convince the reader that they are right. **Persuasive essays** are often meant to get the reader to act. The essayist explains a situation and then suggests what can be done about it. Both facts and opinions are used to persuade. The author tries to get readers to believe that the suggested action will make their own lives better.

Past: What you already know

You may have read a persuasive essay in a magazine or newspaper. What action did the author want the reader to take?

1. _____

_____

Present: What you learn by previewing

You can get a good idea of what you will be reading by looking at the title and reading a few sentences. After you have read a few sentences of the passage, describe the event taking place.

2. _____

_____

Future: What you predict

The passage on pages 151–153 is from an essay titled "Thoughts on Peace in an Air Raid." Based on the title, what do you think the essay will be about?

3. _____

_____

Read the first paragraph. What do you now predict the essay will be about? Read on to find out if you are correct.

4. _____

_____

Thoughts on Peace in an Air Raid by Virginia Woolf

As you read each section, circle the words you don't know. Look up the meanings.

Up there in the sky young Englishmen and young German men are fighting each other. The defenders are men, the attackers are men. Arms are not given to the Englishwoman either to fight the enemy or to defend herself. She must lie weaponless tonight. Yet if she believes that the fight going on up in the sky is a fight for the English to protect freedom, by the Germans to destroy freedom, she must fight, so far as she can, on the side of the English. How far can she fight for freedom without firearms? By making arms, or clothes or food. But there is another way of fighting for freedom without arms; we can fight with the mind. We can make ideas that will help the young Englishman who is fighting up in the sky to defeat the enemy.

Applying Your Skills and Strategies

Distinguishing Fact from Opinion.   A fact is a statement about an event that can be proved true. The statement that men are fighting in the sky is a fact. The air battle can be seen by anyone who looks up. An opinion is a judgment or belief. The Englishwoman's belief that the English are fighting to protect freedom is an opinion. You can't argue about the truth of facts. You can argue about opinions.

In the passage above, the author says that the Englishwoman is not given weapons. But she also says that women can fight with their minds. Which statement is a fact about fighting? Which is an opinion?

_____

_____

A bomb drops. All the windows rattle. The anti-aircraft guns are getting active. Up there on the hill under a net tagged with strips of green and brown stuff to imitate the hues of autumn leaves guns are concealed. Now they all fire at once. On the nine o'clock radio we shall be told "Forty-four enemy planes were shot down during the night, ten of them by anti-aircraft fire." And one of the terms of peace, the loudspeakers say, is to be disarmament. There are to be no more guns, no army, no navy, no air force in the future. No more young men will be trained to fight with arms. That rouses another mind-hornet in the chambers of the brain—another quotation. "To fight against a real enemy, to earn undying honour and glory by shooting total strangers, and to come home with my breast covered with medals and decorations, that was the summit of my hope. . . . It was for this that my whole life so far had been dedicated, my education, training, everything. . . . "

Those were the words of a young Englishman who fought in the last war. In the face of them, do the current thinkers honestly believe that by writing "Disarmament" on a piece of paper at a conference table they will have done all that is needful? Othello's occupation will be gone; but he will remain Othello. The young airman up in the sky is driven not only by the voices of loudspeakers; he is driven by voices in himself—ancient instincts, instincts fostered and cherished by education and tradition. Is he to be blamed for those instincts? Could we switch off the maternal instinct at the command of a table full of politicians? Suppose that imperative among the peace terms was: "Child-bearing is to be restricted to a very small class of specially selected women," would we submit? Should we not say, "The maternal instinct is woman's glory. It was for this that my whole life has been dedicated, my education, training, everything. . . . " But if it were necessary, for the sake of humanity, for the peace of the world, that child-bearing should be restricted, the maternal instinct subdued, women would attempt it. Men would help them. They would honour them for their refusal to bear children. They would give them other openings for their creative power. That too must make part of our fight for freedom. We must help the young Englishmen to root out from themselves the love of medals and decorations. We must create more honourable activities for those who try to conquer in themselves their fighting instinct, their subconscious Hitlerism. We must compensate the man for the loss of his gun.

Understanding Persuasion. Authors of persuasive essays usually do not say directly what they want the reader to do. Instead, an author may use certain words to convince the reader that an action has to be taken. Strong words such as *should*, *must*, and *necessary* suggest that something has to be done. Such words imply that the author feels no other way is possible.

Applying Your Skills and Strategies

What is the first action the author says has to be done as part of the fight for freedom?

_____

_____

What other word does the author use to show that she feels this action has to be taken?

_____

The sound of sawing overhead has increased. All the searchlights are erect. They point at a spot exactly above this roof. At any moment a bomb may fall on this very room. One, two, three, four, five, six . . . the seconds pass. The bomb did not fall. But during those seconds of suspense all thinking stopped. All feeling, save one dull dread, ceased. A nail fixed the whole being to one hard board. The emotion of fear and of hate is therefore sterile, unfertile. Directly that fear passes, the mind reaches out and instinctively revives itself by trying to create. Since the room is dark it can create only from memory. It reaches out to the memory of other Augusts— in Beyreuth, listening to Wagner; in Rome, walking over the Campagna; in

London. Friends' voices come back. Scraps of poetry return. Each of those thoughts, even in memory, was far more positive, reviving, healing and creative than the dull dread made of fear and hate. Therefore if we are to compensate the young man for the loss of his glory and of his gun, we must give him access to the creative feelings. We must make happiness. We must free him from the machine. We must bring him out of his prison into the open air. But what is the use of freeing the young Englishman if the young German and the young Italian remain slaves?

The searchlights, wavering across the flat, have picked up the plane now. From this window one can see a little silver insect turning and twisting in the light. The guns go pop pop pop. Then they cease. Probably the raider was brought down behind the hill. One of the pilots landed safe in a field near here the other day. He said to his captors, speaking fairly good English, "How glad I am that the fight is over!" Then an Englishman gave him a cigarette, and an Englishwoman made him a cup of tea. That would seem to show that if you can free the man from the machine, the seed does not fall upon altogether stony ground. The seed may be fertile.

At last all the guns have stopped firing. All the searchlights have been extinguished. The natural darkness of a summer's night returns. The innocent sounds of the country are heard again. An apple thuds to the ground. An owl hoots, winging its way from tree to tree. And some half-forgotten words of an old English writer come to mind: "The huntsmen are up in America. . . . " Let us send these fragmentary notes to the huntsmen who are up in America, to the men and women whose sleep has not yet been broken by machine-gun fire, in the belief that they will rethink them generously and charitably, perhaps shape them into something serviceable. And now, in the shadowed half of the world, to sleep.

To find out more about this passage, turn to page 240.

Understanding the Author's Purpose.

In a persuasive essay, an author must include facts and examples as well as opinions. The purpose of including facts and examples is to support the stated opinions and make them more persuasive. In the first paragraph of this section, the author states the opinion that fear and hatred are sterile, unfertile emotions. She supports this opinion with the example that creative thought stops during moments of great fear.

Reread the second paragraph of this section. What opinion does the author state in this paragraph?

_____

_____

What facts or examples does the author give to support this opinion?

_____

_____

_____

Thinking About the Essay

Find the numbered words below and underline them in the passage. Study the context in which each word appears. Then match each word with its meaning. Write the letter of the meaning by each word.

_____ 1. disarmament
_____ 2. fostered
_____ 3. imperative
_____ 4. subdued
_____ 5. subconscious
_____ 6. sterile
_____ 7. compensate
_____ 8. access

a. reduced
b. command
c. encouraged
d. lacking creativity or interest
e. the ability to reach
f. not aware of
g. the putting away of weapons
h. give something in place of something taken away

Write your answers in the space provided.

9. Review your predictions on page 150. Were you right about the essay? If you said *yes*, write what you correctly predicted. If not, write two things you did not expect to read about.

_____

_____

10. How did the author feel while waiting for the bomb to fall?

_____

Circle the number of the best answer for each question.

11. Which of the following is the best meaning for the phrase *maternal instinct*?

    (1) love of medals and decorations

    (2) desire to be a mother

    (3) hope for peace

    (4) fight for freedom

    (5) need for power

12. Which of the following is one of the author's opinions?

    (1) "Forty-four enemy planes were shot down during the night . . . "

    (2) " . . . that was the summit of my hope"

    (3) "How glad I am that the fight is over."

    (4) "They point at a spot exactly above this roof."

    (5) "The emotion of fear and hate is therefore sterile . . . "

13. The author includes the example of women giving up child-bearing if it were necessary for world peace

    (1) to suggest that women are better than men.

    (2) to make women aware of the overpopulation problem.

    (3) to compare women's responsibilities with men's.

    (4) to encourage Americans to stay out of the war.

    (5) to urge women to have careers instead of families.

Write your answers in the space provided.

14. The author is concerned with the effects of disarmament. What does she imply would happen if men were not allowed other creative outlets?

    _____

    _____

    _____

15. What do you think would have been your main concern if you had been in the author's situation?

    _____

    _____

16. Have you ever felt strongly enough about an issue that you tried to persuade someone to take action? Or has someone tried to persuade you? What was the issue? What was the action? Were you or the other person persuaded?

    _____

    _____

    _____

    _____

Check your answers on page 229.

Unit 2 Review:
Classical Literature

**Read the following passage from the novel *The Grapes of Wrath*
by John Steinbeck.**

And the migrants streamed in on the highways and their hunger was in their eyes, and their need was in their eyes. They had no argument, no system, nothing but their numbers and their needs. When there was work for a man, ten men fought for it—fought with a low wage. If that fella'll work for thirty cents, I'll work for twenty-five.

If he'll take twenty-five, I'll do it for twenty.

No, me, I'm hungry. I'll work for fifteen. I'll work for food. The kids. You ought to see them. Little boils, like, comin' out, an' they can't run aroun'. Give 'em some windfall fruit, an' they bloated up. Me. I'll work for a little piece of meat.

And this was good, for wages went down and prices stayed up. The great owners were glad and they sent out more handbills to bring more people in. And wages went down and prices stayed up. And pretty soon now we'll have serfs again.

And now the great owners and the companies invented a new method. A great owner bought a cannery. And when the peaches and the pears were ripe he cut the price of fruit below the cost of raising it. And as cannery owner he paid himself a low price for the fruit and kept the price of canned goods up and took his profit. And the little farmers who owned no canneries lost their farms, and they were taken by the great owners, the banks, and the companies who also owned the canneries. As time went on, there were fewer farms. The little farmers moved into town for a while and exhausted their credit, exhausted their friends, their relatives. And then they too went on the highways. And the roads were crowded with men ravenous for work, murderous for work.

And the companies, the banks worked at their own doom and they did not know it. The fields were fruitful, and starving men moved on the roads. The granaries were full and the children of the poor grew up rachitic [with spine problems], and the pustules of pellagra [sores caused by a skin disease] swelled on their sides. The great companies did not know that the line between hunger and anger is a thin line. And money that might have gone to wages went for gas, for guns, for agents and spies, for blacklists, for drilling. On the highways the people moved like ants and searched for work, for food. And the anger began to ferment.

To find out more about this passage, turn to page 240.

Items 1–6 refer to the passage on page 156.

Fill in the blanks with the word or words that best complete the statement.

1. The migrants were competing for _____ so that they could feed their children.

2. The companies and banks did not understand that they would cause their own doom. They did not understand the thin line between

   _____ and _____.

3. One way a great owner increased profits was to buy a

   _____.

Circle the number of the best answer for each question.

4. Which of the following phrases is the best meaning of the word *ferment*?

   (1) slowly to grow dangerously angry

   (2) the process of making beer

   (3) to grow older

   (4) to make people sick

   (5) to die down quickly

5. Which of the following words best describes the mood in this passage?

   (1) calm

   (2) delighted

   (3) forgiving

   (4) uneasy

   (5) quiet

6. What do the words *ravenous* and *murderous* suggest about how the people felt about getting work? The people felt

   (1) uninterested.

   (2) that they deserved work.

   (3) confident.

   (4) desperate.

   (5) that they could always find work.

Go on to the next page.

BEATRICE: Go, Baby, set the table.

CATHERINE: We didn't tell him about me yet.

BEATRICE: Let him eat first, then we'll tell him. Bring everything in. *She hurries* CATHERINE *out.*

EDDIE: *(sitting at the table)* What's all that about? Where's she goin'?

BEATRICE: No place. It's very good news, Eddie. I want you to be happy.

EDDIE: What's goin' on? CATHERINE *enters with plates, forks.*

BEATRICE: She's got a job. *Pause.* EDDIE *looks at* CATHERINE, *then back to* BEATRICE.

EDDIE: What job? She's gonna finish school.

CATHERINE: Eddie, you won't believe it—

EDDIE: No—no, you gonna finish school. What kinda job, what do you mean? All of a sudden you—

CATHERINE: Listen a minute, it's wonderful.

EDDIE: It's not wonderful. You'll never get nowheres unless you finish school. You can't take no job. Why didn't you ask me before you take a job?

BEATRICE: She's askin' you now, she didn't take nothin' yet.

CATHERINE: Listen a minute! I came to school this morning and the principal called me out of the class, see? To go to his office.

EDDIE: Yeah?

CATHERINE: So I went in and he says to me he's got my records, y'know? And there's a company wants a girl right away. It ain't exactly a secretary, it's a stenographer first, but pretty soon you get to be secretary. And he says to me that I'm the best student in the whole class—

BEATRICE: You hear that?

EDDIE: Well why not? Sure she's the best.

CATHERINE: I'm the best student, he says, and if I want, I should take the job and the end of the year he'll let me take the examination and he'll give me the certificate. So I'll save practically a year!

To find out more about this passage, turn to page 239.

Items 7–12 refer to the passage on page 158.

Write your answers in the space provided.

7. What does Eddie think will happen to Catherine if she does not stay in school?

_____

8. What kind of certificate will Catherine get at the end of the year?

_____

9. What is the setting of the play? How do you know?

_____

_____

Circle the number of the best answer for each question.

10. What gave Catherine the idea of taking a job?

    (1) Her school principal suggested it.

    (2) She knew she was failing her classes.

    (3) She needed to pay her rent.

    (4) She knew it would please Eddie.

    (5) She wanted to be able to leave home.

11. How do both Eddie and Beatrice feel about Catherine?

    (1) embarrassed

    (2) resentful

    (3) proud

    (4) worried

    (5) protective

12. How will Eddie probably react next?

    (1) He will give in immediately.

    (2) He will get angry at Catherine and Beatrice.

    (3) He will try to find Catherine a different job.

    (4) He will continue to object to Catherine taking a job.

    (5) He will ignore Catherine and Beatrice.

The instructor said,

> Go home and write
> a page tonight.
> And let that page come out of you—
> Then it will be true.

I wonder if it's that simple?

I am twenty-two, colored, born in Winston-Salem.
I went to school there, then Durham, then here
to this college on the hill above Harlem.
I am the only colored student in my class.
The steps from the hill lead down to Harlem,
through a park, then I cross St. Nicholas,
Eighth Avenue, Seventh, and I come to the Y,
the Harlem Branch Y, where I take the elevator
up to my room, sit down, and write this page:

It's not easy to know what is true for you or me
at twenty-two, my age. But I guess I'm what
I feel and see and hear. Harlem, I hear you:
hear you, hear me—we two—you, me talk on this page.
(I hear New York, too.) Me—who?

Well, I like to eat, sleep, drink, and be in love.
I like to work, read, learn, and understand life.
I like a pipe for a Christmas present,
or records—Bessie, bop, or Bach.

I guess being colored doesn't make me not like
the same things other folks like who are other races.
So will my page be colored that I write?
Being me, it will not be white.
But it will be
a part of you, instructor.
You are white—
yet a part of me, as I am a part of you.
That's American.
Sometimes perhaps you don't want to be a part of me.
Nor do I often want to be a part of you.
But we are, that's true!
As I learn from you,
I guess you learn from me—
although you're older—and white—
and somewhat more free.

*To find out more
about this poem,
turn to page 238.*

This is my page for English B.

Items 13–18 refer to the poem on page 160.

Fill in the blanks with the word or words that best complete each sentence.

13. Hughes lived at the YMCA, which he called the _____.

14. The word *theme* has more than one meaning. You can tell from the context that in this poem the word *theme* means a

_____ for a class.

15. Bessie, bop, and Bach are examples of _____.

Circle the number of the best answer for each question.

16. Which of the following can you conclude about how the speaker feels about himself?

    (1) He dislikes himself.

    (2) He is very different from people of other races.

    (3) He is better than other people.

    (4) He is beginning to understand himself.

    (5) He is out of place at college.

17. From whose point of view does the instructor want the students to write their themes?

    (1) the student's

    (2) a man's

    (3) a woman's

    (4) an African-American person's

    (5) a white person's

18. Which of the following is an opinion the speaker holds about the instructor?

    (1) The instructor is white.

    (2) The instructor is older than the speaker.

    (3) The instructor's assignment is too hard.

    (4) The instructor cannot teach the speaker anything.

    (5) The instructor will learn something from the speaker.

Go on to the next page.

Read the following passage from the essay "I Have a Dream" by Martin Luther King, Jr.

I have a dream today. I have a dream that one day every valley shall be exalted and every hill and mountain shall be made low, the rough places will be made plain and the crooked places will be made straight, and the glory of the Lord shall be revealed, and all flesh shall see it together.

This is our hope. This is the faith that I go to the South with. And with this faith we will be able to hew out of the mountain of despair a stone of hope. With this faith we will be able to transform the jangling discords of our nation into a beautiful symphony of brotherhood. With this faith we will be able to work together, to play together, to struggle together, to go to jail together, to stand up for freedom together, knowing that we will be free one day.

And this will be the day—this will be the day when all of God's children will be able to sing with new meaning:

My country, 'tis of thee,
Sweet land of liberty,
Of thee I sing;
Land where my fathers died,
Land of the Pilgrims' pride,
From every mountainside
Let freedom ring.

And if America is to be a great nation, this must become true.

And so let freedom ring from the prodigious hilltops of New Hampshire. Let freedom ring from the mighty mountains of New York. Let freedom ring from the heightening Alleghenies of Pennsylvania. Let freedom ring from the snow-capped Rockies of Colorado. Let freedom ring from the curvaceous slopes of California.

But not only that. Let freedom ring from Stone Mountain of Georgia. Let freedom ring from Lookout Mountain of Tennessee. Let freedom ring from every hill and molehill of Mississippi. "From every mountainside let freedom ring."

And when this happens—when we allow freedom to ring, when we let it ring from every village and every hamlet, from every state and every city—we will be able to speed up that day when all of God's children, Black men and white men, Jews and Gentiles, Protestants and Catholics, will be able to join hands and sing in the words of the old Negro spiritual: "Free at last! Free at last! Thank God Almighty. We are free at last!"

To find out more about this passage, turn to page 238.

Items 19–23 refer to the passage on page 162.

Items 19–23 refer to the passage on page 162.

Write your answers in the space provided.

19. What two words in the passage have almost the same meaning as *slopes*?

_____

_____

20. What does the writer mean by *a beautiful symphony of brotherhood*?

_____

_____

Circle the number of the best answer for each question.

21. Which of the following pairs of words is a restatement of the word *dream*?

(1) hope and faith

(2) despair and hope

(3) distrust and faith

(4) discord and struggle

(5) exalted and glory

22. Which sentence best states the theme of this passage?

(1) Life is unfair.

(2) Freedom cannot be achieved.

(3) Good things come to those who wait.

(4) People feel more free in the mountains.

(5) By working together, all people can become free.

23. Which of the following methods does the author use to persuade the reader?

(1) a calm presentation of facts

(2) a list of past troubles

(3) angry emotion

(4) hopeful inspiration

(5) an argument with the opposition

COMMENTARY

Peter Jennings is one of the three news anchors discussed in the television review in Section 23.

A **commentary** is a discussion of a work of literature, art, drama, or music. When a commentary makes a judgment about a work, it is called a *critical commentary*. The author thinks about the quality of a work and how it has been put together, and decides whether it is well done. Sometimes an author criticizes one part of a work and praises another part.

One of the most common types of commentary is the review. A review tells the reader what the reviewer thinks about a book, TV program, movie, play, or musical performance. Reviews are usually brief. Reviews are intended to help their readers make choices about what to read, watch, or listen to. Some reviews are written in a serious tone. In others, the tone is humorous. Usually the reviewer's opinion of the subject affects the tone of the review.

Reviewers often tell readers many different things about a work. They may discuss the creators and performers of a work or the history and meaning of the work. But reviewers always give their opinions about the subject. To get the most out of a review, a reader should look for facts that support the reviewer's opinions.

Why do people read reviews? For many people, reviews help them make choices. For example, every fall a number of old TV shows are replaced by new ones. Can you decide what to watch by flipping from channel to channel until something looks good? And every summer a new batch of movies comes to local theaters. Can you choose what to see by looking at the titles? Thousands of books are published every year. Which ones suit your interests? What about all the recordings produced every month? How can you find the ones you want to hear? In your town or city, how can you decide which play to attend? In all these cases, reading reviews can make your choices easier and save time and money. Professional reviewers see, read, or listen to many of the options available. Reading the reviews makes the choices easier.

Reviews usually can be found in newspapers in the entertainment or culture sections. Popular magazines often contain several pages of reviews. Commentaries about older works or artists can be found in books about the specific subjects. Librarians can help you find this kind of information.

This unit presents reviews from several sources. The reviews cover some types of works people often want to know about.

■ The TV review gives opinions about the anchors of the three major network news programs.

■ The movie review explains the ideas behind a popular movie.

■ The book review describes the characters in a crime novel.

■ The music reviews discuss collections of recordings of two well-known musicians.

■ The theater review offers insights into a local theater production.

TV Review

Setting the Stage

Many people watch the news on TV. This is how they learn about what is happening locally, nationally, and around the world. How the news is presented makes a difference in how people react to it. The presentation often depends on the anchor, the person who does most of the talking. Reading a review of the anchors on the major TV channels can help you make a decision about which news program to watch.

Past: What you already know

You may watch a TV news program in the evening or at some other time of day. Do you like the way the anchor reports the news of the day? Why or why not?

1. _____

_____

Present: What you learn by previewing

You can get a good idea of what you will be reading by looking at the title and skimming the article. *To skim* something means to read very quickly, looking for main ideas and main characters. After skimming this article, write the names of the three anchors being reviewed.

2. _____

_____

_____

Future: What you predict

What do you want to learn from a review of a TV news program? Write two questions about anchors you think this review will answer.

3. _____

_____

_____

Check your answers on page 231.

Three Men and a Maybe by Marvin

As you read each section, circle the words you don't know. Look up the meanings.

Who do I, as a critic, watch in times of crisis on the network evening news shows?

It was easy to answer that question when Uncle Walter [Walter Cronkite] was in the anchor chair. He could tell me the world ended this afternoon and it would be OK. I trusted Walter.

But Dan Rather at CBS makes me nervous. I never know when he is going to do something bizarre, like walk off the show. People are always asking him what the frequency is, or he is fighting with cab drivers in Chicago.

And that smile of his can be ghastly, managing a forced grin even after a story about a mine cave-in. On a story about pit bulls, he might say something folksy like "Doggone it."

He looked more relaxed in Saudi Arabia than in the studio. It's as if there are two of them. Dr. Rather and Mr. Angry.

Tom Brokaw on NBC News is about as warm as a fish on camera. He reads the news like his jaws are wired. And he never shows any feeling about the news. He reads each story, picnic or catastrophe, the same way.

Tom is a fabulous reporter, great in the field, a superb ad libber, with a command of fact and authority.

Judging the Author's Qualifications.

Applying Your Skills and Strategies

In a critical commentary, the author's qualifications are very important. The reviewer is making a public statement about whether something is good or bad. The reader wants to be sure that the reviewer knows a lot about the subject. If you wanted a reliable opinion about a TV program, you probably would choose to read a commentary by a professional critic. Your best friends and coworkers don't have as much experience judging the quality of TV news programs. So when you read a review, look for clues about the qualifications of the reviewer.

In addition to stating his personal reactions, the author of this review uses terms that a professional TV reviewer would know. He also shows that he has been watching TV news for some time.

List two ways the author shows the reader that he is an expert in his field.

_____

_____

_____

_____

He has always been at his most comfortable on the road. Yet covering the war from Saudi Arabia, he has been uncomfortable. So would you if your replacement in the studio was Jane Pauley, who is only the best straight news reader in the business today.

Peter Jennings is usually first in the ratings for a good reason. He is good. Jennings is ahead because he is closest to being easygoing, calm, a natural reader.

A few extra Canadianisms [words or expressions used by people from Canada] might creep in. How aboot that! He is a little too handsome, perhaps a little too smooth sometimes. But Jennings is always comfortable.

He is especially good at live events: his off-the-cuff comments on events always seem to be to the point, trenchant, unobtrusive.

And there's a vulnerability to the man. He admits things he doesn't know. But he doesn't try to score points on it, giving us a lecture on good journalism as Rather does.

There is an honest, real quality to Jennings, what I suspect is a human being behind the hair spray and makeup.

Lately, though, he has developed a pained expression with that furrowed brow, as if he has just eaten something that didn't agree with him. Nobody is perfect. Peter could make a great Alka-Seltzer commercial.

If I had my druthers I'd still want Uncle Walter. After 10 years in exile, he is still the most trusted guy in the country. Meanwhile I'll take Peter Jennings, pained expression and all.

Applying Your Skills and Strategies

Comparing and Contrasting. Comparing shows how things or people are similar. Contrasting shows how things are different. You can compare Brokaw, Jennings, and Rather by saying that they are all anchors. However, the reviewer thinks that each one delivers the news in a very different way.

The reviewer compares a particular talent that Brokaw and Jennings have in common. What does the reviewer say they both do especially well?

_____

_____

Which two newscasters does the reviewer think are the best news readers?

_____

What does the reviewer think are the major differences among the ways Brokaw, Jennings, and Rather deliver the news?

_____

_____

_____

Check your answers on page 231.

Thinking About the Review

Find the numbered words below in the passage and underline them. Study the context in which each word appears. Then match each word with its meaning. Write the letter of the meaning by each word.

_____ 1. bizarre

_____ 2. ghastly

_____ 3. catastrophe

_____ 4. ad libber

_____ 5. trenchant

_____ 6. unobtrusive

_____ 7. vulnerability

_____ 8. druthers

a. weakness

b. strange

c. not pushy

d. choices

e. person who says what is not in the script

f. disaster

g. awful

h. clear-cut

Write your answers in the space provided.

9. Review your prediction on page 166. Were your questions answered? If you said _yes_, write the answers to the questions. If not, write two things you learned about.

_____

_____

_____

10. During what special time does the author want to be able to rely on the news?

_____

11. Which of the current news anchors does the reviewer prefer?

_____

12. When the reviewer uses the expression _How aboot that?_, what kind of accent is he describing?

_____

Check your answers on page 231.

13. The reviewer thinks that both Dan Rather and Tom Brokaw are more comfortable outside of the TV studio. What contrast did he see between the two when they were in the field in Saudi Arabia?

    (1) They both seemed more relaxed.

    (2) Dan Rather was more comfortable than Tom Brokaw.

    (3) Tom Brokaw was more relaxed than Dan Rather.

    (4) They were both uncomfortable.

    (5) Neither was as good as Peter Jennings in the field.

14. Why does the reviewer use the simile *as warm as a fish* about Tom Brokaw? He wants to suggest that Tom Brokaw

    (1) is a good news reader.

    (2) is an animal lover.

    (3) does not express much emotion.

    (4) is lovable.

    (5) is not a good-looking man.

15. The reviewer feels it is most important that a news anchor

    (1) is handsome.

    (2) is a good ad-libber.

    (3) can make silly jokes.

    (4) reads every story in the same way.

    (5) can be trusted.

Write your answers in the space provided.

16. Write the statement from the review that summarizes why the reviewer prefers Peter Jennings.

    _____

    _____

17. When you watch a TV news program, what qualities do you like to see in the anchor?

    _____

    _____

Movie Review

Setting the Stage

Sometimes an actor helps to produce a movie. Comedian Billy Crystal appeared in a movie about three men from the city who go out West. As both an actor and one of the producers of the movie, Billy Crystal had an important effect on the whole film. The reviewer of this film takes care to include both the serious and the funny sides of Crystal's influence. The reviewer also uses many of the actor's own words to suggest an opinion about how well the movie works.

Past: What you already know

You may have read a review about a movie you were thinking about seeing. If you decided to see the movie, what did the reviewer say that helped you make up your mind?

1. _____

_____

Present: What you learn by previewing

You can get a good idea of what you will be reading by looking at the title and reading a few sentences. Read the first four paragraphs of the passage. Write the names of the three main characters in the movie.

2. _____

_____

_____

Future: What you predict

The passage on pages 172–173 is a review of the movie *City Slickers*. Reread the first three paragraphs. What do you predict the reviewer will say about the movie? Read on to find out if you are correct.

3. _____

_____

_____

'Slickers' Drives Cattle and Point Home
by Bob Thomas

As you read each section, circle the words you don't know. Look up the meanings.

Its comedy is bright and scenery sunny, but a cloud looms above Billy Crystal's "City Slickers": finding meaning at age 40.

Three longtime friends (Crystal, Bruno Kirby and Daniel Stern) fritter away a few weeks every year taking a vacation-adventure together. Chased by the bulls of Pamplona, Spain, on one such jaunt, the three run for their lives.

Yet for all the legwork they really aren't going anywhere.

Mitch Robbins (Crystal) is stuck selling radio advertising time, and his marriage is filled with static. Grocer Phil Berquist (Stern) feigns catnaps to escape from his shrewish mate. Ed Furillo (Kirby), a sporting goods dealer, stands out as the cheeriest of the trio, and his happiness doesn't run too deeply.

At Furillo's and Berquist's insistence, Robbins joins his playmates at a dude ranch where guests pay to drive cattle. A series of mishaps leaves the three pretty much alone on the range, where they must confront not only storms and pregnant cows but their own insecurities and doubts.

"When I came up with the idea for the movie, it wasn't three funny guys hit the plains," said Crystal, who also served as executive producer and pitched the film's premise to writers Lowell Ganz and Babaloo Mandel ("Parenthood").

Identifying Figurative Language (Metaphor). Like a simile, a metaphor is a figure of speech that compares unlike things. Metaphors are harder to recognize than similes because metaphors do not begin with the word *like* or *as*. For example, a reviewer might write, "The movie galloped forward at breakneck speed." Here the reviewer compares the pace of the movie to a running horse.

Applying Your Skills and Strategies

In the first paragraph of the passage, the reviewer uses the metaphor *a cloud looms* to show that the movie is partly about personal problems. A cloud does not really hang over the movie. By substituting the metaphor of the cloud, the reviewer suggests that the mood of the movie is sometimes gloomy.

Billy Crystal's character in the movie is described as having a marriage *filled with static*. This metaphor refers to the character's job, which is selling radio ads. What does the reviewer suggest about the marriage by using this metaphor?

_____

_____

_____

_____

     Check your answer on page 231.

"It was to tell a story about friendship, and to tell a story about trusting. If friends are friends in good times, they are a better friend if they're there when you're not feeling so good.

"It's also about men and women at a certain age when they enter 'What If?' land, and 'I should have, could have' territories. You sort of forget your purpose in life. You get clouded over. And it's not just an age thing. It's a confusion—a confusion of priorities."

Audiences know Crystal more for his comic reflections than for his insights into the human condition.

Through his work in television's "Soap" and "Saturday Night Live" and the movies "Throw Momma From the Train" and "When Harry Met Sally..." Crystal has avoided heavy issues in favor of light comedy. Nowadays, though, his jokes seem to carry more weight.

Along with Robin Williams and Whoopi Goldberg, Crystal helps feed, care for and house the homeless through the annual benefit concert Comic Relief. "Sessions," a comedy series debuting this fall on cable's Home Box Office, explores the labors and laughs of a man in psychotherapy. And then there's "City Slickers."

"I wanted to make a 'Deliverance' with laughs, and I wanted it to be truthful," Crystal said. "If there's no pain in the movie, then I simply have a funny movie. That's OK, but there's so much more to tell."

Jack Palance co-stars in the film as Curly, a veteran cowboy whose prairie wisdom helps Robbins resolve his crisis.

"When Curly says, 'There's nothing like bringing in the herd,' it's a metaphor for the whole piece—finishing something that you set out to do: raising your family, honoring your commitments.

"It's not about cows. It's about yourself and your priorities in life."

"City Slickers" was filmed on location in New Mexico and Colorado. Crystal, Stern and Kirby all learned to ride for the film. Crystal liked his quarterhorse so much he moved him to Southern California after the movie wrapped.

Recognizing Theme. Even a funny movie can have a serious theme. In addition to summarizing the humorous plot of this movie, the reviewer uses quotes by Billy Crystal to explain the related themes. Crystal describes one theme by saying, "If friends are friends in good times, they are a better friend if they're there when you're not feeling so good." This general truth about human nature describes how people should act toward each other.

Applying Your Skills and Strategies

Another theme is about what happens when people begin to forget their purpose in life. What words does Crystal use to describe this theme?

_____

_____

_____

Thinking About the Review

Find the numbered words below and underline them in the passage. Study the context in which each word appears. Then match each word with its meaning. Write the letter of the meaning by each word.

_____ 1. slickers

_____ 2. fritter

_____ 3. jaunt

_____ 4. feigns

_____ 5. mishaps

_____ 6. priorities

_____ 7. reflections

_____ 8. shrewish

a. accidents

b. trip

c. thoughts

d. things of greater importance than others

e. pretends

f. people not used to rough living

g. spend in a carefree way

h. nagging

Write your answers in the space provided.

9. Review your prediction on page 171. Were you right? If you said *yes*, write what you correctly predicted. If not, write two things you did not expect the reviewer to talk about.

_____

_____

_____

10. What problems do the three friends face?

_____

11. According to the reviewer, Crystal is famous not only for being an actor. For what other reason is Crystal well known?

_____

12. Why does the reviewer mention Crystal's other movies and shows and then follow with the statement, "And then there's 'City Slickers'"?

_____

_____

Check your answers on page 231.

Circle the number of the best answer for each question.

13. Which statement gives the reviewer's opinion about Crystal's jokes in this movie?

    (1) They are not funny.

    (2) They have nothing to do with the theme.

    (3) They deal with heavy issues.

    (4) They are out of place.

    (5) They are better than his old jokes.

14. Which of the following best states the meaning of Curly's metaphor *there's nothing like bringing in the herd*?

    (1) Finishing something gives you a feeling of satisfaction.

    (2) Cattle are the future of the West.

    (3) Everyone could benefit from spending time with cows.

    (4) Westerners are wiser than city folks.

    (5) Caring for animals teaches you about people.

15. Which detail from the passage best suggests the problem that the movie's theme is based on?

    (1) 'What If?' land

    (2) an age thing

    (3) the human condition

    (4) pretty much alone

    (5) funny guys hit the plains

Write your answers in the space provided.

16. How do you think the movie ends?

    _____

    _____

17. If you have not seen *City Slickers,* based on the review would you like to? If you have seen this movie, do you agree with the reviewer's opinions? Why or why not?

    _____

    _____

    _____

Section

25

Book Review

Setting the Stage

A book review usually discusses both the plot and the characters of a book. But the reviewer of a mystery or crime novel doesn't want to give away too much of the plot. So to get the reader's attention the reviewer tries to make the characters sound as interesting as possible. Based mainly on the description of the characters, the reader must make a judgment about reading the book.

Past: What you already know

You may have read a book review that gave more information about the characters than about the plot. If so, what did you learn about the characters?

1. _____

_____

_____

Present: What you learn by previewing

You can get a good idea of what you will be reading by looking at the title and reading a few sentences. Read the first paragraph of the passage. What two types of characters will you be reading about?

2. _____

_____

Future: What you predict

The passage on pages 177–178 is a review of a book called *Get Shorty*. Reread the first paragraph. Based on this paragraph, what do you predict the reviewer will say about the book? Read on to find out if you are correct.

3. _____

_____

_____

176   *Unit 3: Commentary*   *Check your answers on page 232.*

Get Shorty by Elmore Leonard, reviewed by Ralph Novak

As you read each section, circle the words you don't know. Look up the meanings.

A cynic might think old Elmore has revenge on his mind, getting back at what Hollywood has done to a few of his novels by writing this acidic, get-them-laughing-then-punch-them-in-the-gut, splendidly entertaining crime tale. Its moral seems to be that gangsters are a lot like the people who make movies, except crooks are more efficient and have a deeper sense of honor.

Understanding the Author's Tone. How authors feel about a topic influences how they write about it. In turn, an author's tone influences how the reader feels about the topic. Tone is especially important in reviews, since the reviewer's main concern is to express an opinion.

Tone depends a lot on word choice. If an author uses formal or technical words, the tone seems unemotional. The use of slang and humorous words creates a more informal tone.

The reviewer of *Get Shorty* sets an informal tone at once. The use of *old* is an informal way of referring to the author, Elmore Leonard. Also, by using only the writer's first name, the reviewer makes it seem as if Elmore Leonard is a friend. Both word choices are intended to help the reader feel as comfortable with Elmore Leonard's work as the reviewer does.

The informal tone continues with a casual string of hyphenated words. The phrase *get-them-laughing-then-punch-them-in-the-gut* combines both humor and slang. Based on the tone of this phrase, how does the reviewer want the reader to feel about the book?

_____

_____

_____

Leonard's protagonist, Chili Palmer, is an easy-going kind of loan shark, in semiretirement in Florida. But then one of his clients skips off to Las Vegas still owing him, so Chili dutifully takes off after him. It's not long before Palmer is in Los Angeles, hooking up with a has-been horror movie producer, Harry Zimm, a former B-movie actress, Karen Flores, and a current star, Michael Weir. Soon Chili is deciding he knows enough—which isn't all that much—to get into the filmmaking business.

It wouldn't be a Leonard novel without colorful villains, and this one has Ray Bones, an old enemy who has become Chili's boss in the Florida hierarchy, and Bo Catlett, a slick-dressing Angeleno who with his pal Ronnie is a jack-of-all-crimes, including murder.

In this company Chili comes off as a relatively nice guy, and one who knows how to use his expertise. "'What's the guy gonna do, Catlett, take a swing at me?'" he says to Harry. "'He might've wanted to, but he had to consider first, who is this guy? He don't know me. All he knows is I'm looking at him like if he wants to try me I'll . . . take him apart. Does he wanta go for it, get his suit messed up? I mean even if he's good he can see it would be work.'

"'He could've had a gun,' Harry said.

"'It wasn't a gun kind of situation.'"

Harry himself is on the hard-bitten side, recalling one unpleasant literary agent he had dealt with: "'I asked him one time what type of writing brought the most money and the agent says, "Ransom notes."'"

Things fall into place too easily for Chili at times, but Leonard compensates with nice twists, snappy action scenes and more than one blood-drawing zinger. You have to like a Hollywood novel in which a woman studio executive can say, "'Harry, I feel as if I know you. I've been a fan of yours ever since *Slime Creatures*. They remind me of so many people I know in the industry.'"

Recognizing Bias. Bias is a strong preference for a particular point of view. A person can have a bias for or against something. You can recognize a reviewer's bias from words that emphasize either a negative or a positive view of something. Reviewers also show a bias when they tell only one side of a story. When you see clues that suggest a bias, be sure to read carefully to find out whether the reviewer's opinions are supported by the facts.

Applying Your Skills and Strategies

The reviewer uses the words *snappy* and *zinger* to describe the novel. Do these words suggest a bias in favor of, or against, this novel? Why?

_____

_____

Write another phrase or sentence in which the author shows his bias about this novel.

_____

_____

How does the reviewer support his opinion of the novel?

_____

_____

Check your answers on page 232.

Thinking About the Review

Find the words below and underline them in the passage. Study the context in which each word appears. Try to figure out the meaning of each word. Then complete the following sentences by writing the correct words in the blanks provided.

cynic   protagonist   moral

acidic   compensates   zinger

1. If you think that other people often behave selfishly, you might be

    called a _____ .

2. The _____ of *Get Shorty* is named Chili Palmer.

3. The funny, surprise ending of the book was a real

    _____ .

4. The reviewer _____ for his brief discussion of plot by talking a lot about the character.

5. You learn a lesson when you read a story with a _____ in it.

6. The salad dressing had a sharp, _____ flavor because it contained too much vinegar.

Write your answers in the space provided.

7. Review your prediction on page 176. Were you right? If you said *yes*, write what you correctly predicted. If not, write two things that you didn't expect to read about.

    _____

    _____

    _____

8. What detail supports the conclusion that the reviewer has read many of Elmore Leonard's books?

    _____

    _____

9. In comparison to which two characters does Chili look like a nice guy?

    _____

10. Which of the following people is a villain in *Get Shorty*?

    (1) Elmore Leonard

    (2) Harry Zimm

    (3) Chili Palmer

    (4) Ray Bones

    (5) Michael Weir

11. Which of the following words best describes the tone of this review?

    (1) angry

    (2) sympathetic

    (3) humorous

    (4) serious

    (5) worried

12. The reviewer suggests that a cynic might think that Elmore Leonard writes with a bias against

    (1) crooks.

    (2) retired people.

    (3) horror films.

    (4) slick dressers.

    (5) the movie industry.

Write your answer in the space provided.

13. Based on the review, would you like to read this book or one like it? Why or why not?

    _____

    _____

    _____

    _____

Music Review

Setting the Stage

Some musicians become legends in their own time. So when a new collection by a music giant becomes available, fans want to know about it. If the collection covers much of the musician's recording history, the reviewer often discusses how the music has changed over time. This way the reader can compare the new material with the familiar songs.

Past: What you already know

You may have a favorite musician or band who has released a collection of previously unheard material. Name the musician or band. What would you like to see or read about in a review of the recording?

1. _____

_____

Present: What you learn by previewing

You can get a good idea of what you will be reading by looking at the title and skimming a few paragraphs. Skim the passage on page 182. Write the name of the musician and the name of the new recording.

2. _____

_____

Future: What you predict

The passage on pages 182–185 is a review called "Dylan at 50 . . . Remains an Enigma." Reread the first few paragraphs. Based on these paragraphs and the title, what do you predict the reviewer will say about the recording? Read on to find out if you are correct.

3. _____

_____

_____

Dylan at 50. . . Remains an Enigma by Ron Firak

As you read each section, circle the words you don't know. Look up the meanings.

Bob Dylan always has been a measuring stick. A standard of concern and conceit, brilliance and belligerence, innovation and implausible arrangements.

And he's a milepost in the passing of time.

"Blowing in the Wind" . . . "Mr. Tambourine Man" . . . Going electric . . . The motorcycle crash . . . "Nashville Skyline" (and where DID that voice come from?) . . . "Blood on Tracks."

Born Again. Lost Again. Born Again again.

Like a first kiss or last look at a childhood home, his songs provoke the kinds of memories that remind us exactly where we were and what was going on in our lives when Dylan did whatever it was he was doing.

It was 30 years ago that Dylan captured the New York City folk scene and kept it in his thrall for decades. On May 24, it will be 50 years since he was born in Duluth, Minn., as Robert Allen Zimmerman.

Now comes a remarkable three-volume collection of outtakes, rehearsal cuts, demos and concert recordings packaged as "The Bootleg Series," which reminds us of just how much time has passed.

It also reminds us how truly staggering Dylan's work has been, and how astonishing that these 58 cuts would go unpublished for as long as they did. Everything in the set is worth listening to. Even the bad cuts provide valuable insight into the evolution and choices of a major artist.

Recognizing Bias.   Biased writing shows a strong positive or negative attitude. The reviewer shows a positive bias toward Bob Dylan by saying that the collection is remarkable. The reviewer implies that the collection deserves attention. The reviewer is also giving an opinion that is stated as a fact.

Applying Your Skills and Strategies

In the last paragraph above, two biased opinions are stated as fact. Both show the reviewer's positive bias. They support the reviewer's opinion that the recording is worth listening to. Reread the last paragraph above. Write the two words that suggest a strong positive bias.

He was raised in Hibbing, Minn., the son of a Jewish hardware merchant in a town of 17,000 mostly Catholic miners. He started playing the piano at age 8 and the guitar and harmonica at about 10. His heroes were Hank Williams and James Dean, Leadbelly and Little Richard. And, of course, Woody Guthrie. He migrated to New York in part to visit a dying and hospitalized Guthrie.

Dylan is remembered by childhood friends as a loner who didn't seem to mind that almost no one seemed to understand, or like, his music.

Out of it all came the music of America—blues and country and folk—filtered through a blue-eyed, skinny college dropout determined to be noticed.

And noticed he was.

He hit New York City for the first time in January 1961, and right away everyone saw there was something different about him. He was unique. He hadn't yet emerged as a writer (he wasn't quite 20) but the voice that seemed to search for notes, the pounding guitar, the wailing harmonica and uncanny sense of timing and phrasing produced a package perfect for the words he was singing.

"I don't write about things," he said in an interview with The Associated Press. "I write from inside of something, and I sing and play the same way. It's never about that 'something,' hoping to touch it. It's rather from the inside of it reaching out."

In 1961, after rave reviews on the New York coffee house circuit, Dylan signed a three-year deal with Witmark & Sons to publish his songs. It might have been the most creative period for any writer in American music. In three years, Dylan wrote 237 songs for Witmark.

It was the period in which he wrote "Blowin' in the Wind," "A Hard Rain's Gonna Fall," "Masters of War," "With God on Our Side," "It Ain't Me Babe," "Don't Think Twice, It's All Right," "Only a Pawn in Their Game" and "Mr. Tambourine Man."

Says Dylan: "When I'm singin' my songs, it never occurs to me that I wrote them.

"If I didn't have a song like 'Masters of War,' I'd find a song like 'Masters of War' to sing. Same thing with 'Times They Are A-Changin'.' If I didn't have a song like that, I'd go out and look around and I'd search around until I found one like that, you know?"

Summarizing.   Summarizing is not just stating the main idea. To summarize, you tell the most important ideas in a passage in three or four sentences.

Applying Your Skills and Strategies

Reread the passage above, starting on the bottom of page 182. Summarize the important ideas in these paragraphs.

_____

_____

_____

_____

And while Dylan's style and his specific concerns have changed many times, his substance has remained the same.

Throughout "The Bootleg Series" we hear the anger that is as much Dylan as anything—anger at a lover, . . . at the powers that be, at who knows. Sometimes just a shouting anger such as in "Idiot Wind": "You hurt the ones that I love best, cover up the truth with lies"; or in "Let Me Die in My Footstep": "There's always been people that have to cause fear."

But mixed in with the anger is humor, and occasionally hope. There is the determination of the Civil Rights Movement and the fear of a child growing up in the shadow of the atomic bomb, as he sings in "Masters of War." And yet Dylan, who is divorced, has five children.

And always there is a spirituality, a belief that somehow all of the suffering he saw—and all of the pain he felt—make sense.

Dylan remains a work in progress. Each tour has ticket buyers wondering which Dylan they will see: mellow or angry, Born again or lost again, singing old stuff or new. The songs might be the same, but they always sound different. "The Bootleg Series" reinforces the notion of Dylan as a work in progress, changing, evolving.

The early material has a power and intensity too mature for someone just 20 years old. The first three cuts are from late 1961, the next nine from 1962.

"Man on the Street," written in August 1961 and recorded later that year for, but not used on, his first album, "Bob Dylan," is a haunting song about how a police officer tries to arouse a dead man by poking him with his nightstick. Its image of the homeless is as powerful today as the time it was written.

The song Dylan chose to sing in March when he received a lifetime achievement award at the Grammys was "Masters of War." The 1963 song ends with Dylan pledging to "stand o'er your grave 'til I'm sure that you're dead," and was more than an anti-war song. It was an anthem that called for revenge against those who profit from war.

Only Dylan would sing such a brutal tune while battles raged in the Persian Gulf. And only Dylan would perform an arrangement so bizarre that most viewers could not figure out what he was singing.

Recognizing Fact and Opinion. A fact is something that can be proved true. An opinion is a judgment or belief. In the reviewer's opinion, Bob Dylan's work reflects the pain Dylan has felt.

Applying Your Skills and Strategies

The reviewer also says that Dylan's "Man on the Street" is *a haunting song about how a police officer tries to arouse a dead man by poking him with his nightstick.* Which part of this statement is an opinion and which part states a fact?

_____

_____

Thinking About the Review

Find the numbered words below and underline them in the passage. Study the context in which each word appears. Then match each word with its meaning. Write the letter of the meaning by each word.

_____ 1. belligerence

_____ 2. innovation

_____ 3. implausible

_____ 4. uncanny

_____ 5. substance

_____ 6. anthem

a. strange

b. central matter or basic nature of something

c. spiritual song or song of praise

d. anger

e. unbelievable

f. new idea or method

Write your answers in the space provided.

7. Review your prediction on page 181. Were you right? If you said *yes,* write what you correctly predicted. If not, write two things you did not expect the reviewer to say.

_____

_____

_____

8. List the emotions the reviewer hears in "The Bootleg Series."

_____

_____

_____

9. Name four musicians who influenced Bob Dylan's music.

_____

_____

10. On page 182, what metaphor compares Bob Dylan to a standard of excellence?

_____

11. Which of the following suggests that the reviewer has been listening to Bob Dylan for many years?

    (1) like a first kiss

    (2) the kinds of memories that remind us

    (3) Dylan is remembered by childhood friends.

    (4) I'd find a song like "Masters of War" to sing.

    (5) too mature for someone just 20 years old

12. Which fact supports the reviewer's opinion that Bob Dylan's time with Witmark "might have been the most creative period for any writer in American music"? Dylan

    (1) wrote 237 songs during that time.

    (2) wrote "Blowin' in the Wind" then.

    (3) stayed with the company for three years.

    (4) got rave reviews in New York.

    (5) was interviewed by The Associated Press.

13. What does the reviewer imply by saying that only Bob Dylan would *sing such a brutal tune* and *perform an arrangement so bizarre?*

    (1) Bob Dylan doesn't care about other people.

    (2) Bob Dylan is expected to do unusual things.

    (3) People were offended by Bob Dylan's act.

    (4) People do not expect Bob Dylan to entertain them.

    (5) Bob Dylan always tries to please his audience.

Write your answer in the space provided.

14. Based on the review, would you be interested in listening to "The Bootleg Series"? Why or why not?

_____

_____

_____

_____

Theater Review

Setting the Stage

A review of a local theater production is sometimes different from a review of a Broadway play. Often these reviews do not give very much critical commentary on the actors' performances or tell a lot about the plot. The reviewer may give more background information about how the local play was produced. What happens behind the scenes is as important as the quality of the acting. A local review is often designed to get people to come to the theater, instead of making strong artistic judgments.

Past: What you already know

You may have read a review of a local play in a newspaper. Did the reviewer write more about the plot, the actors, or something else?

1. _____

_____

Present: What you learn by previewing

You can get a good idea of what you will be reading by looking at the title and reading a few sentences. Read enough of the passage to write the name of the director and the kind of play.

2. _____

_____

Future: What you predict

The passage on pages 188–189 is a review of a play called "Lend Me a Tenor." Based on the title, what kind of characters do you think will be in the play?

3. _____

Read the first five paragraphs of the passage. What do you predict the review will tell you? Read on to see if you are correct.

4. _____

_____

Lend Me a Tenor by Cara Webster

*As you read each
section, circle the
words you don't
know. Look up the
meanings.*

The action is non-stop, and the characters are bigger than life. But that's the way it has to be if it's a farce, said Christian Moe, director of "Lend Me a Tenor," the second production of Southern Illinois University at Carbondale's Summer Playhouse season.

"This is typical of farce," said Moe, who also chairs the theater department. "A farce should move so quickly that the audience doesn't have time to question the action. If they do, you're in trouble."

The two-act comedy isn't likely to find itself in trouble here anymore than it was when originally produced at the Globe Theater in London by Andrew Lloyd Weber.

And though few modern farces are successful, "Lend Me a Tenor" won seven Tony Awards for the 1989-90 Broadway season.

That might be because audience-goers like to laugh, and this effort gives them plenty of chuckles.

Understanding the Author's Purpose.

*Applying
Your Skills
and
Strategies*

Every fact a reviewer includes is there for a purpose. In this case, the reviewer wants to persuade readers to see the play. So the facts must help to convince readers. One way of influencing a reader is to show that the people who are in the production are qualified. The director of this local production is Christian Moe. The reviewer includes the fact that Christian Moe is the head of the university's theater department. This tells the reader that the director has experience in theater. The reviewer uses this information to imply that the play is well directed.

What two facts does the author give about earlier productions of "Lend Me a Tenor"?

_____

_____

_____

What is the reviewer's purpose for including these facts?

_____

_____

_____

_____

Check your answers on page 233.

From the opening scene, we're treated to typical but overblown characters. There's Saunders, general manager of the Cleveland Opera Company. Played by Robert Kislin, Saunders is overbearing but extremely funny as he awaits the arrival of Tito Merelli, a world-famous tenor who is to make his debut with the company.

His assistant, Max (Timothy Fink) and daughter, Maggie (Anita Rich), wait with him, and each is lost in his or her own world, which revolves around Tito.

But it's after Tito (played by John McGhee) arrives that the fun really begins.

There's a chase scene, slamming doors, a would-be opera singer serenading Tito at the door to the bathroom where the Italian tenor is being sick, and Tito's angry Italian wife. There's shrimp mayonnaise curdling backstage in the 100-degree heat, unexpected visitors, room service intrusions, a presumed death, a note mix-up . . . well, you get the idea.

Everything that happens serves to complicate matters even further.

"It moves a little like a snowball slowly rolling downhill, gaining momentum until finally it hits a big tree and splat! It explodes," Moe said.

In rehearsal one week before the show's debut Thursday, Moe and cast and crew did well to handle the real-life obstacles that sometimes beset a production.

"We're missing Tim Fink tonight," said Moe. "He's out with strep throat."

Stage manager Danny Herbst walked through Fink's part, and assistant manager Jackie Pohlman read the lines from the floor downstage left.

Though Moe said they might be a "little left-footed" in rehearsal without Fink, he later complimented the cast and crew for "carrying on very well."

And carry on they will, beginning Thursday at 8 p.m.

Identifying Details to Support a Conclusion.

Applying Your Skills and Strategies

Sometimes a reviewer draws a conclusion. For the reader to agree with the conclusion, the reviewer must include the facts that led to it. These facts or details support the conclusion.

In the passage above, the reviewer concludes that *Everything that happens serves to complicate matters even further.* Write three details from the play that support this conclusion.

_____

_____

_____

_____

Check your answer on page 233.

Thinking About the Review

Find the words below and underline them in the passage. Study the context in which each word appears. Try to figure out the meaning of the words. Then complete the following sentences by writing the correct words in the blanks provided.

farce	tenor
typical	presumed
overblown	momentum

1. A _____ is a fast-moving comedy with unlikely twists in the plot.

2. The _____ failure of the play will be proved wrong when all goes well on opening night.

3. A sick actor is _____ of the problems that can happen during a rehearsal.

4. The faster something goes, the more _____ it has.

5. The man's high singing voice made him perfect for playing the part of

   the _____.

6. The actor had an _____ idea of his own importance.

Write your answers in the space provided.

7. Review your prediction on page 187. Were you right? If you said *yes,* write what you correctly predicted. If not, write two things you did not expect the review to tell you.

   _____

   _____

   _____

8. When will the momentum of the play probably begin to pick up speed?

   _____

9. Why did the stage manager take part in the rehearsal?

   _____

   _____

190   Unit 3: Commentary   *Check your answers on page 233.*

10. Which of the following is a simile that Christian Moe uses to describe how the action of the play develops?

    (1) nonstop

    (2) bigger than life

    (3) like a snowball

    (4) gaining momentum

    (5) a little left-footed

11. Why does the reviewer include the information about Tim Fink's strep throat? The reviewer wants to

    (1) give an example of the problems that happen during a play.

    (2) show how the play is going downhill.

    (3) explain why Tim Fink will not be in the play.

    (4) make a contrast to the events in the play itself.

    (5) prepare the audience for a poor performance.

12. The reviewer says that audiences like to laugh and that this play will give them plenty of chuckles. Which conclusion do these details support?

    (1) The audience will not enjoy the show.

    (2) The reviewer did not enjoy the rehearsal.

    (3) Modern farces are not successful.

    (4) The show probably will be a success.

    (5) Saunders is the funniest character in the play.

Write your answer in the space provided.

13. Based on this review, would you like to see "Lend Me a Tenor" or a play like it? Why or why not?

    _____

    _____

    _____

    _____

Music Review

Setting the Stage

Sometimes a review seems more like an advertisement than a critical commentary. This happens when the subject of the review is a favorite of the reviewer. The reviewer can't help writing from the point of view of a fan. But these reviews are still valuable to the reader. The reviewer often gives bits of information that only a fan would know. So the reader benefits from the knowledge of a fan who is also a reviewer.

Past: What you already know

You may be a longtime fan of a musician or band. What is the name of the musician or band? What type of background information would you like to give other people?

1. _____

_____

_____

Present: What you learn by previewing

You can get a good idea of what you will be reading by looking at the title and reading a few sentences. Read the first three paragraphs of the passage. Write James Brown's nickname.

2. _____

Future: What you predict

The passage on page 193 is a review of a record collection called *Star Time*. Reread the first three paragraphs. What do you predict the reviewer will say about the collection? Now read on to find out if you are correct.

3. _____

_____

_____

Check your answers on page 233.

Star Time: James Brown by David Hiltbrand

As you read each section, circle the words you don't know. Look up the meanings.

Chuck Berry? Elvis? The Beatles?

When it comes down to who has had the most profound and lasting influence on pop music, no one can touch the Godfather of Soul.

This anthology (four CDs or cassettes) is the Fort Knox of funk. It chronologically traces Brown's evolution from a poor follow-the-crowd R&B singer from Georgia to the absolutely original, superbad superstar.

Disc No. 1 contains the greatest advances. On the earliest tracks, such as "Try Me" and "Bewildered" from the late '50's, Brown is trying to get over as a cookie-cutter pop singer. This smoothed-out doo-wop music isn't all that far from the Ink Spots. But even in this era, there were hints of genius. Mired in the schmaltzy ballad "I Know It's True," Brown still had a flair for using horns and drums.

By the time he recorded "Think" in 1960, James had discovered the funk, and he never decamped. He became a method singer, and that method was madness. His eruptive delivery was completely unpredictable. With "Bring It Up (Hipster's Avenue)" in 1966, lyrics had really become a moot point. A single phrase would suffice.

Brown was always a character. On "Papa's Got a Brand New Bag, Pts. 1, 2, 3," an extended, previously unreleased version of his 1965 hit, you hear the singer exhorting his longtime sax man, Maceo Parker, to play a solo. By the end of the jam, Brown is getting into a dialogue with the horns themselves. (If Brown was, as advertised, "the hardest working man in show business," the guys who worked in his backing bands were tied for second.)

The music is fast and furious the rest of the way. Disc Nos. 2 through 4 present a dizzying cavalcade of hits: "I Got You (I Feel Good)," "I Can't Stand Myself (When You Touch Me) Pt. 1," "Licking Stick-Licking Stick," "Give It Up or Turnit a Loose.". . .

There are many collections of Brown's work, but none so deep or well documented.

Classifying. *To classify* means to sort things into groups, or classes. Music and theater are small classes within a larger group called *the performing arts.* Each class can be divided into even smaller groups. For example, music can be classified as classical, rock, pop, rhythm and blues, or jazz.

Applying Your Skills and Strategies

The reviewer classifies the musical styles of James Brown. What three phrases does the reviewer use to classify Brown's early style of music?

_____

_____

_____

Check your answer on page 233.

Thinking About the Review

Find the numbered words below and underline them in the passage. Study the context in which each word appears. Then match each word with its meaning. Write the letter of the meaning by each word.

_____ 1. profound	a. of little importance
_____ 2. evolution	b. talent
	c. left
_____ 3. schmaltzy	d. sentimental, mushy
_____ 4. flair	e. change
_____ 5. decamped	f. be enough
_____ 6. moot	g. urging strongly
_____ 7. suffice	h. deeply important
_____ 8. exhorting	

Write your answers in the space provided.

9. Review your prediction on page 192. Were you right? If you said *yes,* write what you correctly predicted. If not, write two things you did not expect the reviewer to say.

_____

_____

_____

10. When a musician uses the word *jam,* it does not mean something that is put on bread. Reread the sixth paragraph on page 193. Based on the context, what does *jam* mean?

_____

11. What is the reviewer's overall opinion of the music collection?

_____

12. What does the reviewer think about James Brown's back-up musicians?

_____

     Check your answers on page 234.

Circle the number of the best answer for each question.

13. Why does the reviewer describe the way James Brown encouraged his sax player to do a solo? This reviewer wants to

    (1) give an example of how unusual James Brown is.

    (2) show that James Brown knows how to play a horn.

    (3) suggest that James Brown is selfish.

    (4) criticize James Brown's style.

    (5) give an example of method singing.

14. What does the reviewer call James Brown's latest style?

    (1) pop

    (2) bad

    (3) doo-wop

    (4) funk

    (5) jazz

15. Which of the following best shows the reviewer's bias toward James Brown's musical skill?

    (1) smoothed-out

    (2) completely unpredictable

    (3) fast and furious

    (4) Fort Knox of funk

    (5) flair for using horns

Write your answer in the space provided.

16. If you were a musician like James Brown, would you want a review similar to this one to be written about you? Why or why not?

    _____

    _____

    _____

    _____

Unit 3 Review:
Commentary

**Read the following review, *Is the World Waiting for Ms. Rambo?*
by Ari Korpivaara.**

Sly Stallone and Arnold Schwarzenegger had better get out of town. Sigourney Weaver is ready to take over as the number-one action hero. As Ripley in *Aliens*, she is just as brave and competent with weaponry as the male Rambos. She is also smarter and capable of feeling. She is as close to believable as you can get in science fiction. That's because Weaver can act—more than can be said for the muscle-bound Katzenjammer Kids.

. . . Ripley . . . returns as a consultant with a fighting force of Marines to the planet taken over by the aliens. The human colonists have been wiped out, except for a little girl named Newt.

. . . The "top gun" pilot is a woman. The outfit's best fighting machine is a well-muscled woman named Vasquez, who in barracks-style banter puts the men in their place. A male Marine, eyeing her bulging biceps with envy: "Ever been mistaken for a man?" Vasquez: "No, have you?"

When the going gets rough, a number of the men come apart—panic-stricken, hysterical, cowardly. The women do not. Despite her own fear (something the thickheaded Rambo never feels), Ripley takes control from the mission's commander, paralyzed by the horror of it all, and, driving a space-age tank, rescues the Marines trapped inside the aliens' incubation room. It's a pleasure to root for her.

Items 1–6 refer to the passage on page 196.

Find the numbered words below and underline them in the passage. Study the context in which each word appears. Then match each word with its meaning.

_____ 1. competent

_____ 2. hysterical

_____ 3. paralyzed

a. unable to move

b. able to do something well

c. not in control of one's emotions

Circle the number of the best answer for each question.

4. What is suggested by the metaphor _fighting machine_ that describes Vasquez? Vasquez is

   (1) a mechanical robot.

   (2) a man.

   (3) an excellent soldier.

   (4) a tank.

   (5) a person who causes fights.

5. The author begins his review with the statement _Sly Stallone and Arnold Schwarzenegger had better get out of town_. The author's purpose in doing this is probably to

   (1) set up a comparison between male and female action heroes.

   (2) suggest that the review is about two male movie stars.

   (3) state a fact.

   (4) appeal to fans of the two male movie stars.

   (5) introduce the idea that the movie is science fiction.

6. Which word best describes the tone of this review?

   (1) disapproving

   (2) bored

   (3) angry

   (4) approving

   (5) confused

Read the following music review, "Raitt Again."

Bonnie Raitt is back. And her new album, *Luck of the Draw*, is proof that her recent success is not simply a matter of luck. It is a matter of singing from her soul.

After the success of her 1989 album, *Nick of Time*, no one would have been surprised if Raitt had come out with a collection of cheerful tunes. She has good reason to celebrate after twenty years of struggle. Instead, *Luck of the Draw* presents a series of thoughtful and bittersweet songs. Blues, country, and rhythm and blues combine to produce a picture of insight, sadness, and courage. Raitt's message is about fighting back. The enemy is the bitterness that comes with living.

Raitt's slightly hoarse soprano voice takes off with a smile in the cheerful "Something to Talk About." Her blues background shows up in the powerful "Slow Ride." But beneath the mature control of her voice is the suggestion of past pain.

A lingering distrust of romantic relationships shows up in several of the ballads. A bit of the cynic looks out when she sings, "I kept track of all the love that I gave him / And on paper it looked pretty good." Her "One Part Be My Lover" warns of the problems old memories can bring to a new relationship. Of a couple just coming together she sings, "They remember too much about what went wrong / It might be they should learn to forget."

The real power of Raitt's vocal skill in *Luck of the Draw* is clearest in the ballads. She goes from a moving, quiet understatement to gentle laughter. Her rich, subtle tones capture the despair of a single mother facing the ache of loneliness. "I Can't Make You Love Me," "Luck of the Draw," and "All at Once" alone would be well worth the price of the album.

Raitt's earthy voice and supple slide guitar are not heard alone. Throughout the album, Raitt is backed up superbly by Paul Brady and Richard Thompson. Their harmonies are the perfect support for her songs of sorrow and understanding. The effect is like the swelling chords of an organ.

Listening to Bonnie Raitt has always been a treat. Her latest work is no exception.

Items 7–12 refer to the passage on page 198.

Write your answers in the spaces provided.

7. Reread the fifth paragraph of the passage. According to the context, what does the word *vocal* mean?

_____

8. Which classification of Bonnie Raitt's songs does the reviewer admire most?

_____

9. Is the statement *Listening to Bonnie Raitt has always been a treat* fact or opinion?

_____

Circle the number of the best answer for each question.

10. What does the simile *like the swelling chords of an organ* mean?

    (1) The back-up singers also play organs.

    (2) The three singers sound good together.

    (3) The effect is too loud.

    (4) The effect is unpleasant.

    (5) The back-up singers sing very softly.

11. Which phrase suggests how much the reviewer admires Bonnie Raitt?

    (1) matter of luck

    (2) recent success

    (3) hoarse soprano

    (4) earthy voice

    (5) rich, subtle tones

12. Which detail supports the conclusion that the songs have *the suggestion of past pain*?

    (1) takes off with a smile

    (2) mature control of her voice

    (3) lingering distrust of romantic relationships

    (4) moving, quiet understatement

    (5) rich, subtle tones

Read the following review of the book *Paradise*.

Elena Castedo's first novel is a lot more than it seems at first glance. *Paradise* is the story of a Spanish labor activist's family. Fleeing the oppression of the dictator Franco, the family moves to a Latin American country. At first they live in a refugee ghetto. Then the wife, Pilar, gets herself invited to a large country estate. She tells her daughter, Solita, that the visit will be like paradise. The novel is the story of their visit.

More important, *Paradise* is the story of Solita. It is the story of how a ten-year-old girl learns to survive the cruelties of an unjust world.

The daughters of Pilar's hostess make no move to welcome Solita. In fact, they go out of their way to make her unhappy. They play tricks on her. And, more confusing to Solita, they make fun of her. In the Spanish ghetto, she had had a sort of freedom. She had not been aware of social classes. But the young sisters tell her that they are better than she is. They remind her that she is poor and from a family without social importance. The girls also upset Solita by implying they know a terrible secret about her mother.

Solita puts up with the teasing because she is loyal to her mother. But deep inside she finds a dignity, a sense of self-worth, that keeps her from believing what the sisters say. She learns to deal with the childish cruelty in a day-to-day fashion. She finds that "each minute you had to save your skin right then and there, by yourself, and in ways that wouldn't come back to haunt you."

Solita uncovers the unpleasant truth about the corrupt world of high society. She does not always understand what she reports. But the reader does. It becomes clear to the reader that wealth and power are valued more than individual worth.

Solita finally is freed of the place that was not paradise. She has learned about social injustice. However, she also has learned about the strength of her own character.

Castedo's novel is a powerful criticism of the upper classes. Through the eyes of a child, Castedo reveals the foolishness of people who think only of themselves. The Chilean author makes a disturbing statement about the values of Latin American society. She also comments on human nature in general. The issues she raises apply to all people.

Items 13–18 refer to the passage on page 200.

Fill in the blanks with the word or words that best complete the statements.

13. The novel is written from the point of view of

    _____.

14. The hostess' daughters make fun of Solita because they are

    _____ and she is _____.

15. A summary of the plot of the novel would begin with the family's move

    from _____ to _____.

Circle the number of the best answer for each question.

16. The reviewer implies that she agrees with Elena Castedo's view of the upper classes by using the phrase

    (1) *unpleasant truth.*

    (2) *a sort of freedom.*

    (3) *a sense of self-worth.*

    (4) *a terrible secret.*

    (5) *come back to haunt you.*

17. What general truth about human nature does the reviewer suggest is in the novel?

    (1) Children are crueler than adults.

    (2) Facing difficult situations can teach you about yourself.

    (3) There is no such thing as paradise.

    (4) The rich are better than the poor.

    (5) Poor people are better than rich people.

18. What is the reviewer's opinion of Elena Castedo's novel?

    (1) It is the author's first novel.

    (2) The novel is about a Spanish family.

    (3) The plot is too complicated.

    (4) The novel is a powerful criticism of human nature.

    (5) The point of the novel is not clear.

Check your answers on page 234.

Unit 3 Review 201

POSTTEST

**Read the following passage from the autobiography *The Story of My Life*
by Helen Keller.**

I remember the morning that I first asked the meaning of the word, "love." This was before I knew many words. I had found a few early violets in the garden and brought them to my teacher. She tried to kiss me: but at that time I did not like to have any one kiss me except my mother. Miss Sullivan put her arm gently round me and spelled into my hand, "I love Helen."

"What is love?" I asked.

She drew me closer to her and said, "It is here," pointing to my heart, whose beats I was conscious of for the first time. Her words puzzled me very much because I did not then understand anything unless I touched it.

I smelt the violets in her hand and asked, half in words, half in signs, a question which meant, "Is love the sweetness of flowers?"

"No," said my teacher.

Again I thought. The warm sun was shining on us.

"Is this not love?" I asked, pointing in the direction from which the heat came. "Is this not love?"

It seemed to me that there could be nothing more beautiful than the sun, whose warmth makes all things grow. But Miss Sullivan shook her head, and I was greatly puzzled and disappointed. I thought it strange that my teacher could not show me love.

A day or two afterward I was stringing beads of different sizes in symmetrical groups—two large beads, three small ones, and so on. I had made many mistakes, and Miss Sullivan had pointed them out again and again with gentle patience. Finally I noticed a very obvious error in the sequence and for an instant I concentrated my attention on the lesson and tried to think how I should have arranged the beads. Miss Sullivan touched my forehead and spelled with decided emphasis, "Think."

In a flash I knew that the word was the name of the process that was going on in my head. This was my first conscious perception of an abstract idea.

For a long time I was still—I was not thinking of the beads in my lap, but trying to find a meaning for "love" in the light of this new idea. The sun had been under a cloud all day, and there had been brief showers; but suddenly the sun broke forth in all its southern splendor.

Again I asked my teacher, "Is this not love?"

"Love is something like the clouds that were in the sky before the sun came out," she replied.

*To find out more
about this passage,
turn to page 238.*

Items 1–6 refer to the passage on page 202.

Fill in the blanks with the word or words that best complete the statements.

1. This passage is about how a visually and hearing impaired child learns

   the meaning of _____ from her teacher.

2. The first conversation in the passage takes place in the

   _____.

3. One clue to the fact that the child is visually impaired is that she does

   not understand anything unless she _____ it.

Circle the number of the best answer for each question.

4. Which word or phrase is the best meaning for *abstract*?
   - (1) not warm
   - (2) not physical
   - (3) important
   - (4) hidden
   - (5) confusing

5. What is the first mental process the child realized was going on in her head?
   - (1) stringing beads
   - (2) loving Miss Sullivan
   - (3) thinking about the beads
   - (4) smelling violets
   - (5) being still

6. Miss Sullivan spells words into Helen's hand, and Helen talks partly in sign. These details support which inference?
   - (1) Helen does not like to talk.
   - (2) Helen is not very smart.
   - (3) Miss Sullivan is a good teacher.
   - (4) Miss Sullivan is not a very good teacher.
   - (5) Helen is hearing impaired.

Stuffed animals
mean a lot to Nina Dowley
much more than to some kids
on days
that I run into her house
on any day
to borrow baking soda
last Tuesday
it was pinking shears
and met number 60
she had found him
at the flea market
a dirty pink rabbit
with eyes that moved
by Wednesday
when I returned the shears
Nina had sprayed
and cleaned
and brushed the rabbit
until he looked like new
and placed him
in a wicker basket on glass eggs
that belonged to her mother
she is out of space in the room
bears are lined up
on the chesterfield
and only bears sit there
cats monopolize chairs
of comfort and over-size
and dogs are happy on the floor
guarding stuffed frogs
and crocheted turtles
there is friction
but all agree
they never had a home
like Nina's heart
and never heard a story
like the one
Nina tells them every night
It never changes.

To find out more about this poem, turn to page 239.

Items 7–12 refer to the passage on page 204.

Write your answers in the space provided.

7. What does the number *60* refer to in this poem?

_____

8. What does Nina Dowley collect and love?

_____

9. Why is Nina *out of space in the room*?

_____

Circle the number of the best answer for each question.

10. What is the speaker's tone when she talks about Nina Dowley?

    (1) affectionate

    (2) amused

    (3) embarrassed

    (4) mocking

    (5) superior

11. Which conclusion is supported by the details that the speaker borrowed baking soda and pinking shears? The speaker is

    (1) the neighborhood gossip.

    (2) too poor to buy her own things.

    (3) a salesperson.

    (4) Nina's neighbor.

    (5) avoiding Nina.

12. What would Nina be most likely to do if she found a stuffed animal thrown out in the trash? She would

    (1) leave it there.

    (2) take it home and clean it.

    (3) throw it out again.

    (4) give it to someone as it is.

    (5) tear it up.

He halted at the corner of Grant and Pine and wiped the perspiration on his forehead with a forefinger.

"*Shew*, we have walked a distance of five *li* from the bus station," he said in Mandarin. "Are you tired, May Li?"

"A little," the girl said. She was dressed in a Chinese gown of light blue and wearing a pigtail wound round her head, her pretty face without make-up glowing with health.

"Shall we go visit Mr. Poon now, father?"

"Oh, do not be so foolish. Nobody visits people so early. This is New Year's day, people sleep in the morning with a full stomach of food and wine and do not wish to be disturbed. We shall have our breakfast and rest our legs for a while." He wiped his forehead once more and looked around.

"Here is a teahouse, father," May Li said, pointing at a red signboard saying "Lotus Room."

"Good," Old Man Li said. When he looked at the stairway he frowned. "No, May Li, I shall not climb this with my luggage on my back."

"Let me carry it up for you, father," May Li said.

"No, you are carrying enough of your own."

"I can carry a lot more." She held her father's canvas bag until Li finally yielded it to her, shaking his head. "You are just like your mother, May Li. Forty years ago when she was your age she could carry a hundred catties of flour and walk seventy *li* a day. She was strong as a cow, and just as amiable. . ."

"What shall we eat, father?" May Li asked.

"We shall see," Old Man Li said, trudging up the stairway. "We shall have some New Year dishes. But we must be careful in our selection. The owner of this place might be greedy, otherwise he would not have built a restaurant upstairs. He knows that people will eat more after this climbing, *shew*!"

When he reached the top of the stairs he promptly changed his opinion of the owner. The spacious dining hall with red-lacquered lattice windows was clean and impressive, almost filled with customers. Only a reputable place could be so prosperous, he thought. The smiling manager greeted them and directed them to a vacant table near one of the windows and handed them two copies of the menu with special New Year dishes attached to them. Old Man Li held the menu tensely, swallowing and resisting, his eyes roving among the expensive items. He wanted to eat everything, but he felt his economical nature held him back like an iron chain restraining a dog. He quickly closed the menu and rubbed his neck. "May Li, I shall let you order."

*To find out more
about this passage,
turn to page 239.*

Items 13–18 refer to the passage on page 206.

Write your answers in the space provided.

13. Where did the old man and the girl just come from?

_____

14. What can you conclude about the ethnic origin of the old man and the girl?

_____

15. Why did Old Man Li let May Li order the food?

_____

Circle the number of the best answer for each question.

16. After May Li asks about visiting Mr. Poon, what do she and her father do?

    (1) They try to find Mr. Poon.

    (2) They decide to celebrate New Year's Day.

    (3) They decide to have breakfast.

    (4) They leave the bus station.

    (5) They find a hotel.

17. When Old Man Li compares his wife to a cow, he is suggesting that she was

    (1) ugly.

    (2) very strong.

    (3) fat.

    (4) not very smart.

    (5) a bad mother.

18. What fact changed Old Man Li's opinion about the restaurant?

    (1) The owner was greedy.

    (2) The restaurant was upstairs.

    (3) He was hungry after climbing.

    (4) The restaurant was clean and impressive.

    (5) New Year dishes were on the menu.

Go on to the next page.

Every time he and his brother would be walking somewhere by themselves, Kunta would imagine that he was taking Lamin on some journey, as men sometimes did with their sons. Now, somehow, Kunta felt a special responsibility to act older, with Lamin looking up to him as a source of knowledge. Walking alongside, Lamin would ply Kunta with a steady stream of questions.

"What's the world like?"

"Well," said Kunta, "no man or canoes ever journeyed so far. And no one knows all there is to know about it."

"What do you learn from the arafang?"

Kunta recited the first verses of the Koran in Arabic and then said, "Now you try." But when Lamin tried, he got badly confused—as Kunta had known he would—and Kunta said paternally, "It takes time."

"Why does no one harm owls?"

"Because all our dead ancestors' spirits are in owls." Then he told Lamin something of their late Grandma Yaisa. "You were just a baby, and cannot remember her."

"What's that bird in the tree?"

"A hawk."

"What does he eat?"

"Mice and other birds and things."

"Oh."

Kunta had never realized how much he knew—but now and then Lamin asked something of which Kunta knew nothing at all.

"Is the sun on fire?" Or: "Why doesn't our father sleep with us?"

At such times, Kunta would usually grunt, then stop talking—as Omoro did when he tired of so many of Kunta's questions. Then Lamin would say no more, since Mandinka home training taught that one never talked to another who did not want to talk. Sometimes Kunta would act as if he had gone into deep private thought. Lamin would sit silently nearby, and when Kunta rose, so would he. And sometimes, when Kunta didn't know the answer to a question, he would quickly do something to change the subject.

To find out more about this passage, turn to page 238.

Items 19–24 refer to the passage on page 208.

Fill in the blanks with the word or words that best complete the statements.

19. The two boys in the passage are named _____ and

    _____.

20. The main idea of the passage is that the older brother wants to be

    able to _____ his brother's questions.

21. The arafang the boys talk about is probably a _____.

Circle the number of the best answer for each question.

22. What causes Kunta's conflict with himself?

    (1) He wants to be back at his home.

    (2) He feels his father should be on the journey.

    (3) His brother refuses to learn.

    (4) He does not always know the answers to Lamin's questions.

    (5) He believes he cannot harm an owl.

23. How does the older brother feel about the younger brother?

    (1) He resents the boy.

    (2) He dislikes the boy.

    (3) He cares about the boy.

    (4) He is not interested in his brother.

    (5) He does not want to be responsible for his brother.

24. If Kunta were a boy in the United States today, what would he
    probably teach his brother?

    (1) the verses of the Koran

    (2) how animals behave

    (3) how to behave properly in society

    (4) how to be quiet

    (5) the multiplication tables

Read the following review of the book
Woman Hollering Creek and Other Stories **by Katrina Sepulveda.**

Sandra Cisneros knows her own mind. She knows who she is as a woman. And she knows who she is as a Hispanic. *Woman Hollering Creek and Other Stories*, the author's second collection, presents a powerful vision of the condition of women. This vision is not only of the Latina woman that Cisneros knows so well but of women in general. This new book is compelling and revealing.

At 36, Cisneros was more than ready to write these stories. The problems of Hispanic women are nothing new to her. She is the daughter of a Mexican man. Her mother is Mexican-American. She grew up with traditional roles. From her six brothers she learned that a woman is supposed to be taken care of by a man.

But the women in Cisneros' stories do not need taking care of—not by any means. These are strong characters: young girls, idealistic brides, religious women, and women disappointed in love. The stories of the younger women, like their lives, are short but intense. The older women's longer stories reflect their greater experience. These women are proud of the power they have worked so hard to achieve.

The main character of the title story, "Woman Hollering Creek," is a young Mexican woman. Soap operas have affected her sense of reality. Soon after crossing the border to marry a Texan, she discovers that her new life has little, if any, of the romance and joy enjoyed by her TV idols. Rather than candlelight and roses, she gets snores and bad table manners. The young woman's efforts to rewrite the script of her own real-life soap opera make excellent reading.

Cisneros' view of men is not always complimentary. Men have a definite place in the lives of her characters—preferably at a distance. But the men are always there.

Cisneros' use of language is as balanced as her vision. She blends Spanish and English like spices and subtle flavorings. The effect is twice as nice.

A new breed of writers is demanding attention. Sandra Cisneros is one writer who is sure to get it.

Items 25–29 refer to the passage on page 210.

Write your answers in the space provided.

25. The reviewer divides Sandra Cisneros' characters into groups. What are the four classifications?

_____

_____

26. What simile does the reviewer use to suggest that Sandra Cisneros uses Spanish and English well together?

_____

Circle the number of the best answer for each question.

27. Which statement is the reviewer's opinion of Sandra Cisneros' book?

    (1) It is the best ever written about Hispanic women.

    (2) It is too critical of men.

    (3) It is interesting and balanced.

    (4) It is too revealing.

    (5) It is boring.

28. Which phrase shows the reviewer's bias in favor of the book?

    (1) *traditional roles*

    (2) *longer stories*

    (3) *a soap opera*

    (4) *excellent reading*

    (5) *not always complimentary*

29. How does the reviewer contrast the stories about older women and the stories about young women? The reviewer suggests that

    (1) Cisneros' stories about old and young women are similar.

    (2) the stories about the young women are more interesting.

    (3) all of the stories show women in traditional roles.

    (4) the young and old characters are all powerful women.

    (5) the stories about young women are shorter than those about older women.

Check your answers on pages 235–236.

POSTTEST
Correlation Chart

Literature

The chart below will help you determine your strengths and weaknesses in interpreting literature and the arts.

Directions

Circle the number of each item that you answered correctly on the Posttest. Count the number of items you answered correctly in each row. Write the amount in the Total Correct space in each row. (For example, in the Classical Literature row, write the number correct in the blank before *out of 12*). Complete this process for the remaining rows. Then add the 3 totals to get your Total Correct for the whole 29-item Posttest.

Content Areas	Items	Total Correct	Pages
Popular Literature (Pages 12–105)	7, 8, 9, 10, 11, 12 19, 20, 21, 22 23, 24	_____ out of 12	Pages 38–43, Pages 50–55, 80–85
Classical Literature (Pages 106–163)	1, 2, 3, 4, 5, 6 13, 14, 15, 16 17, 18	_____ out of 12	Pages 138–143 Pages 114–119
Commentary (Pages 164–201)	25, 26, 27, 28, 29	_____ out of 5	Pages 176–180
TOTAL CORRECT FOR INVENTORY _____ out of 29			

If you answered fewer than 26 items correctly, determine which of the three areas of literature you need to study further. Go back and review the passages in those areas. Page numbers to refer to for practice are given in the right-hand column above.

ANSWERS AND EXPLANATIONS

INVENTORY

PAGE 1

1. hurts
2. free
3. smooth
4. **(1) All creatures suffer when they are trapped.** The bird is a symbol for any being that is not free. The poet understands its pain because people feel the same way when they are trapped. Option 2 is incorrect because it is too specific; it is not general enough to apply to cruelty to people. There is no support for options 3 or 4. Option 5 is incorrect because music, or singing, is an expression of pain in the poem, not a way to solve the problem.
5. **(3) yearning** This option is correct because the bird wants what it cannot have. Options 1, 2, and 5 are the opposite of the emotion in the poem. There is no support for option 4.
6. **(4) the blues** This option is correct because the blues express painful emotions and a search for something. Option 1 is incorrect because there is no cause to be thankful. Options 2, 3, and 5 are incorrect because they are generally not songs that express pain.

PAGE 3

7. Joan Rivers, the main writer of the autobiography, is telling the story.
8. The audience was screaming, priests were yelling, and nuns were shaking their fists.
9. **(1) "The biggest scam ever pulled on me was that summer of 1960."** This option is correct because the passage is mainly about the story of this scam. The other options are incorrect because they are details in the story.
10. **(5) embarrassed** This option is suggested by Joan Rivers's description of what she says and does on-stage. Option 1 describes how she felt before going on-stage. Option 3 is the opposite of what is suggested. There is no support in the passage for options 2 and 4.
11. **(1) amused** This option is supported by the author's humorous tone. There is no support for options 2 and 4. Options 3 and 5 are feelings she might have had at the time but does not have now.

PAGE 5

12. They have been married for eight years.
13. Nora will probably leave. The stage directions say that she has put on her cloak, hat, and shawl.
14. **(3) gap** The clue to the meaning is given by the words *opened between us*. There is no support in the passage for the other options.
15. **(2) He does not really understand what Nora wants.** Torvald keeps making the wrong suggestions in his effort to get Nora to stay. Option 1 is incorrect because this is what he offers to do, not what he has done. Options 3 and 5 are the opposite of what is suggested about his character. There is no support for option 4.
16. **(3) treated her like a pet or a toy.** This option is correct because the metaphors suggest how Torvald thought of Nora. Option 1 is incorrect because it is the opposite of what the metaphors suggest. There is no support for options 2 and 4. Option 5 is incorrect because Nora does not like the way Torvald has acted toward her.

PAGE 7

17. bridge, starship
18. opening
19. first contact
20. **(2) glowing** This option is correct because *glowing* means the same as *luminous*. Option 1 refers to the being's face, not just the eyes. There is no support in the passage for options 3, 4, and 5.
21. **(5) He gets excited inside.** This option is supported by the last sentence in the passage. There is no support for options 1, 2, and 3. Option 4 is incorrect because Captain Kirk is only outwardly calm.

22. **(1) suggest an advanced technology.** This option is correct because Jim's words suggest the use of computer images. Jim seems to use the words casually. This helps to create a futuristic setting. Option 2 is incorrect because the phrase does not explain anything. Option 3 is incorrect because the phrase does not suggest anything simple. There is no support for options 4 and 5.

PAGE 9

23. Shirley Horn is known for jazz.
24. Her recordings have not sold enough copies to make money. They have cost her money.
25. **(1) Her new album is near the top of the *Billboard* jazz chart.** This is a fact that can be checked. Options 2, 3, 4, and 5 are incorrect because they are opinions, not facts.
26. **(4) continue to play her music.** This option is based on what the reviewer reveals about Shirley Horn's character. Money is not the reason she loves music. Options 1, 2, and 5 are incorrect because they do not fit Shirley Horn's character. Option 3 is incorrect because carpentry is her hobby, not her career.
27. **(1) She is unforgettable.** This option is suggested in the reviewer's discussion of the new album. He says that she is *indelible*, which means "making a mark that can't be erased." There is no support for options 2 and 4. Option 3 is a fact that has nothing to do with music. Option 5 is incorrect because the reviewer admires both her voice and her piano playing.

UNIT 1: POPULAR LITERATURE
SECTION 1

PAGE 14

1. There are many possible answers.
2. Chee and the horse thief
3. There are many possible answers.
4. There are many possible answers.

PAGE 15

The thief must have tied his horse and then climbed directly up the slope across the arroyo.

PAGE 16

small girl, Navajo, frightened, speaks English

PAGE 17

There are many possible answers. Sample: The girl's face had been forlorn and was now radiant, she looked thoughtful, and she became suspicious.

PAGES 18–19

1. hogan
2. *chindi*
3. gusts
4. plausible
5. tentatively
6. forlorn
7. arroyo
8. ponderosa
9. There are many possible answers.
10. He hears a cough and sniffling from the hogan.
11. The girl comes out of the hogan.
12. The hogan belongs to Hosteen Ashie Begay.
13. **(4) He had died in the hogan.** This option is correct because she knew someone had died in the hogan, and her grandfather was no longer there. There is no evidence for option 1. Option 2 is wrong because she did not know Albert Gorman had died. Option 3 is incorrect because there was no reason for an arrest. Option 5 is wrong because she was the one who stole the horse.
14. Only a person who is not a Navajo would go into a *chindi* hogan.
15. Chee will try to find out how and why Albert Gorman died.
16. The Navajo believe a *chindi* hogan should be avoided. So Begay could no longer live in his old home.

214 *Answers and Explanations*

17. There are many possible answers.
   Samples: Yes, Chee was right to have his
   pistol ready. He thought he would find the
   horse thief, who might be dangerous. No,
   Chee was wrong to have his pistol ready.
   He should have realized there was no
   danger. A dangerous person who was
   hiding would not have coughed and
   sniffled loudly.
18. There are many possible answers.
   Sample: Find a place for the girl to stay.
   Return the horse to its owner. Look for
   Begay, to ask him questions about Albert
   Gorman.
19. There are many possible answers.

SECTION 2

PAGE 20

1. There are many possible answers.
2. Alfred Lanning, Dr. Susan Calvin, The
   Brain
3. There are many possible answers.
4. There are many possible answers.

PAGE 21

The doctors are upset because something is
wrong with The Brain.

PAGE 22

The Brain has sent two men and a space ship
into space.

PAGE 23

The space ship left by itself without any
acceleration. The ship works on an unknown
principle because there are no engines visible.
The ship is being run by remote control.

PAGES 24–25

1. g	2. e	3. c	4. d
5. b	6. f	7. h	8. a

9. There are many possible answers.
10. The Brain is a robot.
11. A robot cannot harm a human being.
12. They are afraid the men will either die or
   be unable to return.
13. She doesn't want to upset The Brain and
   cause it to break communication.

14. **(1) Robots can be a problem if they act
   on their own.** This option is correct
   because it is the basis for the events that
   take place in the story. Option 2 is incorrect
   because The Brain is quite happy; the
   people are angry and upset. There is no
   evidence in the passage for option 3. Option
   4 may be true in many cases, but certainly
   is not true here. Option 5 is incorrect
   because although it is true of The Brain it
   is not the main idea of the story.
15. **(1) The Brain is worth a great deal of
   money.** This is probably true but has
   nothing to do with the main idea. Options
   2, 3, 4, and 5 all give examples of The
   Brain's independent behavior.
16. Dr. Calvin; She is the one in charge of The
   Brain and she keeps telling Dr. Lanning
   to be quiet.
17. There are many possible answers.
   Sample: There is no simple answer. The
   men might be safe, because they are
   protected by the First Law. The men
   might not be safe, because The Brain
   might be out of control.
18. There are many possible answers.

SECTION 3

PAGE 26

1. There are many possible answers.
2. He has left his home and just arrived in
   New York.
3. Harlem, in New York City
4. There are many possible answers.

PAGE 27

good, crazy feeling, breathless, dazzled

PAGE 28

He was happier in the streets of Harlem than
in the classrooms of Columbia. He felt rejected
at school but welcome in Harlem.

PAGE 29

In 1921 African-American men were
discriminated against when looking for jobs.

PAGES 30–31

1. d   2. f   3. b
4. e   5. a   6. c
7. There are many possible answers.
8. He spent his first days exploring the neighborhood of Harlem.
9. His final grades included three *B*s and a *C*.
10. He had few skills and he was an African American.
11. **(2) walking all over Harlem** This answer is correct because the phrase suggests that he could have made a map of Harlem from all the walking he did. There is no support for option 1. Options 3 and 5 are wrong because mapping does not suggest counting or wasting time. Option 4 is wrong because it confuses the verb *mapping* with the noun *map*.
12. **(3) the group that published his poetry.** This answer is correct because of the facts that they had received his poems and that they had readers who enjoyed his work. Option 1 is wrong because Columbia University and *The Crisis* are not related in any way. Also, no one at Columbia took Langston to lunch. Option 2 is wrong because the Negro musical hit is called *Shuffle Along*. Option 4 is wrong because the library had nothing to do with his poetry. Option 5 is wrong because Langston was taken to lunch at the restaurant, but the restaurant did not publish his poems.
13. The Harlem landlords and the Columbia dorms both discriminated against African Americans, the first by charging high rents, the second by not allowing African Americans at all.
14. Langston's father probably was angry because his son was not going on with school. Not replying would be a way to express that anger. *Cultural answer*
15. There are many possible answers. Sample: Langston will probably try to make it on his own as a poet.
16. There are many possible answers.

SECTION 4

PAGE 32

1. There are many possible answers.
2. Don and Jill
3. There are many possible answers.

PAGE 33

Jill is confused by Don. She does not know much about people who are blind, and she does not understand how he can joke about being blind.

PAGE 34

Don and Jill are in Don's apartment. This is first clear from Jill's remark about his apartment and is supported by the stage directions.

PAGE 35

Don and Jill have different opinions about people who are blind. Jill thinks people who are blind are spooky and different from other people. Don thinks of himself as being just like anyone else.

PAGES 36–37

1. braille
2. sinister
3. delicatessen
4. bravura
5. self-consciously
6. There are many possible answers.
7. He realized that most people aren't blind when he was six years old.
8. Jill lives in the apartment next door. The stage directions mention the door to Jill's apartment, blocked by a chest of drawers.
9. Don is making a joke. Having the *market cornered* suggests that Don's mother feels so guilty about his blindness that there is little guilt left to go around.
10. **(2) He is independent and funny.** This option is supported by Don's references to how well he can get around. He also makes a number of jokes. Jill's remarks show that option 1 is wrong. There is no support for option 3. Option 4 is wrong because he makes jokes about himself. Option 5 is wrong because he states that he prefers people to act naturally.

11. **(4) He explains how he feels about being blind.** This option is supported by his responses to Jill's discomfort. Option 1 is wrong because he does talk about blindness. Option 2 is wrong because Don stays calm and in a good mood. There is no support for option 3. Option 5 is wrong because it is the opposite of what Don says.

12. Don's attitude is more positive because he does not feel that being blind gets in his way. Jill, on the other hand, thinks people who are blind must be bitter and a little strange—maybe even to be pitied.

13. There are many possible answers. Sample: Don believes that people have the wrong idea about people who are blind. He thinks that people pay too much attention to the one thing he cannot do. They ignore the fact that he is normal in every other way. He would rather be accepted for who he is and for what he can do.

14. There are many possible answers. Take into account what Don says about how other people act toward him.

SECTION 5

PAGE 38

1. There are many possible answers.
2. a woman who is 38 years old
3. There are many possible answers.
4. There are many possible answers.

PAGE 39

Plain as bread suggests that the speaker does not feel she is pretty. *Round as a cake* suggests that the speaker feels she is chubby, not slim.

PAGE 40

There are many possible answers. Sample: The speaker is 38 years old and is looking at her life. She is not what she had expected to be. She thinks about her mother and her own daughters. She hopes she can face the rest of her life with strength and acceptance.

PAGE 41

The father gives *a knowing nod; tears welled in his eyes.*

PAGES 42–43

1. f   2. e   3. b
4. d   5. c   6. a

7. There are many possible answers.

8. smaller, more beautiful, wiser in African ways (the poet uses the spelling *Afrikan*), more confident

9. There are many possible answers. Sample: The little boy's only remembrance of his mother is a picture. When shopping, the boy sees a woman who looks like the picture. The father apologizes to the woman after the boy stares at her. The woman hugs the boy.

10. **(3) was trying to be like her mother.** Option 3 is supported by the speaker having dreamed dreams for her mother and having made her mother alive again, both of which suggest she wants to be like her mother. Option 1 is wrong because the mother is admired. Options 2 and 4 have no support. There is no evidence for option 5.

11. **(1) accept her own life as it is** This option is supported by her wanting to face the next part of her life without loneliness or fear. Also, the speaker says she wants to go into her own life. Option 2 is wrong because she is bothered by being ordinary. There is no support for option 3. Options 4 and 5 are misreadings of the mentions of Europe and daughters.

12. Both characters' mothers are dead. In each poem, the loss of the mother influences how the character feels and reacts.

13. There are many possible answers. Sample: The boy is looking for a mother's love. The meeting with the woman in the store will not give him what he wants. The woman can fill his need for only a few minutes.

14. There are many possible answers.

SECTION 6

PAGE 44

1. There are many possible answers.
2. Mark. He is a boy, probably in his early teens.
3. There are many possible answers.

PAGE 45

The passage is seen through only one person's eyes. The narrator is Mark.

PAGE 46

The setting is outdoors. There are trees. Nearby is a house. It is sometime in the afternoon.

PAGE 47

Mark's and Sue's fathers know each other. Both Mark and Sue are at this place to kill a vampire.

PAGES 48–49

1. glimpse
2. methodical
3. pondering
4. hunkered
5. incline
6. cylindrical
7. momentarily
8. synchronized
9. There are many possible answers.
10. She moved carefully, and she had guts.
11. **(4) vampires** This is suggested by the reference to killing vampires. There is no support for the other options.
12. **(2) with a wooden stake** Since both of them brought wooden stakes, option 2 is a good conclusion. Option 1 is wrong because only Mark had a pistol. There is no support for options 3, 4, and 5.
13. Sue was frightened. You can tell because she was tense, pale, and ready to scream.
14. Mark thinks he knows about the supernatural, things that are not just everyday events.
15. There are many possible answers. Sample: I wondered what would happen because I was not sure if someone would come out of the house and discover Mark and Sue hiding in the woods.
16. There are many possible answers.

SECTION 7

PAGE 50

1. There are many possible answers.
2. a boy, Mattie, Etta
3. There are many possible answers.
4. There are many possible answers.

PAGE 51

Etta smooths her hair and prances around the table. These actions suggest she understands the boy is flirting and she is flirting a little in return.

PAGE 52

Ciel talks about events that must be from her childhood. Only a child would worry about crayons. She had known Mattie then. Now she and Basil are grown and on their own.

PAGE 53

There are many possible answers. Sample: Etta is a slender, attractive, middle-aged, African-American woman, probably very energetic, maybe nicely dressed.

PAGES 54–55

1. e	2. f	3. a
4. b	5. c	6. d

7. There are many possible answers.
8. San Francisco
9. Ciel has been walking slowly—which suggests that time is passing. More than one person stops Ciel—which means that she stopped several times as she was walking.
10. There are many possible answers. The description of Mattie might be one who acts motherly and responsibly. Mattie's description probably would be very different from the description of Etta.

11. **(3) an outdoor neighborhood party.** This option is supported by mention of dancing in the street, the outdoor grill, and the number of people present. Etta also states that it is a party. Option 1 is wrong because there is no evidence of family relationships. There is no support for option 2. Option 4 is wrong because they are not in San Francisco. The only mention of a wedding refers to the future, so option 5 is wrong.

12. **(1) She had had some kind of personal trouble.** This is suggested by Ciel's references to why she did not write to Mattie. Getting to the ocean was an accident, so option 3 is wrong. There is no support for options 2, 4, and 5.

13. They approve of him because he is both good to her and good for her. They don't care that he isn't black. These ideas are supported by Etta's statement about what a man is and isn't. They are also supported by the way the women volunteer to take part in Ciel's wedding.

14. Yes. Ciel has begun to accept whatever happened in the past. She also has received a warm and loving welcome.

15. There are many possible answers.

SECTION 8

PAGE 56

1. There are many possible answers.
2. Willie Mays. He is in the Army.
3. There are many possible answers.

PAGE 57

The Army had Mays play on baseball teams and teach baseball to other soldiers.

PAGE 58

Frank gives Mays his overcoat. The clue word is *so*.

PAGE 59

Mays uses the tap dancer's comment about his love of dancing to express how he feels about baseball.

PAGES 60–61

1. morale
2. authority
3. technicality
4. suspicious
5. ordeal
6. There are many possible answers.
7. Mays had hoped he could be discharged early to take care of his family. He was sad that he was not discharged, so his last days in the Army were slightly troubled.
8. *The silent treatment* happens when the ball players ignore a good play or something they are pleased about. They do the opposite of what they feel.
9. **(3) were dressed in odd-looking clothes.** This option is supported by the overcoat being too big for Mays and by Forbes using newspapers to stuff his jacket. Option 1 is wrong because the tip had nothing to do with Forbes or Mays. Options 2 and 5 have no support. Option 4 is wrong because it was the way they looked, not the way they acted, that was suspicious.
10. **(3) He took too long getting his snack in New Orleans.** Because he took too long, the train left without him. So he was late for spring training. Option 1 is wrong because he started the trip on time in Washington. There is no support for options 2 and 5. Option 4 is wrong because Leo was only a little annoyed at the delay and had nothing to do with Mays' schedule.
11. There are many possible answers. Answers should reflect Mays' positive attitudes about authority and family. Answers might also deal with Mays' concern about the welfare of his team over his own welfare.
12. Mays shows that his relationship with Leo is close. Leo cares about Mays, and Mays wants Leo's respect and affection.
13. There are many possible answers. Sample: I would be happy because Mays was a great baseball player and the Giants were having a bad season before he returned.
14. There are many possible answers.

SECTION 9

PAGE 62

1. There are many possible answers.
2. Meg, Babe, Lenny
3. There are many possible answers.
4. There are many possible answers.

PAGE 63

Babe had been planning to leave.

PAGE 64

Meg and Babe are impatient with Lenny. Lenny is having trouble deciding whether to blow out the candles. Suspense is created by the reader having to wait for Lenny's decision.

PAGE 65

Meg and Babe watch for Lenny to arrive. Lenny is surprised by the birthday cake. After a delay, they sing "Happy Birthday." Lenny is persuaded into telling her wish. The sisters eat the cake.

PAGES 66–67

1. d
2. c
3. e
4. f
5. a
6. b
7. There are many possible answers.
8. They are sisters.
9. Lenny wishes for a laughing moment with her sisters.
10. Babe means that Meg should watch for Lenny.
11. Babe makes up the traditions about the number of candles and wishing deeply enough.
12. **(1) She takes a long time to make up her mind.** This option is supported by both sisters telling her to hurry up. There is no support for options 2 and 3. Option 4 is wrong because her sister says that the wish is nice. Option 5 is wrong because the sisters enjoy eating the cake.
13. **(5) All the sisters were having problems.** This option is supported by Meg's first statement. Option 1 is the opposite of what is stated. There is no support for options 2 and 4. Option 3 is wrong because Lenny loves birthday celebrations.
14. There are many possible answers. Sample: Babe makes up her beliefs to reassure Lenny. She wants Lenny to feel good about what is happening.
15. Yes. Lenny wants her sisters to laugh with her. In the last minutes of the play, they do. They have gotten to that magical moment.
16. There are many possible answers.

SECTION 10

PAGE 68

1. There are many possible answers.
2. fishing
3. There are many possible answers.
4. There are many possible answers.

PAGE 69

Angry. The word suggests being upset. Angry water would be moving around, not calm.

PAGE 70

The narrator is the young boy. Seeing the action from the narrator's point of view helps you understand how important the story of the carp is to him and the people of the town.

PAGE 71

The people ate the carp; *for a long time, then, finally*

PAGES 72–73

1. furrow
2. churned
3. listlessly
4. abode
5. subsided
6. relent
7. There are many possible answers.
8. He learns about the golden carp after the sun starts to set.
9. Catching carp is bad luck because the carp were the first people.
10. **(2) uncomfortable** This option is supported by the narrator's shivering, his questions, and his thinking about his mother—a source of comfort. Option 1 is wrong because he continues to ask questions. The narrator's reactions do not suggest options 3, 4, and 5.

11. **(3) He wanted to take care of the carp people.** This option is supported by the direct statement that the kind god asked the other gods to turn him into a carp to take care of his people. Option 1 is wrong because the other gods agreed with him. Option 2 is wrong because the disobedience was not connected to the kind god. Option 4 is wrong because looking like the huge golden carp is an effect, not a cause. Option 5 refers to the people, not the god.

12. He is suggesting that many things had happened at the river that no human would ever know. He was about to find out something important.

13. There are many possible answers. Sample: The narrator seems to believe Samuel's story because he asks Samuel what would happen if someone ate a carp.

14. There are many possible answers.

SECTION 11

PAGE 74

1. There are many possible answers.
2. street directions; the dollar, money
3. There are many possible answers.
4. There are many possible answers.

PAGE 75

humorous

PAGE 76

There are many possible answers. Samples: The author exaggerates by suggesting a semester-long course on arrow drawing for sign makers. The author also exaggerates by saying there are cities in America so hard to find your way around in they are not worth figuring out.

PAGE 77

Both essays use a humorous tone. Both authors use the point of view of a narrator.

PAGES 78–79

1. d	2. f	3. b	4. h
5. g	6. a	7. e	8. c
9. There are many possible answers.			

10. The phrase "up and down the island" helps you understand the meaning of *longitudinally*.

11. The government in Washington no longer understands the value of a dollar.

12. A stranger might get confused in New York City because the order of street names changes abruptly.

13. **(5) "I hope they devote a semester to arrow drawing for signmakers."** This option is an exaggerated solution to the problem. Options 1, 2, 3, and 4 are all direct statements.

14. **(2) of some real value to the average American.** This option is supported by the author's introduction and by her reference to putting a punch back into middle America's pocketbook. Option 1 is the opposite of what the author suggests. Option 3 refers to her lessons for Congress, not the value of the dollar. Option 4 has no support. Option 5 refers to what a dollar could buy when the author was young.

15. There are many possible answers. Sample: Yes, I agree. It is very difficult to find your way around a strange city with poorly marked streets.

16. There are many possible answers. Sample: No, I don't think her suggestions would change how the government spends money because they are humorous, unrealistic suggestions.

17. There are many possible answers.

SECTION 12

PAGE 80

1. There are many possible answers.
2. a mother and a daughter named Waverly
3. Chinese and American
4. There are many possible answers.

PAGE 81

The differences are the way she walks and her facial expression.

PAGE 82

You can infer that the Chinese believe in not wasting what one has been given.

PAGE 83

The mother wants her daughter to learn Chinese values. The daughter wants to be Chinese only in appearance; her other values are American.

PAGES 84–85

1. pursuing
2. opportunities
3. blend
4. fabulous
5. advantage
6. circumstances
7. There are many possible answers.
8. American circumstances and Chinese character
9. The Chinese face shows her real emotions. The American face conceals her real emotions.
10. **(2) They look directly at each other.** The mother's criticism implies that Americans do the opposite of the Chinese. Option 1 refers to Americans. There is no support for options 3, 4, and 5.
11. **(1) She doesn't believe her mother understands American ways.** She feels her mother might make a mistake if left on her own. Option 2 is wrong; it refers to the daughter's voice, which the mother objects to. Option 3 may be true, but it does not matter, because the mother speaks English. Option 4 is wrong because the mother seems to know quite well what she wants. There is no support for option 5.
12. **(3) ". . . her famous Mr. Rory . . ."** This option suggests that the mother doesn't think much of the hairdresser. She is making fun of how well known he is. Options 1 and 4 are statements about how the mother thinks Waverly feels. Option 2 is a comment by Waverly. Option 5 is a judgment unrelated to the daughter's ideas.
13. There are many possible answers. Sample: Waverly may understand what she has in common with her mother when she has children of her own. She may understand that all parents and children have some conflicting values.
14. There are many possible answers.

SECTION 13
PAGE 86

1. There are many possible answers.
2. Smith and Carlos
3. There are many possible answers.

PAGE 87

The numbers stand for the time it took to run the race. *Semi* is a shortened form of *semifinal*.

PAGE 88

The two effects are that Smith came in first and that Norman came in second.

PAGE 89

There are many possible answers. Sample: Smith and Carlos may have been punished by sports authorities in the United States. Their protest may have caused people around the world to consider the problem of racism in sports and in society.

PAGES 90–91

1. e
2. b
3. a
4. f
5. d
6. c
7. g
8. There are many possible answers.
9. Smith is referring to the fact that the Olympic audience was made up of people from many countries. They would not all understand a protest spoken only in English.
10. Norman wore an Olympic Project for Human Rights button.
11. Smith had injured his leg two hours earlier.
12. Carlos thinks that he would have won the race and set a new world record.
13. **(5) he was going to raise his gloved right hand.** This option can be inferred from his statement that he took the right glove and later raised that hand. There is no support for options 1, 3, and 4. Option 2 is wrong because he accepted the symbolism of the olive tree.
14. **(2) He slowed down.** This option is a figurative way of saying what is later stated about Carlos. There is no support for options 1, 3, and 5. Option 4 is the opposite of what is stated in the passage.

15. **(1) the excellence of African-American athletes** This option can be inferred from the whole article. It is also supported by several statements by Smith and Carlos. There is no support for the other options.
16. There are many possible answers. Sample: They are proud of what they did.
17. There are many possible answers.

SECTION 14

PAGE 92

1. There are many possible answers.
2. The biography is about Luis W. Alvarez. He was a scientist.
3. There are many possible answers.

PAGE 93

The detail *an accidental explosion would cause a terrible disaster* supports the main idea of the paragraph.

PAGE 94

There are many possible answers. Sample: The second shock wave happened because the first shock wave bounced off the ground back into the air.

PAGE 95

The Alvarezes concluded that the dinosaurs died after the earth was hit by a large body from outer space. They starved and froze to death.

PAGES 96–97

1. d
2. e
3. c
4. h
5. g
6. a
7. f
8. b
9. There are many possible answers.
10. after
11. explosion or bomb
12. **(3) his work as a geologist** This option is stated in the passage as the work he *may be best remembered for.* Options 1 and 2 are incorrect because he was just part of a team and was not directly responsible for either one. Option 4 is incorrect because he is better known for something else. There is no support for option 5.

13. **(2) A clay layer formed on Earth.** This option is correct because there is no evidence of fossils in the layer. Option 1 is a hypothesis, not a fact. Option 4 is true but does not support the conclusion. Option 3 does not discuss the differences between the layers and why they are significant. Option 5 does not help to explain the animals' death.
14. **(2) Future wars would be avoided.** Alvarez referred to this possible cause-and-effect relationship in his letter to his son. There is no support in the passage for the other options.
15. There are many possible answers.

UNIT 1 REVIEW

PAGE 99

1. c   2. a   3. b
4. **(1) proud.** This option is supported by Marsha's comments about how beautiful her baby is. Options 2 and 3 are wrong because they refer to the way Victor feels. There is no support for options 4 and 5.
5. **(3) The baby is not normal.** This option is supported by the fact that the baby clearly focuses on Victor's eyes. Option 1 is wrong because the passage states that the baby is a newborn. There is no support for options 2, 4, and 5.
6. **(5) shock and fear** These words are used to describe Victor's feelings as he looks into the infant's eyes. Option 1 is wrong because the words refer to reactions of the resident and the mother. Option 2 is wrong because the baby's eyes are blue. Option 3 is wrong because the words refer to Marsha's and Victor's observations. Option 4 is wrong because eye color does not affect how Victor feels.

PAGE 101

7. divorced
8. nights
9. woman
10. torn up/shredded

11. **(1) arguing bitterly** This option is correct because it suggests that the two tried to hurt each other's feelings with words in the same way they might hurt each other physically by throwing furniture. Option 2 is wrong because the couple did not really throw furniture. There is no support for options 3, 4, and 5.

12. **(3) The man and woman now live in different parts of the country.** This option is correct because it is implied that the two are separated by distance. There is no support for options 1, 2, 4, and 5.

13. **(5) held on tight, and let go** This option is correct because it summarizes the sadness the couple felt about the divorce. It also refers to the fact that they finally decided to end the marriage. Option 1 is wrong because it refers to how the couple acted before the end of the marriage. There is no support for options 2, 3, and 4.

PAGE 103

14. The story is told by Tammy Wynette, whose real name is Wynette Byrd.
15. She thinks Billy felt sorry for her.
16. There are many possible answers. Sample: It pays to keep trying.
17. **(1) The woman enters the office and sees the man.** This option is correct because it is the first action. Options 2, 3, 4, and 5 all occur later.
18. **(2) nervous.** This option is supported by her own statement in paragraph 2. Options 1, 3, and 4 are wrong because they do not describe how she felt. Option 5 describes how Billy acted, not Wynette.
19. **(4) the casual way Billy offered to record her.** This option is supported by Wynette's statement. There is no support for options 1, 2, 3, and 5.

PAGE 105

20. science fiction
21. radio signals
22. Friday
23. **(3) were expecting to receive signals from outer space.** This answer is supported by the narrator's introduction which describes Adela's and Marcos' work. There is no support for options 1, 2, and 5.

Option 4 is the opposite of what is stated in the play.

24. **(4) she is afraid the police will think she and Marcos are crazy.** This option is supported by Adela's statement ". . . they'll think we're a couple of UFO freaks who have gone off the deep end." There is no support for options 1 and 2. Option 3 is incorrect because she and Marcos are both convinced that the radio is giving news that is a day ahead of them. Option 5 is incorrect because Marcos says they have until "tomorrow at five o'clock."

25. **(4) go to the authorities and try to convince them that the bridge will collapse.** Option 1 is incorrect because the discovery is too important to ignore. Option 2 is incorrect because they could make more money if they kept the radio. There is no support for option 3. Option 5 may be true in the future, but it is not the first thing they would do.

UNIT 2: CLASSICAL LITERATURE

SECTION 15

PAGE 108

1. There are many possible answers.
2. He is very nervous.
3. a thriller
4. There are many possible answers.

PAGE 109

very gradually

PAGE 110

The mood is tense. There are many possible answers. Sample: The action happens very slowly, and the author repeats many things. For example, "cautiously—oh, so cautiously—cautiously."

PAGE 111

He probably will act quickly in anger. He will get rid of the evil eye by killing the old man immediately.

PAGES 112–113

| 1. g | 2. j | 3. c | 4. b | 5. d |
| 6. i | 7. h | 8. a | 9. e | 10. f |

11. There are many possible answers.
12. the old man's strange-looking eye
13. "first the idea entered my brain"
14. **(5) waiting to see the vulture eye.** The eye is what terrifies the narrator and causes him to murder. Option 1 is not mentioned by the narrator. Option 2 is the opposite of what is stated in the story. Option 3 is wrong because the eye can't be seen while the old man is asleep. Option 4 doesn't seem to matter to the narrator.
15. **(5) nervous pride** The narrator is boasting about how clever he was, but he is still nervous about what he did. There is an element of fear in the story, but the narrator does not feel enough fear to support option 1. There is no support for options 2 and 4. Option 3 seems to be the opposite of his emotion.
16. There are many possible answers. Sample: No. He is crazy. His reason for killing the old man is not the thinking of a sane man.
17. There are many possible answers.

SECTION 16

PAGE 114

1. There are many possible answers.
2. Alessandro and Ramona
3. There are many possible answers.

PAGE 115

a horse; *trotting, snort* and *whinny*

PAGE 116

reiterated

PAGE 117

There are many possible answers. Sample: Ramona asks Alessandro to give her a name he likes.

PAGES 118–119

1.	f	4.	g	7.	b
2.	a	5.	c	8.	h
3.	d	6.	e		

9. There are many possible answers.
10. They are running off to get married.

11. **(4) He thought they might be stopped.** He thinks that Ramona's family will follow them and take Ramona back. There is no support for options 1 and 5. Option 2 is wrong because the horse and pony do not seem to be in a hurry. Option 3 is wrong because it is the opposite of what Ramona wants.
12. **(3) Ramona's family does not approve of Alessandro.** This option is supported by Ramona's discussion of the Señora and Felipe. Options 1 and 4 are wrong because the opposites are suggested. There is no mention of Alessandro's parents, so option 2 is wrong. Option 5 is wrong because he is clearly devoted to her.
13. **(1) Love conquers all problems.** The couple's love gives them the courage to break away from Ramona's family and to ignore class differences. There is no suggestion of hesitation, so option 2 is wrong. There is no support for options 3 and 5. The question of names is only a portion of the passage, so option 4 is wrong.
14. The Baba passage is humorous. Seeing Ramona and Alessandro through the horse's eyes emphasizes the happiness they feel.
15. There are many possible answers. Sample: Ramona and Alessandro might try to reason with Ramona's family before running away to get married.
16. There are many possible answers.

SECTION 17

PAGE 120

1. There are many possible answers.
2. The speaker is trying to choose which one of two roads to take.
3. There are many possible answers.
4. There are many possible answers.

PAGE 121

There are many possible answers. Sample: *Wanted wear* means the road has not been used very much. Some context clues are *less traveled by* and *no step had trodden.*

PAGE 122

There are many possible answers. Samples: The people of the town envied Richard Cory because he looked as though he had everything. Richard Cory was probably very unhappy and felt there were many important things he did not have. The theme of the poem could be "No one can know how another person feels inside from the way that person looks on the outside."

PAGE 123

Grandma thinks that the old ways were good, and she wishes that today's young people could feel the way she did.

PAGES 124–125

1. minuet
2. trodden
3. diverged
4. arrayed
5. schooled
6. claim
7. There are many possible answers.
8. He stood and looked down the two roads.
9. She was pretty, with bright and sunny hair and dimpled cheeks.
10. The words *crown* and *imperially* suggest that Richard Cory was like a king.
11. **(2) *really about the same*** This option is correct because the restatement suggests that one road is as good as the other. Options 1 and 5 are wrong because they make a contrast between the two roads. There is no support for options 3 and 4.
12. **(3) You can't judge a book by its cover.** This option is correct because the saying means that you should not make a decision based on appearances. Looking at the outside of something does not always tell you what the inside is like. There is no support for options 1, 2, and 4. Option 5 is wrong because there is no suggestion that Richard Cory was evil.

13. **(1) Both poems discuss individual choice.** This option is correct because both poems focus on the choices that people make about their lives. Options 2, 4, and 5 are wrong because success, failure, and social issues are talked about or hinted at only in "Richard Cory." Option 4 is wrong because only "A Road Not Taken" talks about the future.
14. There are many possible answers.

SECTION 18
PAGE 126

1. There are many possible answers.
2. a white man named Karl Lindner, Beneatha, her brother Walter, and Ruth
3. There are many possible answers. Sample: a problem affecting African Americans
4. There are many possible answers.

PAGE 127

Walter sees himself as the head of the household, as being in control of the situation. Ruth and Beneatha do not take Walter seriously as the head of the house.

PAGE 128

People can become uncomfortable when dealing with other people whom they consider different.

PAGE 129

There are many possible answers. Sample: There have been racial problems in other neighborhoods. This neighborhood wants to find a peaceful way to avoid conflict.

PAGES 130–131

1. e	2. h	3. g	4. f
5. d	6. c	7. a	8. b

9. There are many possible answers.
10. Lindner becomes uncomfortable after Walter offers him a drink. The stage direction is *"Upset for some reason."*
11. There are many possible answers. Sample: The association looks after the neighborhood, greets new people, and handles any problems that come up.

12. The Youngers are an African-American family. This is supported by the early reference to Lindner as white and his later reference to colored people.

13. **(4) suspicious** Option 4 is supported by the stage directions that say "BENEATHA *is watching the man carefully.*" Option 1 is incorrect because all three of the Youngers act in a friendly manner toward Lindner. Option 2 is incorrect because Beneatha listens carefully to everything Lindner says. Option 3 refers to Ruth's attitude, not Beneatha's. There is no support for option 5.

14. **(1) The association does not want an African-American family in the neighborhood.** The implication is that the Youngers are a "special community problem." This is supported by Lindner's reference to "incidents" involving "colored people." There is no mention of the house itself, so option 2 is wrong. There is no support for options 3 and 4. It is unlikely that the Youngers would protest against themselves, so option 5 is wrong.

15. **(3) suggest in a nice way that they sell the house** This option is supported by Lindner's awkward way of getting to the idea that there is a problem. He is gentle and hesitant and thinks he is being reasonable. Option 1 does not fit with Lindner's personality so far. Options 2 and 4 would mean that the association had no problem with African-American families. There is no support for option 5.

16. There are many possible answers.

SECTION 19
PAGE 132
1. There are many possible answers.
2. Lark
3. There are many possible answers.
4. There are many possible answers.

PAGE 133
Lark drew her horse to a walk. She reached a boulder. She rode her horse slowly down the slope.

PAGE 134
The setting is a thicket. It is dark. There are pine saplings and leafless brush. The ground is covered with pine needles.

PAGE 135
Lark feels nervous, scared, and excited.

PAGES 136–137
1. aperture
2. reconnoiter
3. dubious
4. liberate
5. pondering
6. elaborated
7. tortuous
8. There are many possible answers.
9. Lark wants to free the wild horses.
10. The phrase describes the group of moving horses.
11. **(5) the wild-horse catchers** This option is supported by Lark looking for Blanding's men before she frees the wild horses. Options 1, 2, and 3 are wrong because they are the opposite of what is suggested. There is no mention of the law, so option 4 is wrong.
12. **(1) cautious** This option is supported by the fact that Lark thinks about every move she makes. She also moves slowly to avoid making a mistake. Options 2 and 5 are wrong because they are the opposite of what is described in the passage. There is no support for options 3 and 4.
13. **(2) The trap will be ruined.** This option is supported in the passage. Burning the fence will destroy the trap, which cannot be easily rebuilt. Option 1 is wrong because Lark does not want to frighten the horses. There is no support for options 3 and 4. Option 5 is wrong because there is no nearby timber.
14. There are many possible answers. Sample: Lark would stand up to them and shoot if necessary.
15. There are many possible answers.

SECTION 20

PAGE 138

1. There are many possible answers.
2. the start of a journey
3. the narrator, who is Black Elk
4. There are many possible answers.

PAGE 139

The nation's hoop means the Sioux nation as a harmonious whole.

PAGE 140

He sees the *Wasichus'* world as too crowded and too fenced in.

PAGE 141

The ship left New York. It passed through bad weather and high seas. First the Native Americans, and then the crew members, became very ill. The Native Americans prepared to die. Some of the animals died and were thrown overboard. The ship finally reached London. It was searched by Customs before everyone could leave.

PAGES 142–143

1. d   2. c   3. e
4. a   5. f   6. b
7. There are many possible answers.
8. The train stopped three times.
9. The weather was rough and stormy.
10. Black Elk felt homesick and in despair.
11. The sailors looked down on the Native Americans and were amused by them.
12. **(3) cloth hammocks** This option is supported by the fact that they should have been hung up for sleeping. Black Elk's description does not support options 1, 4, and 5. Option 2 refers to a later description by Black Elk and so is wrong.
13. **(4) a spiritual experience** This option is supported by the fact that Black Elk is a holy man. Option 1 is wrong because it refers to another meaning of the word *vision*. Options 2 and 3 have no support. Option 5 is wrong because he faces death bravely.

14. **(4) the animals represented the Native American way of life.** This option is supported by Black Elk saying that throwing the animals away was like throwing part of the power of his people away. There is no support for options 1, 2, and 5. Option 3 is incorrect because it was the voyage, not the animals, that made the passengers sick.
15. There are many possible answers.

SECTION 21

PAGE 144

1. There are many possible answers.
2. a dog and a man
3. There are many possible answers.
4. There are many possible answers.

PAGE 145

He thought his cheeks might freeze.

PAGE 146

The man is compared to a horse.

PAGE 147

There are many possible answers. Samples: He has dressed warmly, has brought matches, and has brought the dog. If he were going across a desert, he might bring water and food and wear light clothing to keep himself cool.

PAGES 148–149

1. crypts   4. devised
2. intervened   5. instinct
3. automatically   6. floundered
7. There are many possible answers.
8. The man and dog are going to a camp.
9. The main threat is the effect of extreme cold on the body.
10. **(4) He strikes his fingers against his leg.** This is stated in the passage. Option 1 is wrong because he doesn't put on his mitten until later. Option 2 is wrong because building a fire is the last thing he does. Option 3 is wrong because he checks the numbness in his toes later. Option 5 is wrong because he unbuttons his jacket before his fingers become numb.

11. **(2) The dog acts on instinct, but the man thinks.** This option is supported by the author's statement that the dog did not know why it licked the water off its paws, but the man knew. Options 1 and 4 have no support. Options 3 and 5 are opposite to what is stated about the dog.

12. **(3) It is even colder than he thought it would be.** This option is supported by the man remembering that he laughed at the person who told him how cold it gets in the country. There is no support for options 1 and 5. Option 4 is wrong because the man comments that it is noontime. Option 2 is wrong because the man doesn't hesitate to use the dog in dangerous situations.

13. There are many possible answers. Sample: I think he will have difficulty reaching his goal because it is colder than he expected.

14. There are many possible answers.

SECTION 22

PAGE 150

1. There are many possible answers.
2. An air fight between the English and the Germans is taking place.
3. There are many possible answers.
4. There are many possible answers.

PAGE 151

That women are not given weapons is a fact. That they can fight with their minds is an opinion.

PAGE 152

Young Englishmen must be helped to get rid of their love of medals and decorations; *must*

PAGE 153

If men are freed from the machines of war, they will become more caring. This opinion is supported by the example of the English man and woman giving the captured pilot cigarettes and tea.

PAGES 154–155

1. g	2. c	3. b	4. a
5. f	6. d	7. h	8. e

9. There are many possible answers.

10. She describes the feeling as dull dread.

11. **(2) desire to be a mother.** This option is supported by the reference to child-bearing. Option 1 is wrong because it refers to young men. Options 3 and 4 are wrong because they refer to the reasons why maternal instinct might be given up. Option 5 has no support.

12. **(5) "The emotion of fear and hate is therefore sterile . . ."** This option is a judgment and cannot be proved true. Options 1 and 4 are wrong because they are facts about what is happening. Options 2 and 3 are wrong because they are other people's opinions.

13. **(3) to compare women's responsibilities with men's.** This option is correct because the point of the passage is to show what men and women would be willing to do to achieve peace. Option 1 is wrong because there is no suggestion of one being better than the other. Options 2 and 5 have no support. Option 4 has no link to the example.

14. The author implies that young men might find their lives empty in peacetime if they were directed away from their warlike instincts.

15. There are many possible answers. Sample: I would have been concerned about my personal safety and the possibility of being killed.

16. There are many possible answers.

UNIT 2 REVIEW

PAGE 157

1. jobs
2. hunger, anger
3. cannery
4. **(1) slowly to grow dangerously angry** This option is suggested by the fact that the people's hunger was slowly turning into anger. Option 2 has nothing to do with the passage. There is no support for options 3 and 4. Option 5 is the opposite of what is meant.

5. **(4) uneasy** The migrants are restless, and the author suggests that the situation will soon change for the worse. Options 1 and 2 are too positive for the situation described. There is no support for options 3 and 5.

6. **(4) desperate.** The two words suggest the extremes of hunger and violence. Options 1 and 3 are the opposite of what is suggested. There is no support for options 2 and 5.

PAGE 159

7. He thinks that Catherine will not get ahead in life if she quits school.

8. Catherine will get a certificate from the school, showing that she has passed a test. The certificate probably will be the equivalent of a high school diploma.

9. The setting is a kitchen or dining room. This is indicated by the stage directions, which say that Catherine is bringing in plates and forks and Eddie is sitting at the table.

10. **(1) Her school principal suggested it.** This option is stated in the passage. Options 2 and 4 are the opposite of what can be learned from the passage. There is no support for options 3 and 5.

11. **(3) proud** This option is supported by their reaction to Catherine saying that she is the best student in the class. There is no support for options 1 and 2. Options 3 and 4 are wrong because only Eddie seems worried or protective.

12. **(4) He will continue to object to Catherine taking a job.** In the passage so far, his character does not seem to be one that would give in easily without more persuasion. Option 1 does not follow from what has been said. There is no support for options 2 and 5. Option 3 is wrong because he objects to Catherine having any job.

PAGE 161

13. Y
14. page of original writing
15. records

16. **(4) He is beginning to understand himself.** This is supported by his thoughts about what makes him the way he is and what he will learn. There is no support for options 1, 3, and 5. Option 2 is the opposite of what he states.

17. **(1) the student's** This option is supported by the way the assignment is stated, which is *let that page come out of you*. There is no support for the other options.

18. **(5) The instructor will learn something from the speaker.** The speaker seems to believe this option, but he has no factual support, so it is an opinion. Options 1 and 2 are facts, not opinions. Options 3 and 4 are not mentioned in the poem.

PAGE 163

19. mountains, hilltops
20. There are many possible answers. Sample: *A beautiful symphony of brotherhood* means a society in which people of all races live in harmony.

21. **(1) hope and faith** This option is correct because the author is talking about a positive idea that he has. He also says that he has hope and faith. Options 2 and 3 are wrong because his dream is the opposite of despair and distrust. There is no support for options 4 and 5.

22. **(5) By working together, all people can become free.** This is the general truth suggested by Martin Luther King's examples. Options 1 and 2 are too negative to be the theme of this uplifting speech. Options 3 and 4 may be true, but they are not suggested by this passage.

23. **(4) hopeful inspiration** Martin Luther King's emotional appeal is based on hope for the future. Option 1 is wrong because he does not cite facts. Option 2 is wrong because there are no details about the past. There is no evidence of anger or of arguments with the other side, so options 3 and 5 are wrong.

UNIT 3: COMMENTARY

SECTION 23

PAGE 166

1. There are many possible answers.
2. Dan Rather, Tom Brokaw, and Peter Jennings
3. There are many possible answers.

PAGE 167

The reviewer begins the review by saying that he is a critic. He also shows he has been watching TV news for a long time by referring to Walter Cronkite.

PAGE 168

The reviewer says that both Brokaw and Jennings are good at delivering unrehearsed material. The reviewer thinks that Peter Jennings and Jane Pauley are the best news readers. He thinks that Rather smiles at the wrong moments and is unpredictable. The reviewer thinks that Brokaw is a good journalist, but that he delivers the news without enough emotion. The reviewer thinks that Jennings is good at live events and delivers the news comfortably and calmly.

PAGES 169–170

1. b   2. g   3. f
4. e   5. h   6. c
7. a   8. d
9. There are many possible answers.
10. The author wants to be able to rely on the news during a time of crisis.
11. The reviewer prefers Peter Jennings.
12. He is giving an example of a Canadian accent.
13. **(2) Dan Rather was more comfortable than Tom Brokaw.** This option is correct because the reviewer states that Dan Rather looked relaxed, but Tom Brokaw looked uncomfortable. Options 1, 3, and 4 are the opposite of what is stated. There is no support for option 5.
14. **(3) does not express much emotion.** The simile suggests that Tom Brokaw is cold. That is, he does not show emotion. There is no support for the other options.

15. **(5) can be trusted.** This option is supported by the reviewer's references to Walter Cronkite and why he thinks Cronkite is still the best news anchor. Options 1 and 2 are not important considerations to the author. There is no support for option 3. Option 4 is the opposite of what the author states he likes in a news anchor.
16. "There is an honest, real quality to Jennings, what I suspect is a human being behind the hair spray and makeup."
17. There are many possible answers.

SECTION 24

PAGE 171

1. There are many possible answers.
2. Mitch Robbins, Phil Berquist, Ed Furillo
3. There are many possible answers.

PAGE 172

The reviewer is suggesting that there are problems in the marriage.

PAGE 173

He calls this theme *a confusion of priorities*.

PAGES 174–175

1. f   2. g   3. b   4. e
5. a   6. d   7. c   8. h
9. There are many possible answers.
10. The three friends face storms, pregnant cows, insecurities, and doubts.
11. The reviewer says that Crystal is best known for his comedy.
12. The reviewer mentions the other movies and shows to point out the contrast between Billy Crystal's comic background and the more serious nature of the movie *City Slickers*.
13. **(3) They deal with heavy issues.** This option is correct because it is stated in the review. Also, this statement can be taken only as opinion, not fact, because the reviewer gives no examples. There is no support for the other four options.

14. **(1) Finishing something gives you a feeling of satisfaction.** This option is supported by the explanation the reviewer gives. The other options are not suggested by the metaphor, which implies an emotional response to an action.

15. **(1) 'What If?' land** This option is correct because it points out a question that many people ask themselves when they reach a certain stage of life. Option 2 is wrong because there is more to the problem than age. Option 3 is wrong because it is too general. There is no support for options 4 and 5.

16. There are many possible answers. Sample: The movie has a happy ending, with the three men taking what they have learned back home to improve their lives.

17. There are many possible answers.

SECTION 25

PAGE 176
1. There are many possible answers.
2. gangsters and people who make movies
3. There are many possible answers.

PAGE 177

The reviewer probably wants the reader to expect a funny book written in a casual, informal way.

PAGE 178

There are many possible answers. Samples: These words suggest a bias in favor of the novel because they make the reader feel the book would be fun to read. The reviewer uses the phrase *You have to like a Hollywood novel* to show his bias in favor of the novel. The reviewer supports his opinion by using quotations from the novel.

PAGES 179–180
1. cynic
2. protagonist
3. zinger
4. compensates
5. moral
6. acidic
7. There are many possible answers.

8. The detail *It wouldn't be a Leonard novel without colorful villains* shows that the reviewer has read many of Elmore Leonard's books.

9. Chili looks like a nice guy in comparison with Ray Bones and Bo Catlett.

10. **(4) Ray Bones** This option is correct because Ray Bones is named as a villain. Option 1 is wrong because Elmore Leonard is the author. Options 2, 3, and 5 are not villains.

11. **(3) humorous** This option is supported by the word choices and use of exaggeration throughout the review (examples: He is a jack-of-all-crimes, he knows enough—which is not all that much—to get into the filmmaking business, "I've been a fan of yours ever since *Slime Creatures*"). There is no support for options 1, 2, 4, and 5.

12. **(5) the movie industry.** This option is suggested in the first sentence and is supported in the last sentence of the review. Option 1 is wrong because the "hero" of the novel is a crook. There is no support for options 2, 3, and 4.

13. There are many possible answers.

SECTION 26

PAGE 181
1. There are many possible answers.
2. Bob Dylan, "The Bootleg Series"
3. There are many possible answers.

PAGE 182

staggering, astonishing

PAGE 183

There are many possible answers. Sample: Bob Dylan, who grew up in the Midwest, was interested in music at an early age. He went to New York to write and sing his music. He became successful and wrote many songs.

PAGE 184

The word *haunting* is an opinion. The rest of the statement is fact.

PAGES 185–186
1. d	2. f	3. e
4. a	5. b	6. c

7. There are many possible answers.
8. The reviewer hears anger, humor, hope, and spirituality.
9. Hank Williams, Leadbelly, Little Richard, and Woody Guthrie are the four musicians who influenced Bob Dylan.
10. *A measuring stick* is the metaphor that compares Bob Dylan to a standard of excellence.
11. **(2) the kinds of memories that remind us** This phrase suggests that the songs are from a time the reviewer remembers. There is no support for options 1 and 5. Option 3 refers to Bob Dylan's childhood, not the reviewer's. Option 4 is a quote by Bob Dylan.
12. **(1) wrote 237 songs during that time.** The fact that Bob Dylan wrote 237 songs in only three years clearly means that this was a creative period. Option 2 refers to only one song and does not support the opinion. Option 3 refers only to the length of time, not to what was done during that time. Options 4 and 5 do not support an opinion about a creative period.
13. **(2) Bob Dylan is expected to do unusual things.** This option is correct because the reviewer suggests that other people would act in a more ordinary way. There is no support for options 1, 3, and 4. Option 5 is incorrect because Bob Dylan sometimes seems to puzzle his audiences.
14. There are many possible answers.

SECTION 27
PAGE 187
1. There are many possible answers.
2. The director is Christian Moe. The play is a farce. A farce is a humorous play featuring unlikely situations.
3. There are many possible answers. Sample: The characters are probably singers.
4. There are many possible answers.

PAGE 188
"Lend Me a Tenor" was well received in London and won seven Tony Awards. The reviewer wants to show that other performances of the play have been successful.

PAGE 189
There are many possible answers. Samples: chase scene, slamming doors, Tito's angry wife, curdling mayonnaise, unexpected visitors, room service, a presumed death

PAGES 190–191
1. farce
2. presumed
3. typical
4. momentum
5. tenor
6. overblown
7. There are many possible answers.
8. The momentum will probably pick up speed when Tito Merelli arrives.
9. The stage manager had to read the part played by Tim Fink, who was sick.
10. **(3) like a snowball** This simile suggests how the action goes faster and becomes more complex as the play moves along. None of the other options is a simile.
11. **(1) give an example of the problems that happen during a play.** This option is correct because it is stated in the review. There is no evidence for options 2, 4, and 5. Option 3 is wrong because there is no mention of Tim Fink being absent from anything but rehearsal.
12. **(4) The show probably will be a success.** Because the play will give people what they want, it will succeed. Options 1 and 2 are the opposite of what is suggested. Option 3 is wrong because this play is the stated exception. There is no support for option 5.
13. There are many possible answers.

SECTION 28
PAGE 192
1. There are many possible answers.
2. the Godfather of Soul
3. There are many possible answers.

PAGE 193
Brown's early style is classified as *follow-the-crowd R&B*, *cookie-cutter pop*, and *doo-wop*.

1. h 2. e 3. d 4. b
5. c 6. a 7. f 8. g
9. There are many possible answers.
10. The word *jam* means a performance or recording session in which musicians play improvised, unrehearsed material.
11. There are many possible answers. Sample: In the reviewer's opinion, the collection is complete and well documented.
12. The reviewer thinks that the back-up musicians tie for second as the hardest-working people in show business.
13. **(1) give an example of how unusual James Brown is.** This option is supported by the first sentence in the paragraph about the sax player: *Brown was always a character*. Options 2, 4, and 5 have no support. Option 3 is the opposite of what is suggested.
14. **(4) funk** This option is supported by the fact that James Brown did not leave this style. Options 1 and 3 refer to earlier styles. Options 2 and 5 are not mentioned.
15. **(4) Fort Knox of funk** The reviewer is comparing the anthology of James Brown's music to the place where the U.S. gold treasury is stored. So he believes that James Brown is a musical treasure. Options 1, 2, and 3 are wrong because they do not support the positive bias. Option 5 is wrong because it is only a mild suggestion about how the reviewer feels.
16. There are many possible answers.

UNIT 3 REVIEW

PAGE 197

1. b 2. c 3. a
4. **(3) an excellent soldier.** This option is supported by references to the Marines and to the fact that Vasquez is a pilot. Option 1 is wrong because Vasquez is a human being. Option 2 is the opposite of what is stated. There is no support for options 4 and 5.

5. **(1) set up a comparison between male and female action heroes.** This option is supported by the entire passage. There is no support for options 2 and 4. Option 3 is wrong because the author's statement is an opinion, not a fact. Option 5 is wrong because no connection between the two movie stars and science fiction is made.
6. **(4) approving** The reviewer is clearly in favor of the movie and the actresses. Options 1 and 2 are the opposite of the reviewer's tone. There is no support for options 3 and 5.

PAGE 199

7. The word *vocal* refers to the way the singer uses her voice.
8. The songs classified as ballads are most admired by the reviewer.
9. The statement is an opinion.
10. **(2) The three singers sound good together.** The chords of an organ are pleasant sounds. Options 1, 3, and 4 have no support. Option 5 is wrong because the word *swelling* indicates that they are singing loudly.
11. **(5) rich, subtle tones** The words *rich* and *subtle* suggest a positive bias. Option 1 has nothing to do with admiration. Option 2 is a fact, not an opinion. Options 3 and 4 are descriptions, not opinions.
12. **(3) lingering distrust of romantic relationships** This option is correct because the word *distrust* supports the idea of past pain. Options 1, 2, 4, and 5 are wrong because they have nothing to do with past pain.

PAGE 201

13. Solita, or a ten-year-old girl
14. rich; poor
15. Spain; a Latin American country

16. **(1) unpleasant truth** This option is correct because it is a biased phrase that presents an opinion as if it were fact. It shows agreement with Elena Castedo's idea that there is something wrong with the upper classes. Options 2, 3, 4, and 5 are wrong because they do not refer to Elena Castedo's view of the upper classes.

17. **(2) Facing difficult situations can teach you about yourself.** This theme refers to how Solita learned from her situation. Options 1, 4, and 5 are wrong because they are comparisons that are not suggested in the review. Option 3 has no support.

18. **(4) The novel is a powerful criticism of human nature.** This option is supported by the final paragraph in the review. Options 1 and 2 are wrong because they are facts, not opinions. Options 3 and 5 are wrong because they are not opinions expressed by the reviewer.

POSTTEST

PAGE 203

1. love
2. garden
3. touches
4. **(2) not physical** The clue that this option is correct is in the sentences that tell how Helen Keller understood what thinking is. Thinking is not physical. It cannot be touched. Options 1 and 5 have no support. Options 3 and 4 are true in part, but they do not fit the overall idea.
5. **(3) thinking about the beads** Thinking is what Miss Sullivan was trying to help Helen Keller understand. Options 1, 4, and 5 refer to physical, not mental, processes. Option 2 is incorrect because it does not happen until later.
6. **(5) Helen is hearing impaired.** Having to communicate by hand signs suggests that Helen is hearing impaired. There is no support for the other options.

PAGE 205

7. The number *60* refers to the number of stuffed animals in Nina Dowley's house.
8. Nina Dowley collects and loves stuffed animals.
9. Stuffed animals take up all the space in the room.
10. **(1) affectionate** This is suggested by the whole poem. There is no support for the other options.
11. **(4) Nina's neighbor.** Neighbors often borrow things from each other. There is no support for the other options.
12. **(2) take it home and clean it.** This option is correct because of what she did with the rabbit. The other options are incorrect because they would not be in character.

PAGE 207

13. The old man and the girl have just come from the bus station.
14. They are Chinese.
15. Old Man Li was afraid that he would order too much if he ordered the meal.
16. **(3) They decide to have breakfast.** This is stated in the passage. Option 1 is the opposite of what is stated. There is no support for options 2 and 5. Option 4 is incorrect because they have already left the station.
17. **(2) very strong.** This is clear from the simile in the passage *She was strong as a cow.* There is no suggestion in the passage that supports the other options.
18. **(4) The restaurant was clean and impressive.** This is stated as the reason Old Man Li changed his mind. Options 1, 2, and 3 refer to his first opinion. Option 5 did not affect his decision.

PAGE 209

19. Kunta, Lamin
20. answer
21. school, book, or teacher

22. **(4) He does not always know the answers to Lamin's questions.** This option is suggested in the last paragraph. The other options have no support.

23. **(3) He cares about the boy.** This option is clear from Kunta's willingness to take on the responsibility of teaching him and from the pleasure he seems to feel being with him. The other options are the opposite of what is suggested.

24. **(3) how to behave properly in society** This option is correct because Kunta is trying to teach the boy what he needs to know about the world around him. Options 1 and 2 refer only to the place where Kunta and Lamin live. There is no support for options 4 and 5.

PAGE 211

25. The four classifications are young girls, idealistic brides, religious women, and women disappointed in love.

26. The simile *like spices and subtle flavorings* suggests that Sandra Cisneros uses Spanish and English well together.

27. **(3) It is interesting and balanced.** These opinions are stated in the passage. There is no support for the other options.

28. **(4) *excellent reading*** The word *excellent* shows a positive bias. Option 1 is a fact about Sandra Cisneros's life. Options 2, 3, and 5 are phrases used in describing the book but do not show a bias.

29. **(5) the stories about young women are shorter than those about older women.** This option is stated by the reviewer in the passage. Options 1 and 4 are incorrect because they compare the two kinds of stories. They do not contrast them. There is no support for options 2 and 3.

Annotated Bibliography

Most of the passages you have read in this book are parts of larger works such as novels, magazine articles, essays, biographies, and plays. On the following pages you will find more information about the passages you have read. Use this information to help you find these works in your local library.

Anaya, Rudolfo A. *Bless Me Ultima.* Berkeley: Tonatiuh-Quinto Sol International, 1972, reprinted 1988. An award-winning Hispanic novelist tells the story of a boy growing up in a traditional culture.

Arkins, Diane C. "Back When a Dollar Was a Dollar." *USA Today,* November 2, 1989, p. 10A. A newspaper columnist uses a humorous tone to write about modern economic problems.

Asimov, Isaac. "Escape," in *I, Robot.* Garden City, New York: Doubleday and Co., Inc., 1950. A short story about the role of computers in the future as told by a respected scientist and science-fiction author.

Clifton, Lucille. "The Thirty Eighth Year of My Life," in *Women in Literature: Life Stages Through Stories, Poems, and Plays.* Englewood Cliffs, New Jersey: Prentice Hall, Inc., 1988. An African-American woman expresses her feelings about getting older.

Codye, Corinn. *Luis W. Alvarez.* Austin, Texas: Steck-Vaughn Co., 1991. The discoveries of an Hispanic scientist who won the Nobel Prize for physics in 1968 are described in this biography.

Cook, Robin. *Mutation.* New York: G.P. Putnam's Sons, 1989. This novel is a medical thriller about genetic engineering.

Dodge, Mary Mapes. "The Minuet," in *One Hundred and One Famous Poems,* ed. Roy J. Cook. Chicago: The Cable Company, 1928. A poet recalls her grandmother's tales of what it was like to be a young woman in America in the nineteenth century.

Dunbar, Paul. "Sympathy," in *Black Writers of America.* New York: Macmillan and Co., 1972. Dunbar, the son of a slave, reflects on the idea of freedom in a moving poem.

Frost, Robert. "The Road Not Taken," in *An Introduction to Robert Frost.* New York: Holt Rinehart Winston, 1971. A poet considers making an important decision at a crossroads in life.

Gershe, Leonard. *Butterflies Are Free.* New York: Random House, 1969. This play tells the story of a visually impaired young man living independently in New York City.

Grey, Zane. *Horse Heaven Hill.* New York: Grosset & Dunlap, 1959. The challenges of life in the Old West are described in exciting detail by the author of many western novels and short stories.

Haley, Alex. *Roots: The Saga of An American Family.* New York: Dell Publishing Co., 1976. This fiction novel tells the story of Kunta Kinte. Kinte is the ancestor of the African-American author who has traced his ancestry back to Africa.

Hansberry, Lorraine. *A Raisin in the Sun.* New York: Random House, 1958. The experiences of an African-American family living in a predominantly white neighborhood in the 1950s are dramatized in this play.

Henley, Beth. *Crimes of the Heart.* New York: Viking Press, 1982. This play is a comedy in which three sisters work out some of their differences and re-establish their family ties.

Hillerman, Tony. *The Ghostway.* New York: Avon Books, 1984. In one of a series of mystery novels, a well-known fiction author relates the investigations of a Navajo detective.

Hughes, Langston. "Theme for English B," in *Literature: An Introduction to Reading and Writing,* eds., Edgar V. Roberts and Henry E. Jacobs. Englewood Cliffs, New Jersey: Prentice Hall, 1986. A prominent member of the Harlem Renaissance literary movement writes about one of his early educational experiences.

Ibsen, Henrik. *A Doll's House,* in *Four Great Plays,* translated by R. Farquharson Sharp. New York: Bantam Books, 1959, reprinted 1962. This play, written in the mid-nineteenth century, is a social drama. It tells about the tensions in a marriage and is an early example of a drama dealing with women's rights.

Jackson, Helen Hunt. *Ramona.* Boston: Little, Brown and Company, 1884, reprinted 1939. This novel tells the story of a romance between an Hispanic woman and a Native American man during the time when the West was being settled. It was one of the earliest literary works to examine the mistreatment of Native Americans.

Keller, Helen. *The Story of My Life.* Garden City, New York: Doubleday and Company, Inc., 1954. This autobiography is the inspiring story of a woman who achieved international fame and success in spite of the physical disabilities of being blind and deaf.

King, Martin Luther, Jr. "I Have a Dream," in *The Writer's Craft,* eds. Sheena Gillespie, Robert Singleton, and Robert Becker. Glenview, Illinois: Scott, Foresman and Company, 1986. A leading civil-rights activist made this famous speech during a protest march on Washington, D.C. in 1963.

King, Stephen. *'Salem's Lot.* New York: A Signet Book, New American Library, 1975. This novel tells the story of a small town terrorized by vampires. Stephen King is one of the United States' most popular thriller writers.

Lee, C. Y. *The Flower Drum Song*. New York: Grosset and Dunlap, 1957. The conflicts between cultures and generations are played out in this fiction novel about a Chinese-American family.

London, Jack. "To Build a Fire," in *The Best Stories of Jack London,* ed. Eugene Burdick. Greenwich, Connecticut: Fawcett Publications, Inc., 1962. This gripping story tells about a man's struggle to survive in the hostile conditions of Alaska and the Yukon Territory.

Mathis, Cleopatra. "Getting Out," in *Sound and Sense,* ed. Laurence Perrine, 7th edition. New York: Harcourt Brace Jovanovich, 1987. The break-up of a marriage is described from a woman's point of view.

Mays, Willie, with Lou Sahdie. *Say Hey.* New York: Simon and Schuster, 1988. A legendary baseball player tells the story of his life and his experiences in major-league baseball.

McDaniel, Wilma. "That Woman," in *The Red Coffee Can.* Fresno, California: Valley Publishers, 1974. This poem describes how a lonely woman finds a way to spend her time and the love she has to offer.

McIntyre, Vonda N. *Enterprise: The First Adventure.* New York: Pocket Books, 1986. The challenges of space exploration are described in this science-fiction novel based on the TV series *Star Trek.*

Meltzer, Milton. *Langston Hughes: A Biography.* New York: Thomas Y. Crowell Company, 1968. The life story and struggles of the African-American poet Langston Hughes are described in this biography. *See also* Hughes, Langston.

Miller, Arthur. *A View From the Bridge*. New York: Bantam Books, 1967. An American playwright tells of the struggles of a working-class family.

Moore, Kenny. "A Courageous Stand," in *Sports Illustrated.* Vol. 75:6, August 5, 1991, pp. 62–73. This magazine article recounts a protest against racial discrimination made by two American athletes at the 1968 Olympics.

Naylor, Gloria. *The Women of Brewster Place.* New York: Penguin Books, 1982. This novel follows the lives and complex relationships of several women in an inner-city neighborhood.

Neihardt, John G. *Black Elk Speaks.* Lincoln, Nebraska: The University of Nebraska Press, 1961. A holy man of the Oglala Sioux tells the dramatic true story of his travels in the United States and Europe.

Poe, Edgar Allan. "The Tell-Tale Heart," in *Complete Tales and Poems.* New York: The Modern Library, 1938. One of the earliest mystery and thriller writers sends chills up the reader's spine with this story of murder and obsession.

Reeves, Robyn, *The Tomorrow Radio*, in *On Stage, A Readers' Theater Collection*. Austin, Texas: Steck-Vaughn Co., 1992. In this modern science-fiction drama, two scientists accidently discover a way to know what will happen in the future. The play also shows the difficulty they face convincing other people to believe in their discovery.

Rivers, Joan, with Richard Meryman. *Enter Talking*. New York: Delacorte Press, 1986. The autobiography of Joan Rivers shows that the life of a comedienne is not all laughs. Rivers recounts the struggles of her early career as she tries to break into show business.

Robinson, Edwin A. "Richard Cory," in *Sound and Sense,* ed., Laurence Perrine. 7th edition. New York: Harcourt Brace Jovanovich, 1987. This poem was written by the first winner of a Pulitzer Prize for poetry. The poem suggests that people are not always what they seem to be.

Rooney, Andy. "Street Directions," in *And More by Andy Rooney.* New York: Atheneum, 1982. A TV commentator takes a humorous look at giving, receiving, and trying to follow directions.

Steinbeck, John. *The Grapes of Wrath.* New York: Penguin, 1939, reprinted 1987. The terrible effects of the Great Depression of the 1930s are described in this novel. It is about an Oklahoma farming family who was forced to leave their farm and move to California.

Tan, Amy. *The Joy Luck Club*. New York: Ivy Books/Ballantine Books, 1989. This popular novel describes how the conflicts between people of different generations can be complicated by changes in cultural values.

Walker, James. "A Picture on the Mantel," in *Contemporary Poets of America*. Bryn Mawr, Pennsylvania: Dorrance and Company, Inc., 1985. A modern poet tells about the emotions of a little boy whose mother has died.

Woolf, Virginia. "Thoughts on Peace in an Air Raid," in *The Death of a Moth and Other Essays*. New York and London: Harcourt Brace Jovanovich, 1942. An English novelist expresses her opinions on war and peace.

Wynette, Tammy. *Stand by Your Man*. New York: Simon and Schuster. 1979. This autobiography describes the life and career of a country-and-western singer.

Acknowledgments *(continued from page ii)*

pp. 15–17
Excerpts from THE GHOSTWAY by Tony Hillerman. Copyright © 1984 by Tony Hillerman. Reprinted by permission of HarperCollins Publishers.

pp. 21–23
Excerpt from I, ROBOT by Isaac Asimov. Copyright 1950 by Isaac Asimov. Used by permission of Doubleday, a division of Bantam Doubleday Dell Publishing Group, Inc.

pp. 27–29
Excerpt from LANGSTON HUGHES, A BIOGRAPHY by Milton Meltzer. Copyright © 1968 by Milton Meltzer. Selection reprinted by permission of HarperCollins Publishers.

pp. 33–35
Excerpts from BUTTERFLIES ARE FREE by Leonard Gershe. Copyright as an unpublished work, 1969 by Leonard Gershe. Copyright © 1970 by Leonard Gershe. Reprinted by permission of Random House, Inc.

pp. 39–40
LUCILLE CLIFTON. "The Thirty Eighth Year of My Life" copyright © 1987 by Lucille Clifton. Reprinted with the permission of BOA Editions, Ltd., 92 Park Ave., Brockport, NY 14420.

p. 41
James Lafayette Walker, "A Picture on the Mantel" copyright © 1985. Reprinted by permission of Dorrance and Company.

pp. 45–47
Excerpt from, 'SALEM'S LOT by Stephen King. Copyright © 1975 by Stephen King. Used by permission of Doubleday, a division of Bantam Doubleday Dell Publishing Group, Inc.

pp. 51–53
Excerpt from THE WOMEN OF BREWSTER PLACE by Gloria Naylor. Copyright © 1980, 1982 by Gloria Naylor. Used by permission of Viking Penguin, a division of Penguin Books USA Inc.

pp. 57–59
From SAY HEY: THE AUTOBIOGRAPHY OF WILLIE MAYS, by Willie Mays with Lou Sahadi. Copyright © 1968 by Willie Mays. Reprinted by permission of Simon & Schuster, Inc.

pp. 63–65
Excerpt from CRIMES OF THE HEART by Beth Henley. Copyright © 1981, 1982 by Beth Henley. Used by permission of New American Library, a division of Penguin Books USA Inc.

pp. 69–71
Excerpt from BLESS ME, ULTIMA by Rudolfo A. Anaya. © 1972 Rudolfo A. Anaya. TQS Publishers, P. O. Box 9725, Berkeley, CA 94709. Reprinted by permission of the author.

pp. 75–76
Excerpt from AND MORE by Andrew A. Rooney. Reprinted with the permission of Atheneum Publishers, an imprint of Macmillan Publishing Company, from AND MORE by Andrew Rooney. Copyright © 1982 by Essay Productions, Inc.

p. 77
"Back When A Dollar Was A Dollar" by Diane C. Arkins. Copyright © 1989. Reprinted by permission of the author.

pp. 81–83
Reprinted by permission of the Putnam Publishing Group from THE JOY LUCK CLUB by Amy Tan. Copyright © 1989 by Amy Tan.

pp. 87–91
The following excerpts are reprinted courtesy of SPORTS ILLUSTRATED from the October 5, 1991 issue. Copyright © 1991, the Time Inc. Magazine Company. "A Courageous Stand" by Kenny Moore. All Rights Reserved.

pp. 93–95
LUIS W. ALVAREZ by Corinn Codye. © 1991, Steck-Vaughn Company.

p. 98
Reprinted by permission of the Putnam Publishing Group from MUTATION by Robin Cook. Copyright © 1989 by Robin Cook.

p. 100
"Getting Out" by Cleopatra Mathis. Reprinted by permission of the poet.

p. 102
Excerpt from STAND BY YOUR MAN by Tammy Wynette. Copyright © 1979 by Tammy Wynette. Reprinted by permission of Simon & Schuster, Inc.

p. 104
Excerpt from "The Tomorrow Radio" in ON STAGE, A READER'S THEATER COLLECTION by Robyn Reeves. © 1992 by Steck-Vaughn Company.

pp. 109–111
"The Tell-Tale Heart" by Edgar Allan Poe.

pp. 115–117
Excerpt from RAMONA by Helen Hunt Jackson. Published by Little, Brown & Co., Inc.

p. 121
"The Road Not Taken" from THE POETRY OF ROBERT FROST edited by Edward Connery Lathem, and published by Henry Holt & Co.

p. 122
"Richard Cory" from THE CHILDREN OF THE NIGHT by Edwin Arlington Robinson (New York: Charles Scribner's Sons, 1897).

p. 123
"The Minuet" by Mary Mapes Dodge.

pp. 127–129
Excerpts from A RAISIN IN THE SUN by Lorraine Hansberry. Copyright © 1958 by Robert Nemiroff as an unpublished work. Copyright © 1959, 1966, 1984 by Robert Nemiroff. Reprinted by permission of Random House, Inc.

pp. 133–135
Excerpt from HORSE HEAVEN HILL by Zane Grey. Copyright © 1959 by Zane Grey, Inc. Reprinted by permission of Dr. Loren Grey, 4417 Coloma Ave., Woodland Hills, CA 91364.

pp. 139–141
Reprinted from BLACK ELK SPEAKS, by John G. Neihardt, by permission of University of Nebraska Press. Copyright 1932, 1959, 1972, by John G. Neihardt. Copyright © 1961 by the John G. Neihardt Trust.

pp. 145–147
"To Build a Fire" by Jack London. The Jack London Ranch, Box 327, Glen Ellen, CA 95442.

pp. 151–153
Excerpts from "Thoughts on Peace in an Air Raid" in DEATH OF THE MOTH AND OTHER ESSAYS by Virginia Woolf, copyright 1942 by Harcourt Brace Jovanovich, Inc. and renewed 1970 by Marjorie T. Parsons, Executrix, reprinted by permission of the publisher, The Executors of the Estate of Virginia Woolf, the source, and The Hogarth Press as publishers.

p. 156

From THE GRAPES OF WRATH by John Steinbeck. Copyright 1939, renewed © 1967 by John Steinbeck. Used by permission of Viking Penguin, a division of Penguin Books USA Inc.

p. 158

From A VIEW FROM THE BRIDGE by Arthur Miller. Copyright © 1955, 1957, renewed 1983, 1985 by Arthur Miller. Used by permission of Viking Penguin, a division of Penguin Books USA Inc.

p. 160

"Theme From English B" by Langston Hughes. Reprinted by permission of Harold Ober Associates Incorporated. Copyright © 1951 by Langston Hughes. Copyright renewed 1979 by George Houston Bass.

p. 162

Excerpt from "I Have A Dream" speech by Martin Luther King, Jr. Reprinted by permission of Joan Daves Agency. Copyright © 1963 by Dr. Martin Luther King, Jr.

pp. 167–169

From "Three Men and a Maybe" by Marvin Kitman. Reprinted with permission from TV GUIDE® Magazine. Copyright © 1991 by News America Publications, Inc., Radnor, Pennsylvania.

pp. 172–173

"Slickers Drive Cattle and Point Home" by Bob Thomas. Reprinted by permission of The Associated Press.

pp. 177–179

GET SHORTY (Elmore Leonard) by Ralph S. Novak from PEOPLE WEEKLY © 1990 Ralph Novak.

pp. 182–183

"Dylan at 50 . . . " by Ron Firak. Reprinted by permission of The Associated Press.

pp. 188–190

"Lend Me A Tenor" by Cara Webster. Reprinted by permission of THE SOUTHERN ILLINOISAN.

pp. 193–194

"Star Time: James Brown" by David Hiltbrand from PEOPLE WEEKLY © 1991 David Hiltbrand.

p. 196

Excerpt from "Roll Over, Rambo" by Ari Korpivaara from MS. Magazine © 1986. Reprinted by permission of the author.

p. 202

THE STORY OF MY LIFE by Helen Keller.

p. 204

"That Woman" by Wilma Elizabeth McDaniel. Reprinted by permission of the poet.

p. 206

THE FLOWER DRUM SONG by C. Y. Lee. By permission of The Ann Elmo Agency.

p. 208

From ROOTS by Alex Haley. Copyright © 1976 by Alex Haley. Used by permission of Doubleday, a division of Bantam Doubleday Dell Publishing Group, Inc.

Glossary

adventure story a story that tells about people facing danger from the unknown

anthology a collection of poems, stories, or other writings

autobiography the true story of a real person's life written by that person

bias a strong preference for a particular point of view

biographer the writer of a biography

biography the true story of a real person's life written by another person

cause a person, thing, or event that brings about a result

cause-and-effect relationship a situation in which one event happens as a result of something else

character a person in a story or a play

classical literature literature that has set a high standard of excellence, remains meaningful, and continues to be read after many years

classify to sort things into groups or classes

comedy a play that is meant to be funny

commentary a discussion of a work of literature, art or music

compare to find the ways things are alike

conclusion a judgment or opinion based on facts and details

conflict a struggle or problem between characters or forces

context the words and sentences surrounding a word or phrase. The context of a word helps show what that word means.

contrast to find the ways things are different

critical commentary a discussion of a work of literature, art, or music that makes a judgment about the quality of the work

detail a fact about a person, place, thing, event, or time. Details answer the questions *who, what, when, where, why,* and *how.*

drama a story written in dialogue that is meant to be acted on stage

effect the result of a cause

essay a short piece of nonfiction writing that gives the author's opinion about something

fact a statement that can be proved true

figurative language words used in a special way to make a point. Similes, metaphors, and personification are examples.

folktale a story that people tell over and over for many generations. Folktales often explain how people believe things began.

implied main idea a main idea that is not directly stated but is suggested by the author

inference an idea that the reader figures out based on clues an author suggests and what the reader already knows

main idea the most important point in a paragraph or passage

metaphor a directly stated figurative comparison of unlike things. Example: She is a ray of sunshine.

mood how a reader feels about a written work based on the atmosphere the author has created

mystery novel a story about solving a puzzle. The main character of a mystery is usually a detective who has to figure out who committed a crime.

narrator the character telling the story

nonfiction writing that is about real people, places, and events

novel a long work of fiction that can include many events, people, and experiences

opinion a judgment or belief

personification a type of figurative language that gives human qualities to something that is not human. Example: The leaves danced in the wind.

persuasive essay an essay that gives an author's opinion and is meant to get the reader to think a certain way

play a story that is written in dialogue and is meant to be acted on a stage

plot the series of events that create the action of a story

poet a writer of poetry

poetry literature that uses words in special ways to show feelings and create images. Poetry is usually arranged in short lines.

point of view the way the action is seen by the narrator or author of a story

popular fiction recently written works including short stories, novels, plays, and poems. Fiction comes from the author's imagination.

popular literature recently written works whose topics may include ordinary day-to-day things or ideas that can only be imagined

popular novel a recently written book about people and events that are not real

predict to tell what one thinks will happen in the future

problem play a drama that deals with a major social issue

purpose the reason why something is done

qualification skill, experience, or special training

review a short commentary that tells what the author thinks of a book, movie, TV program, musical performance, or work of art

romantic novel a fictional story about love

science fiction fictional stories based on the possibilities found in science. Science fiction shows what life and people might be like in another time or place.

sequence the order in which events occur

setting the time and place in which the events of a story take place

short story a work of fiction that is shorter than a novel but has a full plot and a single theme

simile a figure of speech that compares unlike things using the word *like* or *as*. Example: My love is like a red, red rose.

skim to read something quickly, looking for main ideas and main characters

social drama a play that deals with a major social issue

stated main idea a statement that tells clearly the most important point of a paragraph or story

summary a short statement of the main idea and most important supporting details of a passage.

synonyms words that have the same or nearly the same meaning. Examples: *paste* and *glue*

theme a general truth about life or human nature that is suggested in a work of literature

thriller novel a work of fiction that is meant to scare the reader; also called a horror novel

tone the author's attitude or feeling about a subject

tragedy a serious play with a sad ending

visualize to form a picture in the mind

western novel a fiction story about the challenges people faced on the western frontier of the United States

Index